THE EVERYTHING® LARGE-PRINT TRAVEL WORD SEARCH BOOK

Dear Reader,

I think this book can be the perfect travel companion. These word search puzzles are always there for you, and they never complain or talk back! Sure, at times they can be challenging, but with enough dedication, all the words can be found. And in the process, your brain will light up with word-searching joy. What a nice way to pass the time as you fly to an exotic destination or just commute to work.

I've given each word search puzzle a fun travel-related theme. These themes cover the places we travel to, how we get to those places, and what we do once we arrive. We've printed this book with large letters to make the solving less tedious. Your word-finding abilities will be tested, not your vision. So I hope you'll take this book with you on your next journey; I promise it will be a delightful companion!

Welcome to the EVERYTHING® Series!

These handy, accessible books give you all you need to tackle a difficult project, gain a new hobby, comprehend a fascinating topic, prepare for an exam, or even brush up on something you learned back in school but have since forgotten.

You can choose to read an Everything® book from cover to cover or just pick out the information you want from our four useful boxes: e-questions, e-facts, e-alerts, and e-ssentials. We give you everything you need to know on the subject, but throw in a lot of fun stuff along the way, too.

We now have more than 400 Everything® books in print, spanning such wide-ranging categories as weddings, pregnancy, cooking, music instruction, foreign language, crafts, pets, New Age, and so much more. When you're done reading them all, you can finally say you know Everything®!

PUBLISHER Karen Cooper

DIRECTOR OF ACQUISITIONS AND INNOVATION Paula Munier

MANAGING EDITOR, EVERYTHING® SERIES Lisa Laing

COPY CHIEF Casey Ebert

ACQUISITIONS EDITOR Lisa Laing

EDITORIAL ASSISTANT Ross Weisman

EVERYTHING® SERIES COVER DESIGNER Erin Alexander

LAYOUT DESIGNERS Colleen Cunningham, Elisabeth Lariviere, Ashley Vierra, Denise Wallace

THE EVERYTHING® LARGE-PRINT TRAVEL WORD SEARCH BOOK

Find your way through 150 easy-to-read puzzles

Charles Timmerman
Founder of Funster.com

Adams Media
New York London Toronto Sydney New Delhi

Adamsmedia

Adams Media
An Imprint of Simon & Schuster, Inc.
100 Technology Center Drive
Stoughton, MA 02072

Manufactured in the United States of America

16 2022

Library of Congress Cataloging-in-Publication Data has been applied for.

ISBN 978-1-4405-2736-4
ISBN 978-1-4405-2739-5 (ebook)

Dedicated to
Suzanne, Calla, & Meryl

Acknowledgments

I would like to thank each and every one of the more than half a million people who have visited my website, *www.funster.com*, to play word games and puzzles. You have shown me how much fun puzzles can be and how addictive they can become!

It is a pleasure to acknowledge the folks at Adams Media who made this book possible. I particularly want to thank my editor, Lisa Laing, for so skillfully managing the many projects we have worked on together.

Contents

Introduction

The puzzles in this book are in the traditional word search format. Words in the list are hidden in the grid in any direction: up, down, forward, backward, or diagonally. The words are always found in a straight line, and letters are never skipped. Words can overlap. For example, the letters at the end of the word "MAST" could be used as the start of the word "STERN." Only the letters A to Z are used, and any spaces in an entry are removed. For example, "TROPICAL FISH" would be found in the grid as "TROPICALFISH." Apostrophes and hyphens are also omitted in the grids. Draw a circle around each word that you find in the grid. Then cross the word off the list so that you will always know what words remain to be found.

A favorite strategy is to look for the first letter in a word, then see if the second letter is in any of the eight neighboring letters, and so on until the word is found. Or, instead of searching for the first letter in a word, it is sometimes easier to look for letters that stand out, like Q, U, X, and Z. Double letters in a word will also stand out and be easier to find in the grid. Another strategy is to simply scan each row, column, and diagonal looking for any words.

Puzzles

ACTIVITY
ADVENTURE
BAR
BOARDING
CHAIRLIFT
COUNTRY
EQUIPMENT
GONDOLA
GUESTS
HAT
HILLS
HOTELS
ICE
LIFTS
LODGING
MOUNTAIN
PASS
RESORT
RESTAURANT
RUNS
SKI AREA
SKI LIFT
SKI PATROL
SKIERS
SKIING
SLEDDING
SLOPES
SNOWBOARD
SPORT
TOURIST
TRAILS
TRAVEL
VACATION
VAIL
VILLAGE
WINTER

Ski Resort

T	I	C	E	N	J	V	T	C	L	O	W	L	I
R	E	T	N	I	W	H	S	R	E	I	K	S	C
A	E	R	A	I	K	S	K	I	L	I	F	T	S
V	V	A	C	A	T	I	O	N	U	R	R	S	L
E	C	G	T	N	E	M	P	I	U	Q	E	E	O
L	G	N	I	D	R	A	O	B	J	M	S	U	P
P	N	I	V	I	L	L	A	G	E	O	T	G	E
A	I	G	I	R	E	S	O	R	T	U	A	R	S
S	D	D	T	A	H	T	S	F	S	N	U	G	N
S	D	O	Y	I	S	K	I	P	A	T	R	O	L
L	E	L	L	I	I	L	O	X	N	A	A	N	I
I	L	L	R	I	R	R	S	E	B	I	N	D	F
A	S	U	N	I	T	N	V	S	S	N	T	O	T
R	O	G	A	M	U	D	V	H	O	T	E	L	S
T	C	H	D	R	A	O	B	W	O	N	S	A	F
S	C	O	U	N	T	R	Y	L	I	A	V	L	B

Solution on Page 304

BANK
CHANNEL
CONGO
DANUBE
DEEP
ELBE
EROSION
FLOWING
GANGES
GULLY
HUDSON
JORDAN
LEVEE
LOIRE
MOUTH
MURRAY
NIGER
NILE
OHIO
ORINOCO
OTTAWA
PATH
POTOMAC
RAFT
RAPIDS
RHINE
SANDBAR
SEINE
SHALLOW
SHORE
SOURCE
STREAM
THAMES
TIBER
TIGRIS
URAL
VOLGA
WATERWAY
YANGTZE
ZAMBEZI

River Trip

D	A	Z	I	M	X	T	T	I	B	E	R	E	K
O	T	T	A	W	A	S	D	I	P	A	R	B	F
H	T	U	O	M	W	E	H	E	G	U	L	L	Y
P	S	A	N	D	B	A	R	A	E	R	Z	E	P
R	O	T	H	S	Y	E	T	T	L	P	I	Z	C
N	N	T	H	G	F	A	Z	E	S	L	R	S	H
H	A	O	O	A	H	L	N	I	R	E	O	J	D
P	R	H	E	M	M	N	O	G	J	W	I	W	V
E	I	U	V	J	A	E	I	W	T	B	A	N	K
L	H	D	D	H	M	C	S	L	I	Z	V	Y	E
I	V	S	C	A	J	U	O	E	P	N	E	S	R
N	O	O	C	O	N	I	R	O	G	O	G	H	A
Y	L	N	R	I	R	U	E	R	G	N	I	M	F
O	G	D	G	E	C	D	B	X	A	N	A	H	T
R	A	E	S	O	U	R	C	E	E	Y	O	G	O
N	R	Q	C	E	E	V	E	L	A	R	U	C	N

Solution on Page 304

AXLES
BALANCE
BASKET
BELL
BMX
BRAKES
CHAINS
COMMUTE
CRUISER
CYCLING
FAST
FITNESS
FRAME
FUN
GEARING
HEALTH
HELMETS
LOCK
MIRROR
OIL
PATCH
PEDALS
PUMP
RACING
RIDING
ROAD
SADDLE
SAFETY
SEAT
SPEEDS
SPORTS
STEERING
STREET
TANDEM
TIRES
TOURING
TRICYCLE
UNICYCLE
VEHICLE
WHEELS

Bikes

L	Q	T	L	L	Q	A	A	Y	M	Y	P	X	S
S	T	E	E	R	I	N	G	H	T	G	T	V	P
D	E	L	L	E	B	F	I	T	N	E	S	S	E
P	E	C	W	C	C	U	R	I	E	S	F	B	E
E	R	Y	W	H	Y	H	L	A	E	K	A	A	D
D	T	C	A	L	E	C	T	R	M	L	S	L	S
A	S	I	V	O	Y	E	I	L	A	E	T	A	Q
L	N	R	E	C	X	T	L	N	A	N	S	R	B
S	P	T	H	K	M	P	C	S	U	E	E	O	F
T	G	N	I	R	A	E	G	F	K	S	H	R	P
R	N	E	C	S	E	A	T	A	I	P	S	R	A
O	I	O	L	G	N	I	R	U	O	T	R	I	T
P	C	D	E	D	X	B	R	P	M	U	P	M	C
S	A	A	I	M	D	C	S	T	E	M	L	E	H
P	R	O	B	N	T	A	N	D	E	M	O	I	N
L	Y	R	D	M	G	T	S	E	L	X	A	C	O

Solution on Page 304

AIRPORT
ALA MOANA
ALOHA
AMERICAN
BAY
BEACH
BUSINESS
CAPITAL
CITY
CLIMATE
COCONUT
COUNTY
CULTURE
HAWAIIAN
HISTORY
HOTELS
ISLANDS
LARGE
LEI
MOUNTAINS
OAHU
OCEAN
PACIFIC
POLYNESIAN
RESORT
SAND
STATE
SUNSHINE
TOURISTS
TRAVEL
TRIP
TROPICAL
UNIVERSITY
URBAN AREA
VENUES
WAIKIKI
WATER

Honolulu

W	C	I	T	Y	A	B	I	L	A	S	C	G	L
A	N	W	Y	R	S	D	N	A	L	S	I	J	G
T	N	A	T	O	H	A	F	C	O	E	A	S	L
E	R	I	I	T	O	E	T	I	H	N	O	T	P
R	E	K	S	S	T	R	I	P	A	I	C	A	A
L	K	I	R	I	E	A	M	O	Y	S	E	T	C
M	R	K	E	H	L	N	M	R	T	U	A	E	I
I	O	I	V	M	S	A	Y	T	N	B	N	N	F
T	T	U	I	E	L	B	H	L	U	Y	A	I	I
R	R	O	N	A	N	R	C	E	O	U	I	H	C
A	O	O	U	T	U	U	A	L	C	P	I	S	U
V	P	A	S	R	A	M	E	R	I	C	A	N	L
E	R	K	H	E	I	I	B	S	Z	M	W	U	T
L	I	W	N	U	R	S	N	B	D	N	A	S	U
L	A	T	I	P	A	C	T	S	L	B	H	T	R
T	U	N	O	C	O	C	T	S	L	A	R	G	E

Solution on Page 304

ABAFT
ABEAM
ABOARD
ADRIFT
AFLOAT
AHOY
ANCHOR
BATTEN
BEACON
BERTH
BILGE
BOAT
BRIDGE
BUOY
CABIN
COMPASS
CREW
DOCK
FORE
GALLEY
GANGWAY
HARBOR
HELM
HULL
JIB
KEEL
KNOTS
LEEWARD
MAST
MATE
OCEAN
PORT
RIGGING
RUDDER
SAILS
SEA
SHIP
STERN
WHEEL
YAW

Nautically Speaking

A	N	I	B	A	C	W	W	G	W	I	T	T	F
H	T	D	S	B	K	T	H	A	S	A	Q	O	R
W	T	F	L	O	C	N	S	E	Y	N	R	D	R
D	Y	H	I	A	O	F	O	A	E	E	U	K	Q
C	B	P	A	R	D	D	W	T	M	L	D	H	J
X	U	S	S	D	D	G	T	W	S	E	D	H	W
D	O	P	S	R	N	A	O	E	H	N	E	P	S
B	Y	O	H	A	B	J	A	R	O	B	R	A	H
B	A	R	G	W	P	G	T	C	T	F	A	B	A
O	I	T	N	E	Z	M	A	N	C	H	O	R	N
A	R	L	I	E	V	E	O	L	H	G	E	I	G
T	Q	K	G	L	B	O	L	C	L	T	H	D	L
U	R	E	G	E	E	C	F	L	A	E	R	G	J
K	I	V	I	A	B	E	A	M	L	Y	Y	E	I
S	T	E	R	N	A	A	K	M	G	U	A	A	B
V	K	V	D	H	L	N	P	K	G	S	H	I	P

Solution on Page 305

BAROMETER
BLIZZARD
CLIMATE
CLOUDY
COLD
CONDITIONS
COOL
CYCLONE
DROUGHT
DUST
FLOOD
FORECASTS
HAIL
HEAT WAVE
HOT
HUMIDITY
HURRICANES
ICE
JET STREAM
LIGHTNING
LOW
NATURE
NEWS
PREDICTIONS
PRESSURE
RAINFALL
SKY
SNOW
STATION
STORMS
SUNSHINE
TEMPERATURE
TORNADO
TROPICS
TROPOSPHERE
WARM
WET
WINTER
ZONE

Travel Forecast

E	S	C	I	P	O	R	T	H	D	B	Y	K	S
E	U	M	R	A	I	N	F	A	L	L	T	N	N
E	N	W	R	C	O	N	D	I	T	I	O	N	S
R	S	O	E	O	A	N	Z	L	S	W	H	C	N
U	H	F	Z	T	T	Z	T	T	E	U	E	X	O
S	I	O	U	X	A	S	A	T	R	R	J	J	I
S	N	R	E	R	U	T	A	R	E	P	M	E	T
E	E	E	D	D	I	M	I	H	E	D	C	T	C
R	H	C	G	O	I	C	P	V	R	Y	L	S	I
P	U	A	N	L	A	S	A	O	C	O	O	T	D
R	M	S	C	N	O	W	U	L	O	W	U	R	E
E	I	T	E	P	T	G	O	C	D	T	D	E	R
T	D	S	O	A	H	N	E	W	S	O	Y	A	P
N	I	R	E	T	E	M	O	R	A	B	O	M	I
I	T	H	L	I	G	H	T	N	I	N	G	L	S
W	Y	W	A	R	M	T	O	R	N	A	D	O	F

Solution on Page 305

BATHROOM
BELLHOP
BREAKFAST
BUILDING
CHAIN
CLERK
CONCIERGE
EXCLUSIVE
FLOOR
FUN
GIFT SHOP
GUESTS
HILTON
INN
KEY
KING
LARGE
LODGING
LUXURY
MANAGEMENT
MARRIOTT
MOTEL
RATES
RESORT
RESTAURANT
ROOMS
SERVICE
SLEEP
SPA
STAY
SUITES
TALL
TELEVISION
TEMPORARY
TIP
TOURIST
TRAVEL
TRIP
VACATION
VIEW

Staying at a Hotel

Y	T	F	D	R	O	O	M	S	L	E	E	P	Q
U	R	M	K	B	R	E	A	K	F	A	S	T	Y
I	O	A	D	I	S	I	N	N	T	L	R	P	U
R	S	B	R	E	N	I	A	L	N	D	O	G	A
A	E	U	T	O	A	G	G	E	O	Z	L	O	E
T	R	I	T	H	P	V	E	V	I	L	E	N	R
E	U	L	C	L	I	M	M	A	S	U	T	V	B
S	I	D	V	E	L	H	E	R	I	X	O	A	E
H	T	I	W	G	T	A	N	T	V	U	M	C	L
Q	T	N	A	R	U	A	T	S	E	R	O	A	L
Y	O	G	U	E	S	T	S	U	L	Y	O	T	H
E	I	E	C	I	V	R	E	S	E	Q	R	I	O
K	R	E	L	C	L	G	I	F	T	S	H	O	P
T	R	I	P	N	T	S	I	R	U	O	T	N	I
H	A	K	L	O	D	G	I	N	G	N	A	A	T
V	M	E	X	C	L	U	S	I	V	E	B	S	Y

Solution on Page 305

ARMY
BALLOON
BICYCLE
BLIMP
BOAT
BRIDGES
BUS
CABLE
CAMEL
CANAL
CARGO
DIESEL
DRIVING
ENGINE
FERRY
FUEL
GAS
GOODS
HORSE
HUMAN
HYBRID
LAND
LOAD
MODES
MOVING
NAVY
PLANE
PRIVATE
PUBLIC
ROCKET
ROUTES
SEA
SHUTTLE
SPACE
SUBWAY
SYSTEM
TRACTOR
TRAVEL
TRUCK
VAN

Transport

B	S	P	A	C	E	F	D	N	A	L	O	A	D
G	G	Y	U	N	S	R	T	R	A	V	E	L	F
N	A	V	S	J	M	A	M	N	O	B	L	W	E
A	S	A	G	T	O	Y	A	Y	P	U	G	A	R
S	G	N	B	G	E	C	T	R	A	C	T	O	R
T	R	N	R	N	G	M	I	N	S	W	C	E	Y
E	J	A	I	S	L	V	X	H	A	P	B	Q	S
J	C	G	D	V	A	X	U	D	U	M	P	U	V
M	N	O	G	T	I	T	I	B	P	I	U	Q	S
E	O	K	E	E	T	R	L	G	L	L	L	H	C
G	I	D	S	L	B	I	D	L	A	B	D	R	A
E	B	R	E	Y	C	T	Q	G	N	I	V	O	M
Z	O	S	H	S	R	Y	O	A	E	A	T	C	E
H	A	M	E	U	R	A	C	S	U	B	S	K	L
F	T	V	C	A	B	L	E	I	V	F	U	E	L
N	J	K	N	O	O	L	L	A	B	P	E	T	K

Solution on Page 305

AFRICA
ALEXANDRIA
ASWAN DAM
BASIN
BLUE NILE
BOATS
CAIRO
CROSSING
CRUISE
DELTA
DESERT
DRAINAGE
ETHIOPIA
FLOODING
GEOGRAPHY
HEADWATERS
HISTORY
HUGE
HYDROLOGY
IRRIGATION
KHARTOUM
LUXOR
NAVIGATION
NORTH
PHARAOH
PYRAMIDS
RIVERS
RWANDA
SAHARA
SUDAN
TANZANIA
TRAVEL
UGANDA
WHITE NILE

Down the Nile

A	M	A	D	N	A	W	S	A	Y	I	H	S	P
N	U	L	E	V	A	R	T	A	F	R	I	C	A
T	O	E	W	A	N	A	D	U	S	Y	S	R	D
R	T	X	S	H	O	M	V	R	H	B	T	U	N
E	R	A	T	O	I	Z	E	P	S	L	O	I	A
S	A	N	A	N	T	T	A	R	L	U	R	S	W
E	H	D	O	Y	A	R	E	U	S	E	Y	E	R
D	K	R	B	W	G	V	X	N	D	N	H	M	W
K	R	I	D	O	I	O	I	A	I	I	U	P	C
S	D	A	E	R	R	F	L	G	M	L	G	H	R
A	E	G	I	X	R	U	R	O	A	E	E	A	O
H	L	X	G	N	I	S	A	B	R	T	G	R	S
A	T	A	N	Z	A	N	I	A	Y	D	I	A	S
R	A	A	D	N	A	G	U	E	P	A	Y	O	I
A	I	P	O	I	H	T	E	X	C	D	M	H	N
Z	N	O	R	T	H	F	L	O	O	D	I	N	G

Solution on Page 306

AIR FORCE
ASPEN
AVALANCHE
BEER
BOULDER
BRONCOS
CANYONS
CATTLE
COLD
COORS
DENVER
FORESTS
GOLD
HISTORY
LANDSCAPE
MESAS
MILE HIGH
MINING
MOUNTAINS
NUGGETS
PIKES PEAK
PLAINS
PUEBLO
RESORTS
RIVERS
ROCKIES
SCENIC
SETTLERS
SKI
SNOW
TOURIST
VACATION
VAIL
WEATHER
WESTERN
WILDERNESS
WILDLIFE

Come to Colorado

P	I	K	E	S	P	E	A	K	N	E	P	S	A
U	H	E	Z	C	S	N	I	A	T	N	U	O	M
E	N	V	L	B	R	E	D	L	U	O	B	H	T
B	R	F	S	T	E	O	N	L	J	Y	S	G	S
L	E	S	V	E	T	E	F	R	O	K	N	I	I
O	T	P	O	A	T	A	R	R	E	C	I	H	R
F	S	H	A	C	C	T	C	E	I	D	A	E	U
M	E	E	H	C	N	A	L	A	V	A	L	L	O
I	W	U	P	E	S	O	T	E	N	N	P	I	T
N	S	R	O	O	C	D	R	I	R	Y	E	M	W
I	S	T	E	G	G	U	N	B	O	S	O	D	S
N	H	I	S	T	O	R	Y	A	L	N	K	N	A
G	O	L	D	E	F	I	L	D	L	I	W	I	S
W	O	N	S	T	R	O	S	E	R	H	A	H	E
S	R	E	V	I	R	O	C	K	I	E	S	V	M
R	E	H	T	A	E	W	F	C	I	N	E	C	S

Solution on Page 306

AMERICAN
ATLANTIC
BRITISH
CAPE COD
CHURCHES
COLONIST
CORNUCOPIA
DISEASE
ENGLAND
ENGLISH
FEAST
FISHING
FREEDOM
HATS
HISTORY
INDIAN
JAMESTOWN
MAIZE
MAYFLOWER
NATIVE
OCEAN
OLD
PILGRIMS
PROTESTANT
PURITANS
RELIGIOUS
SCURVY
SEPARATIST
SETTLEMENT
SHIP
SICKNESS
SQUANTO
TRAVEL
TURKEY
VOYAGE

Pilgrim's Journey

C	H	U	R	C	H	E	S	C	U	R	V	Y	T
A	H	I	S	T	O	R	Y	Z	A	T	T	T	K
P	E	R	E	L	I	G	I	O	U	S	N	S	S
E	N	G	L	A	N	D	E	Z	I	A	M	I	I
C	G	T	N	E	M	E	L	T	T	E	S	N	C
O	L	O	C	E	A	N	A	S	C	F	T	O	K
D	I	N	A	C	I	R	E	M	A	N	A	L	N
S	S	U	O	N	A	T	I	V	E	W	H	O	E
A	H	A	I	P	O	C	U	N	R	O	C	C	S
B	F	I	E	R	I	P	U	R	I	T	A	N	S
V	R	S	P	I	L	G	R	I	M	S	T	A	T
O	E	I	M	A	Y	F	L	O	W	E	R	I	U
Y	E	O	T	N	A	U	Q	S	D	M	A	D	R
A	D	L	C	I	T	N	A	L	T	A	V	N	K
G	O	D	D	I	S	E	A	S	E	J	E	I	E
E	M	P	F	I	S	H	I	N	G	J	L	X	Y

Solution on Page 306

- AIRBOAT
- BARGE
- BASS BOAT
- CANOE
- CARAVEL
- CATAMARAN
- DHOW
- DINGHY
- DORY
- FERRY
- FREIGHTER
- GONDOLA
- HOUSEBOAT
- JUNK
- KAYAK
- KETCH
- LIFEBOAT
- MOTORBOAT
- OUTRIGGER
- PADDLE
- PONTOON
- POWER
- PUNT
- RAFT
- REED BOAT
- RIVERBOAT
- ROWBOAT
- SAILBOAT
- SCHOONER
- SKI BOAT
- SLOOP
- STEAMBOAT
- SUBMARINE
- TRAWLER
- TRIMARAN
- TUGBOAT
- U-BOAT

All Kinds of Boats

T	U	G	B	O	A	T	R	O	W	B	O	A	T
E	R	O	R	T	T	A	O	B	E	F	I	L	R
L	E	N	I	R	A	M	B	U	S	R	C	Z	A
D	N	D	V	A	O	O	I	U	B	O	A	T	W
D	O	O	E	F	B	N	B	O	P	U	N	T	L
A	O	L	R	T	S	Y	A	R	G	J	O	R	E
P	H	A	B	T	S	T	T	R	O	T	E	T	R
O	C	T	O	N	A	R	A	M	A	T	A	C	E
N	S	D	A	E	B	O	O	O	H	M	O	H	W
T	L	C	T	O	E	D	B	G	B	C	I	M	O
O	O	A	D	G	B	L	I	M	Y	D	T	R	P
O	O	R	R	O	I	E	K	K	A	R	E	E	T
N	P	A	X	A	R	G	S	N	A	E	R	E	K
X	B	V	S	F	S	Y	B	U	U	Y	T	E	R
P	R	E	G	G	I	R	T	U	O	J	A	S	F
Z	I	L	W	O	H	D	I	N	G	H	Y	K	Q

Solution on Page 306

ALPS
ALTITUDE
ANDES
ANIMALS
BLUE RIDGE
CLIMATE
CLIMBING
COLORADO
ELEVATION
EROSION
EVEREST
FACE
FOREST
HEIGHTS
HIGH
HIKING
HILL
HIMALAYAS
ICE
LAKES
LANDFORM
NATURE
PEAKS
RANGE
RIVERS
ROCKIES
ROPE
ROUGH
SKIING
SNOW
STEEP
SUMMIT
TALL
TREES
VIEW
VOLCANO
WATERFALL
WEATHER

On a Mountain

F	N	S	B	L	P	R	N	E	A	Q	N	X	O
H	I	M	A	L	A	Y	A	S	L	I	O	K	T
J	Y	C	S	A	U	W	T	D	T	H	I	G	H
C	S	I	T	F	S	E	U	G	I	I	T	N	D
E	U	S	E	R	Q	A	R	N	T	K	A	I	W
G	M	D	E	E	A	T	E	I	U	I	V	I	E
N	M	V	P	T	N	H	H	B	D	N	E	K	I
A	I	N	M	A	I	E	G	M	E	G	L	S	V
R	T	W	R	W	M	R	U	I	C	E	E	E	O
F	P	Z	O	D	A	R	O	L	O	C	T	I	L
I	E	E	F	N	L	O	R	C	S	S	A	K	C
G	A	S	D	D	S	P	K	E	E	M	M	C	A
A	K	E	N	W	W	E	E	R	O	S	I	O	N
Y	S	K	A	F	O	R	E	S	T	Y	L	R	O
M	T	A	L	L	T	V	O	P	C	E	C	A	F
H	I	L	L	H	E	I	G	H	T	S	P	L	A

Solution on Page 307

ABIDJAN
AIRPORTS
ATHENS
ATLANTA
BAGHDAD
BANGKOK
BEIJING
BERLIN
BOSTON
BRUSSELS
BUDAPEST
CAIRO
CHICAGO
DUBLIN
LIMA
LONDON
MADRID
MIAMI
MILAN
MONTREAL
MOSCOW
NAIROBI
OTTAWA
PARIS
RIO
ROME
SEATTLE
SEOUL
SHANGHAI
SINGAPORE
STOCKHOLM
SYDNEY
TOKYO
TORONTO
TRAFFIC
TRAVEL
URBAN
VENICE
VIENNA

Major Cities

N	R	M	V	T	B	U	D	A	P	E	S	T	A
L	E	V	A	R	T	G	N	I	J	I	E	B	N
S	E	O	U	L	A	E	R	T	N	O	M	I	N
K	D	U	B	L	I	N	X	G	C	Y	U	M	E
T	I	E	R	O	M	E	A	B	H	K	R	A	I
R	R	T	U	S	L	P	A	O	I	O	B	I	V
A	D	O	S	T	O	A	B	S	C	T	A	M	E
F	A	R	S	R	H	R	I	T	A	H	N	S	N
F	M	O	E	O	K	I	D	O	G	G	N	N	I
I	A	N	L	P	C	S	J	N	O	E	M	O	C
C	B	T	S	R	O	B	A	G	H	D	A	D	E
A	H	O	N	I	T	H	N	T	S	S	P	N	M
I	O	I	R	A	S	E	A	T	T	L	E	O	I
R	N	A	M	I	L	M	O	S	C	O	W	L	L
O	T	T	A	W	A	T	S	Y	D	N	E	Y	A
S	J	K	O	K	G	N	A	B	E	R	L	I	N

Solution on Page 307

AMERICAN
CLINTON
COUNTRY
DELTA
DIAMONDS
ECONOMY
FARMING
FISHING
FORESTS
FORT SMITH
GEOGRAPHY
HISTORY
HOT
HUMID
HUNTING
INDIANS
JONESBORO
MAP
MIKE BEEBE
MISSOURI
MOUNTAINS
NATURAL
OKLAHOMA
OZARKS
POOR
PRESIDENT
RELIGIOUS
RIVER
SIOUX
SOUTHERN
STATE
TENNESSEE
TEXARKANA
TOURISM
UNIVERSITY

Visit Arkansas

T	A	F	O	R	E	S	T	S	H	U	M	I	D
I	N	T	D	J	N	A	T	U	R	A	L	R	I
N	A	E	L	S	O	U	T	H	E	R	N	U	A
D	M	R	D	E	S	N	I	A	T	N	U	O	M
I	O	Y	I	I	D	I	E	E	T	A	T	S	O
A	H	R	W	V	S	V	T	S	T	S	E	S	N
N	A	T	M	P	E	E	U	Y	B	U	X	I	D
S	L	N	I	A	E	R	R	H	G	O	A	M	S
O	K	U	K	M	S	S	M	P	N	I	R	N	G
G	O	O	E	E	S	I	S	A	I	G	K	O	N
N	Z	C	B	R	E	T	I	R	M	I	A	T	I
I	A	X	E	I	N	Y	R	G	R	L	N	N	H
T	R	U	E	C	N	N	U	O	A	E	A	I	S
N	K	O	B	A	E	N	O	E	F	R	D	L	I
U	S	I	E	N	T	P	T	G	T	O	H	C	F
H	I	S	T	O	R	Y	M	O	N	O	C	E	X

Solution on Page 307

AIRCRAFT
AIRPLANES
BALLISTIC
BALLOON
BIRDS
BLIMP
DIRECT
DRAG
ENGINE
FLYING
FORCE
FUEL
GLIDERS
GLIDING
GRAVITY
HELICOPTER
HISTORY
HYPERSONIC
INSECTS
JETS
LANDING
LAUNCH
LIFT
NAVIGATION
PHYSICS
PILOT
ROCKETS
SAFETY
SKY
SOARING
SPACECRAFT
SPEED
SUPERSONIC
TAIL
TAKEOFF
TRAVEL
WINGS
WRIGHT

Flight

T	T	H	C	N	U	A	L	A	N	D	I	N	G
Y	C	L	F	F	O	E	K	A	T	B	G	L	U
S	T	E	K	C	O	R	V	T	R	A	V	E	L
H	A	I	R	G	L	I	D	E	R	S	N	U	L
G	I	S	V	I	G	S	E	D	H	G	B	F	V
L	L	S	C	A	D	C	G	N	I	R	A	O	S
I	N	C	T	I	R	E	G	N	I	Y	L	F	W
D	O	I	I	O	N	G	E	L	I	A	L	Q	R
I	O	N	F	N	R	O	O	P	I	W	I	P	I
N	L	O	Y	K	S	Y	S	R	S	F	S	H	G
G	L	S	P	A	C	E	C	R	A	F	T	Y	H
P	A	R	I	W	W	R	C	I	E	G	I	S	T
M	B	E	L	S	A	F	E	T	Y	P	C	I	S
I	O	P	O	F	B	I	R	D	S	A	U	C	T
L	Q	Y	T	A	I	R	P	L	A	N	E	S	E
B	P	H	E	L	I	C	O	P	T	E	R	U	J

Solution on Page 307

ADVANCED
ASTRONOMICAL
BACTERIA
BEYOND
BIOCHEMISTRY
CARL SAGAN
CONSPIRACY
CONTACT
EARTH
EVIDENCE
EXOBIOLOGY
GALAXY
INTELLIGENT
JUPITER
LIFE ON MARS
MARTIANS
MOON
NASA
OUTER SPACE
PLANETS
PROBE
SATURN
SETI
SIGHTINGS
SOLAR SYSTEM
STARS
TELESCOPE
THEORIES
TITAN
TRAVEL
VENUS
WATER
XENOBIOLOGY

Alien Travelers

L	H	T	R	A	E	C	N	E	D	I	V	E	X
O	A	S	M	Y	G	O	L	O	I	B	O	X	E
U	Y	C	A	R	I	P	S	N	O	C	P	P	N
T	C	A	I	R	E	T	C	A	B	M	L	W	O
E	N	L	Q	M	S	N	A	I	T	R	A	M	B
R	A	E	I	C	O	N	T	A	C	T	N	E	I
S	G	V	G	F	D	N	O	Y	E	B	E	T	O
P	A	A	S	I	E	B	O	R	P	T	T	S	L
A	S	R	E	I	L	O	R	R	E	N	S	Y	O
C	L	T	T	W	G	L	N	L	T	A	S	S	G
E	R	B	I	O	C	H	E	M	I	S	T	R	Y
S	A	T	U	R	N	S	T	T	A	A	A	A	X
U	C	B	P	F	C	A	U	I	N	R	R	L	A
S	E	I	R	O	E	H	T	N	N	I	S	O	L
W	J	U	P	I	T	E	R	I	E	G	S	S	A
T	D	E	C	N	A	V	D	A	T	V	S	I	G

Solution on Page 308

AIR PUMP
ATTENDANT
CAR WASH
CASHIER
CLERKS
DIESEL
ETHANOL
FILL UP
FLUIDS
FOOD
FUEL
GALLONS
GARAGE
GAS PUMPS
GASOLINE
HIGHWAY
HOSE
MAPS
MECHANIC
MONEY
NOZZLE
OCTANE
OIL
PAY
PETROLEUM
PREMIUM
PRICES
REGULAR
REPAIRS
RESTROOMS
SERVICE
STATION
STORE
TANKS
TIRES
TRAVEL
TRUCK
UNLEADED
VEHICLES
WATER

Filling Stations

Y	A	W	H	G	I	H	K	C	U	R	T	J	Q
N	O	I	T	A	T	S	S	R	I	A	P	E	R
L	E	V	A	R	T	R	G	A	L	L	O	N	S
U	C	A	P	A	Y	T	A	N	W	A	T	E	R
S	L	F	R	G	M	U	E	L	O	R	T	E	P
D	E	D	A	E	L	N	U	N	U	Z	A	S	K
I	R	R	S	L	S	A	P	H	D	G	Z	C	O
U	K	E	I	E	S	T	V	M	O	A	E	L	N
L	S	U	I	T	R	E	R	C	U	S	N	R	E
F	M	F	S	H	H	V	T	O	F	P	E	T	E
T	U	I	E	I	S	A	I	V	O	U	R	O	T
A	I	L	C	I	N	A	H	C	E	M	E	I	H
N	M	L	I	E	M	M	C	J	E	P	S	L	A
K	E	U	R	A	E	N	I	L	O	S	A	G	N
S	R	P	P	Y	E	N	O	M	F	O	O	D	O
N	P	S	E	R	O	T	S	D	I	E	S	E	L

Solution on Page 308

AZTECS
BAJA
BEANS
BORDER
CANCUN
COUNTRY
COZUMEL
CUISINE
CULTURE
FESTIVAL
FIESTA
FOOD
GULF
HISPANIC
HOT
MARIACHI
MAYANS
MEXICANS
MOLE
OAXACA
OLMEC
PESOS
PYRAMIDS
RESORTS
RICE
SHOPPING
SOCCER
SOUTH
SPANISH
TACOS
TAMALES
TEQUILA
TEXAS
TIJUANA
TORTILLA
TOURISM
TRAVEL
TROPICAL
VACATION
YUCATAN

Tour of Mexico

M	A	Z	T	E	C	S	N	A	E	B	A	J	A
S	E	L	A	M	A	T	I	J	U	A	N	A	F
I	T	Y	I	X	E	N	I	S	I	U	C	Z	I
R	A	R	E	U	C	S	O	A	X	A	C	A	E
U	C	T	O	F	Q	G	N	I	P	P	O	H	S
O	O	N	E	S	E	E	Z	A	T	F	L	F	T
T	S	U	Z	H	E	S	T	V	C	A	O	G	A
S	S	O	C	C	E	R	T	O	C	I	C	O	N
K	D	C	I	N	A	P	S	I	H	T	X	A	D
H	S	I	N	A	P	S	P	C	V	R	T	E	V
X	C	E	M	L	O	O	A	O	E	A	F	S	M
W	S	X	L	A	R	I	W	Z	C	V	L	O	A
A	L	L	I	T	R	O	T	U	I	E	U	U	Y
N	U	C	N	A	C	Y	Y	M	R	L	G	T	A
Q	I	Z	M	O	L	E	P	E	S	O	S	H	N
B	O	R	D	E	R	U	T	L	U	C	W	S	S

Solution on Page 308

ADVENTURER
ANTARCTIC
BASE CAMP
BEEKEEPER
BOOTS
BRITISH
CLIMBING
COLD
DISCOVERY
EVEREST
EXPEDITION
EXPLORING
FIRST
HERO
HIGH
HIMALAYAS
HISTORY
ICE
KNIGHTHOOD
MOUNTAINS
NAVIGATOR
NEPAL
NORTH POLE
PEAK
ROPE
SHERPA
SIR
SNOW
SOUTH POLE
SUMMIT
TIBET
TRAVEL

Sir Edmund Hillary

S	A	N	T	A	R	C	T	I	C	O	L	D	E
A	O	D	P	Z	U	D	W	R	V	N	I	G	D
Y	R	E	V	O	C	S	I	D	Q	F	I	A	Y
A	O	X	U	E	L	O	P	H	T	U	O	S	D
L	T	P	Y	S	N	I	A	T	N	U	O	M	C
A	A	L	C	K	T	T	C	P	B	D	R	E	L
M	G	O	E	N	S	D	U	E	A	I	X	S	I
I	I	R	L	I	E	H	S	R	S	P	L	H	M
H	V	I	O	G	R	E	P	E	E	K	E	E	B
S	A	N	P	H	E	R	H	D	C	R	V	R	I
I	N	G	H	T	V	O	I	B	A	O	A	P	N
T	E	S	T	H	E	T	S	O	M	P	R	A	G
I	P	N	R	O	I	H	T	O	P	E	T	B	F
R	A	O	O	O	P	G	O	T	I	M	M	U	S
B	L	W	N	D	F	I	R	S	T	I	B	E	T
F	R	M	S	J	Z	H	Y	K	A	E	P	Q	P

Solution on Page 308

ADDRESS
ART
CARDBOARD
CHEAP
COLLECTOR
DELTIOLOGY
EMBOSSED
ENVELOPE
GREETING
HISTORY
IMAGE
LETTER
MAILING
MESSAGES
NOTES
NOVELTY
OLD
PAPER
PERSONAL
PHOTOGRAPH
PICTURES
PLACE
POSTMARK
QUICK
SCENIC
SENT
SOUVENIR
STAMPS
TOURIST
TRAVEL
VIEW
WRITING

Postcards

B	Y	P	P	I	C	T	U	R	E	S	S	Y	P
E	V	U	H	O	T	O	U	R	I	S	T	R	A
Y	G	O	L	O	I	T	L	E	D	S	E	I	P
L	E	V	A	R	T	Y	T	L	E	V	O	N	E
K	R	A	M	T	S	O	P	L	E	T	T	E	R
M	G	U	Q	L	W	D	G	D	P	C	U	V	L
E	N	V	E	L	O	P	E	R	L	G	T	U	D
S	I	N	O	T	E	S	I	A	A	V	S	O	G
S	T	R	A	L	S	B	N	O	C	P	L	S	R
A	I	Y	T	O	L	O	Y	B	E	D	H	P	E
G	R	S	B	S	S	E	R	D	D	A	L	A	E
E	W	M	P	R	G	P	O	R	T	P	F	E	T
S	E	A	E	A	M	S	T	A	M	P	S	H	I
E	I	P	M	D	D	K	S	C	E	N	I	C	N
N	V	I	M	A	I	L	I	N	G	I	Y	M	G
T	O	U	P	T	Q	Q	H	Q	U	I	C	K	S

Solution on Page 309

ANNUAL
BIKES
CIRCUITS
CLIMBING
CYCLISTS
DISTANCE
DOPING
ENDURANCE
EUROPE
EVENT
FANS
FRANCE
GRAND TOURS
GREG LEMOND
HILLS
JERSEYS
JULY
KILOMETERS
MARATHON
MILES
MOUNTAINS
PEDAL
POPULAR
RACING
RIDERS
ROADS
ROUTE
SPEED
STAGES
STEROIDS
STRENGTH
SUMMER
TEAMS
THREE WEEKS
TRAINING
VICTORY
WINNERS

Tour de France

J	N	A	N	N	U	A	L	G	N	I	C	A	R
S	E	G	A	T	S	E	K	I	B	Z	R	V	O
W	Y	R	O	U	T	E	A	M	S	U	I	I	A
S	R	E	T	E	M	O	L	I	K	C	D	C	D
U	K	V	S	S	J	S	D	I	O	R	E	T	S
M	G	E	V	R	N	E	T	S	M	D	R	O	D
M	S	N	E	N	E	I	P	I	N	P	S	R	I
E	G	T	I	W	O	J	A	O	U	A	E	Y	S
R	N	Y	S	N	E	H	M	T	R	C	F	G	T
W	I	U	L	I	I	E	T	W	N	U	R	N	A
I	P	O	P	U	L	A	R	A	S	U	E	I	N
N	O	P	J	G	J	C	R	H	R	L	O	B	C
N	D	E	E	P	S	U	Y	T	T	A	L	M	E
E	P	R	P	E	D	A	L	C	T	U	M	I	G
R	G	R	A	N	D	T	O	U	R	S	L	L	H
S	T	R	E	N	G	T	H	F	R	A	N	C	E

Solution on Page 309

ARCHITECTURE
ATTRACTIONS
CHICAGO
COUNTRIES
CULTURE
EIFFEL TOWER
EVENTS
EXHIBITIONS
EXPOSITION
FERRIS WHEEL
FUN
HOST CITY
HYDE PARK
INDUSTRY
INNOVATION
INVENTIONS
LARGE
NAO DE CHINA
NEW YORK
PARIS
PEOPLE
PRINCE ALBERT
RIDES
SCIENCE
SPACE NEEDLE
SPECIALIZED
ST. LOUIS
UNIVERSAL
WORLD

World's Fair

O	E	X	H	I	B	I	T	I	O	N	S	H	K
S	K	N	I	N	V	E	N	T	I	O	N	S	R
P	U	R	E	X	P	O	S	I	T	I	O	N	O
E	L	D	E	E	N	E	C	A	P	S	I	K	Y
C	I	B	A	O	G	A	C	I	H	C	T	R	W
I	N	F	U	N	E	R	U	T	L	U	C	A	E
A	N	N	F	P	I	C	B	S	I	R	A	P	N
L	O	E	L	E	E	H	W	S	I	R	R	E	F
I	V	C	A	O	L	I	C	I	Z	G	T	D	H
Z	A	N	R	P	S	T	N	E	V	E	T	Y	O
E	T	E	G	L	T	E	O	D	D	Q	A	H	S
D	I	I	E	E	I	C	D	W	U	O	S	H	T
L	O	C	O	U	N	T	R	I	E	S	A	L	C
R	N	S	T	L	O	U	I	S	R	R	T	N	I
O	A	K	L	A	S	R	E	V	I	N	U	R	T
W	P	R	I	N	C	E	A	L	B	E	R	T	Y

Solution on Page 309

ALPINE
ALTITUDE
ASCENT
ATHLETIC
BELAY
BOOTS
CAMPING
CAVES
COLD
CRAMPONS
DESCENT
EVEREST
EXERCISE
GEAR
GLACIERS
GUIDE
HEIGHTS
HIKING
HILLARY
HIMALAYAS
HOBBY
ICE AXE
MOUNTAINS
NEPAL
OXYGEN
PEAKS
ROCKY
ROPES
SAFETY
SKIING
SNOW
SPORT
STEEP
SUMMITS
TENT
TIBET
TRAINING
TRAVEL
WEATHER
WHITEOUTS

Climb a Mountain

Y	T	E	F	A	S	T	H	G	I	E	H	Y	Y
S	R	O	C	K	Y	X	S	O	D	F	E	B	V
K	A	W	H	I	T	E	O	U	T	S	N	B	M
I	V	E	I	I	V	I	T	S	I	E	U	O	S
I	E	A	X	A	M	I	K	C	P	E	U	H	E
N	L	T	C	A	T	A	R	A	T	N	B	W	P
G	S	H	R	L	E	E	L	R	T	I	E	O	O
U	T	E	A	P	X	C	A	A	O	P	L	N	R
I	E	R	M	E	S	I	I	T	Y	L	A	S	N
D	N	E	P	T	N	N	S	T	G	A	Y	U	E
E	T	Q	O	I	S	E	N	N	E	R	S	M	G
S	E	O	N	S	R	E	I	C	A	L	G	M	Y
T	B	G	S	E	C	P	O	L	R	G	H	I	X
E	I	M	V	S	M	L	L	S	P	O	R	T	O
E	T	E	E	A	D	I	Z	T	N	E	C	S	A
P	E	D	C	T	H	I	K	I	N	G	Y	Q	E

Solution on Page 309

ACADIA
ARCHES
BADLANDS
BEARS
BIG BEND
BISCAYNE
BRYCE
CARLSBAD
COLORADO
DENALI
EVERGLADES
FORESTS
GLACIER
HALEAKALA
HIKING
HISTORIC
LASSEN
MESA VERDE
MOUNTAINS
NATIONAL
OLYMPIC
PARKS
PROTECTED
REDWOOD
RIVER
SAGUARO
SHENANDOAH
TRAIL
VALLEY
WILDERNESS
WILDLIFE
WIND CAVE
YOSEMITE
ZION

Scenic National Parks

C	C	M	O	U	N	T	A	I	N	S	N	I	Y
I	A	I	D	A	C	A	R	L	S	B	A	D	E
R	P	R	O	T	E	C	T	E	D	R	A	S	C
O	A	R	C	H	E	S	N	R	L	L	A	H	Y
T	D	K	S	F	V	R	G	L	A	C	I	E	R
S	V	A	L	L	E	Y	S	K	S	I	D	N	B
I	R	N	R	D	R	A	A	D	S	R	L	A	S
H	E	O	L	O	G	E	E	M	E	O	D	N	Y
S	D	I	I	U	L	N	V	V	N	L	N	D	O
T	W	Z	A	A	A	O	A	F	A	Y	E	O	S
S	O	R	H	L	D	S	C	N	T	M	B	A	E
E	O	R	I	V	E	R	D	I	I	P	G	H	M
R	D	W	F	M	S	S	N	R	O	I	I	Q	I
O	E	N	Y	A	C	S	I	B	N	C	B	Y	T
F	G	N	I	K	I	H	W	P	A	R	K	S	E
Q	E	Y	Q	E	F	I	L	D	L	I	W	Q	B

Solution on Page 310

AIDS
BABY DOC
CARIBBEAN
CATHOLIC
CHARITY
CHILDREN
CHOLERA
COFFEE
COLUMBUS
COUNTRY
CREOLE
CULTURE
DISASTER
DISEASE
DOMINICAN
FLOOD
FRENCH
HAITIAN
HELP
HOMELESS
HURRICANE
ISLAND
MALARIA
MANGOES
NATION
OCEAN
PAPA DOC
PLANTAIN
POLITICS
PORT
POVERTY
RED CROSS
REPUBLIC
SOCCER
SUGAR
TROPICAL
WATER

Haiti

S	D	N	A	L	S	I	C	S	D	H	E	L	P
C	S	A	Y	A	R	E	L	O	H	C	N	H	O
I	S	E	O	G	N	A	M	C	U	W	A	C	V
T	O	B	L	E	B	I	H	C	Q	N	I	N	E
I	C	B	S	E	N	A	H	E	W	A	T	E	R
L	E	I	F	I	M	A	B	R	B	C	I	R	T
O	A	R	C	L	R	O	C	Y	D	S	A	F	Y
P	N	A	T	I	O	N	H	I	D	S	H	C	M
T	N	C	T	G	X	O	S	T	R	O	P	I	A
R	C	Y	P	A	P	A	D	O	C	R	C	L	L
O	U	V	D	I	S	E	A	S	E	C	U	O	A
P	L	A	N	T	A	I	N	A	I	D	S	H	R
I	T	W	E	C	H	I	L	D	R	E	N	T	I
C	U	R	C	I	L	B	U	P	E	R	A	A	A
A	R	A	G	U	S	U	B	M	U	L	O	C	S
L	E	E	F	F	O	C	R	E	O	L	E	Q	L

Solution on Page 310

ADMISSION

AUTOPIA

CALIFORNIA

CASTLE

CHARACTERS

CHILDREN

CROWDS

DREAM

DUMBO

EARS

FAMILY

FIREWORKS

FOOD

FUN

GOOFY

GUESTS

HOTELS

LINES

MATTERHORN

MEMORIES

MONORAIL

MUSIC

ORIGINAL

PARADES

PRINCESS

RESORT

RIDES

SHOWS

SNOW WHITE

SOUVENIRS

TICKETS

VACATION

Let's Go to Disneyland

S	U	S	T	E	K	C	I	T	M	U	S	I	C
T	H	O	T	E	L	S	Z	Y	L	I	M	A	F
S	C	U	O	B	M	U	D	E	A	R	S	C	V
E	R	V	N	R	O	H	R	E	T	T	A	M	X
U	M	E	M	O	R	I	E	S	L	L	R	Y	L
G	O	N	T	T	S	B	A	E	I	E	K	A	X
R	N	I	P	C	R	N	M	F	S	J	N	E	P
I	O	R	X	T	A	D	O	O	F	I	O	F	C
D	R	S	V	P	L	R	R	W	G	B	I	Z	H
E	A	D	A	R	N	T	A	I	W	R	S	J	I
S	I	W	C	I	Y	X	R	H	E	H	S	E	L
H	L	O	A	N	P	O	Q	W	C	F	I	N	D
O	I	R	T	C	G	O	O	F	Y	X	M	T	R
W	N	C	I	E	L	R	T	O	U	E	D	Y	E
S	E	Y	O	S	K	M	U	U	E	N	A	K	N
W	S	H	N	S	Z	P	A	R	A	D	E	S	L

Solution on Page 310

AUTOMATIC
BATTERY
BMW
BRAKES
BUMPER
CADILLAC
CHEVROLET
CHRYSLER
DIESEL
DRIVER
ELECTRIC
ENGINE
EXHAUST
FUEL
GASOLINE
HENRY FORD
HIGHWAY
HYBRID
INSURANCE
LICENSE
MECHANIC
MOTOR
OIL
PASSENGERS
POLLUTION
ROADS
SEAT BELT
SEDAN
SPEED
SUV
TIRES
TOYOTA
TRAFFIC
TRUNK
VAN
VEHICLE
WHEELS
WINDOWS
WINDSHIELD

Autos

T	Z	D	I	E	S	E	L	C	I	H	E	V	T
C	L	O	I	L	I	C	E	N	S	E	W	Y	I
W	I	E	C	H	R	Y	S	L	E	R	H	R	R
B	I	F	B	T	S	U	A	H	X	E	E	E	E
R	W	N	F	T	R	D	E	E	P	S	E	T	S
A	E	B	D	A	A	N	S	U	V	L	L	T	N
K	C	P	N	S	R	E	G	N	E	S	S	A	P
E	H	C	M	Y	H	T	S	C	A	P	V	B	C
S	E	H	F	U	C	I	T	A	M	O	T	U	A
W	V	O	I	X	B	R	E	O	S	L	E	A	L
O	R	T	R	G	I	M	T	L	E	L	N	T	L
D	O	R	E	C	H	O	W	U	D	U	I	O	I
N	L	U	V	V	R	W	F	F	A	T	G	Y	D
I	E	N	I	L	O	S	A	G	N	I	N	O	A
W	T	K	R	D	I	R	B	Y	H	O	E	T	C
R	O	A	D	S	M	E	C	H	A	N	I	C	I

Solution on Page 310

AMTRAK
BOGIES
BOXCAR
CARS
COAL
CONDUCTOR
CONNECT
CROSSING
DEPOT
DIESEL
DINING CAR
DISTANCE
ELECTRIC
ENGINE
EXPRESS
FREIGHT
HIGH SPEED
LIGHT RAIL
LINE
LOCOMOTIVE
LONG
MAGLEV
METRO
MONORAIL
PASSENGERS
PULLMAN
RAILCAR
RAILROADS
RAILWAYS
SCHEDULE
SEATS
STATION
STEAM
TRAVEL
TUNNELS
VEHICLES

Train Travel

M	A	G	L	E	V	G	C	O	N	N	E	C	T
B	G	O	E	C	O	N	D	U	C	T	O	R	K
O	N	D	V	L	E	S	E	I	D	A	L	O	A
G	J	P	I	L	F	R	E	D	L	K	F	S	R
I	E	U	T	N	I	E	P	E	M	R	E	S	T
E	L	L	O	B	I	G	S	P	O	A	C	I	M
S	U	L	M	O	M	N	H	O	N	I	N	N	A
E	D	M	O	X	A	E	G	T	O	L	A	G	C
L	E	A	C	C	E	S	I	C	R	C	T	E	F
C	H	N	O	A	T	S	H	Z	A	A	S	N	N
I	C	H	L	R	S	A	P	R	I	R	I	I	O
H	S	O	A	E	L	P	S	A	L	F	D	L	I
E	V	V	R	J	C	I	R	T	C	E	L	E	T
V	E	P	C	T	S	Y	A	W	L	I	A	R	A
L	X	S	T	A	E	S	F	R	E	I	G	H	T
E	N	I	G	N	E	M	T	U	N	N	E	L	S

Solution on Page 311

AXLE
BIG RIG
BRAKING
CARGO
CB RADIO
CONVOY
COUPLING
DIESEL
DISTANCE
DRIVER
ENGINE
FREIGHT
FUEL
HAULING
HEAVY
HIGHWAY
JACKKNIFE
LARGE
LICENSE
LIGHTS
LOAD
LONG HAUL
LORRY
PETERBILT
RIGS
ROAD
ROUTE
SEMI
SLEEPER
SPEED
TANKER
TIRES
TRACTOR
TRAILER
TRANSPORT
TRAVEL
TRUCKER
VEHICLE
WEIGH
WHEELS

Semi Trucks

L	O	R	R	Y	S	E	M	I	V	T	R	S	T
S	C	W	W	E	I	G	H	E	A	V	Y	R	I
P	A	D	C	T	L	A	R	G	E	A	U	R	R
E	R	R	W	H	E	E	L	S	W	C	E	E	E
E	G	I	R	G	I	B	S	H	K	P	U	L	S
D	O	V	E	I	N	C	G	E	E	K	E	I	P
R	T	E	C	E	B	I	R	E	I	U	F	A	E
C	O	R	N	R	H	G	L	O	F	D	I	R	T
O	G	U	A	F	S	S	N	P	A	H	N	T	E
N	N	D	T	N	E	E	G	I	U	D	K	F	R
V	I	A	S	E	S	T	N	I	L	O	K	S	B
O	K	O	I	L	N	P	A	I	R	U	C	M	I
Y	A	L	D	X	E	L	O	N	G	H	A	U	L
F	R	T	R	A	C	T	O	R	K	N	J	H	T
K	B	V	E	H	I	C	L	E	T	E	E	Z	E
S	T	H	G	I	L	I	L	E	V	A	R	T	C

Solution on Page 311

ALMONDS
APPLES
BAG
BREAK
CAKE
CANDY BAR
CARROTS
CHEETOS
CHOCOLATE
COOKIES
CORN CHIPS
CRACKERS
DOUGHNUTS
DRINK
FRESH
FRUIT
HEALTHY
ICE CREAM
JERKY
JUNK FOOD
NOODLES
PACKAGED
POPCORN
PORTABLE
PRETZELS
PROCESSED
QUICK
SANDWICH
SATISFYING
SEEDS
SMALL
SNICKERS
SWEET
TRAIL MIX
VEGETABLES

Travel Snack

T	S	E	I	K	O	O	C	V	J	E	R	K	Y
C	T	E	G	A	B	M	A	E	R	C	E	C	I
R	O	S	L	Q	D	O	U	G	H	N	U	T	S
A	R	R	W	P	R	O	C	E	S	S	E	D	A
C	R	U	N	E	P	S	N	T	E	N	Y	E	N
K	A	P	E	C	E	A	R	A	R	I	H	G	D
E	C	C	T	E	H	T	O	B	F	C	T	A	W
R	D	P	A	C	H	I	C	L	X	K	L	K	I
S	P	O	L	N	D	S	P	E	I	E	A	C	C
Q	S	R	O	K	D	F	O	S	M	R	E	A	H
U	D	T	C	F	N	Y	P	J	L	S	H	P	E
I	N	A	O	R	K	I	B	Z	I	D	B	L	E
C	O	B	H	U	M	N	R	A	A	E	C	L	T
K	M	L	C	I	F	G	U	D	R	E	A	A	O
S	L	E	Z	T	E	R	P	J	T	S	K	M	S
K	A	E	R	B	N	N	O	O	D	L	E	S	G

Solution on Page 311

ANCHOR
BALCONY
BEACHES
BEDS
BUFFETS
CABINS
CAPTAIN
CASINO
CREW
DANCING
DINING
DOCK
DRINKING
EXCURSIONS
FUN
GAMBLING
LIFE VEST
LIFEBOAT
LUGGAGE
MEAL
PORTHOLE
READING
RELAXATION
SAILING
SALT AIR
SEA BREEZE
SEASICK
SHOPPING
STERN
SUN TANS
SUNBATHING
SUNSHINE
TOURISTS
TUGBOAT
VACATION
WATER

Pleasure Cruise

R	S	W	S	U	N	T	A	N	S	K	C	O	D
E	T	E	H	N	D	A	N	C	I	N	G	W	I
A	S	R	O	R	E	L	A	X	A	T	I	O	N
D	I	C	P	E	X	K	C	I	S	A	E	S	I
I	R	L	P	T	C	A	P	T	A	I	N	R	N
N	U	I	I	S	U	N	B	A	T	H	I	N	G
G	O	F	N	C	R	C	A	B	I	N	S	W	X
J	T	E	G	K	S	E	A	B	R	E	E	Z	E
B	P	B	G	N	I	L	B	M	A	G	R	B	N
E	S	O	E	O	O	N	I	S	A	C	B	A	I
A	T	A	R	D	N	E	G	A	G	G	U	L	H
C	E	T	L	T	S	E	V	E	F	I	L	C	S
H	F	C	A	T	H	V	A	C	A	T	I	O	N
E	F	Y	E	T	A	O	B	G	U	T	G	N	U
S	U	U	M	S	A	I	L	I	N	G	F	Y	S
I	B	A	N	C	H	O	R	E	T	A	W	A	H

Solution on Page 311

AFRICA
ARABIAN
ARIZONA
ATACAMA
BARREN
BEDOUIN
CACTUS
CALIFORNIA
CLIMATE
COLD
COYOTE
DIURNAL
DROUGHT
DUNES
EGYPT
EXTREME
GOBI
HEAT
HOT DESERTS
HUMID
KALAHARI
LANDSCAPE
LIFE
LIZARDS
MOJAVE
MOUNTAINS
NEVADA
RAINFALL
REGION
SAHARA
SANDSTORM
SCORPIONS
SNAKES
SONORAN
SUN
TEMPERATURE
WATER
WIND

Desert Journey

T	N	E	V	A	D	A	S	E	K	A	N	S	Y
S	A	A	R	I	Z	O	N	A	R	O	N	O	S
S	A	E	I	R	L	A	N	D	S	C	A	P	E
K	E	H	H	B	K	I	Z	H	U	M	I	D	N
T	M	N	A	S	A	N	D	S	T	O	R	M	S
H	E	A	U	R	L	R	W	L	C	R	M	N	D
G	R	M	F	D	A	O	A	I	A	A	O	E	I
U	T	A	P	X	H	F	T	Z	C	I	U	R	U
O	X	C	F	E	A	I	E	A	P	N	N	R	R
R	E	A	C	R	R	L	R	R	K	F	T	A	N
D	E	T	N	O	I	A	O	D	K	A	A	B	A
E	T	A	M	I	L	C	T	S	N	L	I	W	L
G	O	B	I	X	S	D	A	U	Y	L	N	I	I
Y	Y	H	O	T	D	E	S	E	R	T	S	N	F
P	O	X	P	B	N	I	U	O	D	E	B	D	E
T	C	M	O	J	A	V	E	R	E	G	I	O	N

Solution on Page 312

ACCIDENTS
ANGER
BUSES
CARS
CITIES
CONGESTION
DIRECTION
DRIVERS
DRIVING
EXIT
FAST
FREEWAYS
GRIDLOCK
HEAVY
HIGHWAYS
INTERSTATE
JAMS
LANES
LATE
MOVING
NEW YORK
PASSING
PEOPLE
POLICE
RED LIGHTS
ROAD RAGE
ROADWAY
RULES
RUSH HOUR
SIGNS
SLOW
SPEED
STOP SIGN
STREETS
TICKET
TRAVEL
TRUCKS
VEHICLES

Driving

D	K	R	O	A	D	W	A	Y	E	T	A	L	M
R	E	G	N	A	C	C	I	D	E	N	T	S	O
U	L	E	C	O	N	G	E	S	T	I	O	N	V
L	T	A	P	H	I	G	H	W	A	Y	S	T	I
E	E	S	N	S	T	E	E	R	T	S	T	D	N
S	K	V	R	E	J	H	P	A	S	S	I	N	G
G	C	C	A	A	S	H	O	H	R	R	S	S	I
N	I	S	O	R	C	T	I	X	E	T	R	V	R
I	T	N	M	L	T	I	H	C	T	A	E	V	E
V	T	G	S	A	D	F	T	G	N	H	V	C	N
I	R	I	Y	L	J	I	B	I	I	Y	I	Y	E
R	U	S	H	H	O	U	R	C	E	L	R	D	W
D	C	P	E	N	S	W	L	G	O	S	D	Q	Y
K	K	O	X	E	P	E	O	P	L	E	P	E	O
W	S	T	S	H	S	E	G	A	R	D	A	O	R
H	Z	S	Y	A	W	E	E	R	F	A	S	T	K

Solution on Page 312

ANCHOR
ARTIFICIAL
BARGES
BOATS
BOSTON
CARGO
CITIES
COAST
DOCK
DREDGING
HARBOR
HAVEN
INLAND
JETTY
LOADING
LONG BEACH
MARINA
NATURAL
NEW YORK
PIER
PORTS
PROTECT
SAN DIEGO
SEA
SHELTER
SHIPS
STORM
TIDE
TRADE
WATER
WAVES
WEATHER
WHARF

Harbor

S	R	K	L	C	T	S	A	O	C	R	W	B	P
K	R	V	F	A	N	C	H	O	R	B	N	I	F
C	B	S	N	R	R	Y	D	E	O	A	E	V	F
K	T	A	T	G	A	U	W	A	L	R	N	Q	S
E	I	S	R	O	S	H	T	M	S	T	R	O	P
U	N	P	E	G	R	S	W	A	G	I	E	G	I
W	L	R	H	D	E	M	E	R	N	F	L	R	H
H	A	O	T	L	A	S	D	I	I	I	H	C	S
M	N	T	A	F	G	R	I	N	D	C	H	I	E
N	D	E	E	Y	W	N	T	A	A	I	S	T	A
F	O	C	W	R	T	O	I	E	O	A	E	I	N
A	T	T	D	Y	Z	T	B	G	L	L	V	E	E
L	T	K	S	D	O	G	E	I	D	N	A	S	V
W	A	U	C	O	N	R	V	J	Z	E	W	U	A
C	B	F	I	O	B	W	K	R	O	B	R	A	H
Y	M	L	L	M	D	U	O	S	Z	K	W	D	B

Solution on Page 312

APPAREL
BELTS
BLOUSE
BUTTONS
CASUAL
CLOAK
COATS
COTTON
DRESSES
FABRIC
FIT
GLOVES
HATS
HEM
JACKET
JEANS
JUMPER
MODELS
PAJAMAS
PANTS
PONCHO
PURSES
SCARVES
SEWING
SHAWL
SHIRTS
SHORTS
SILK
SIZE
SKIRTS
SLEEVE
SOCKS
STYLE
SWEATER
T SHIRT
TIE
UNIFORM
WARMTH
WOOL
ZIPPER

Clothes to Pack

G	L	Q	S	W	O	S	J	L	O	O	W	S	P
S	W	U	T	O	W	A	R	M	T	H	I	A	L
N	A	L	Y	N	C	A	S	U	A	L	N	U	S
N	H	B	L	K	C	K	P	C	K	T	S	T	N
R	S	G	E	E	O	T	S	P	S	R	E	N	O
E	T	T	B	L	T	J	G	Z	A	N	S	P	T
P	R	I	R	L	T	L	X	X	M	R	S	R	T
P	O	N	C	H	O	S	S	R	A	R	E	A	U
I	H	M	R	V	N	U	O	C	J	T	R	L	B
Z	S	S	E	T	I	F	S	C	A	G	D	F	Z
F	L	S	P	H	I	N	O	E	P	R	A	S	M
D	E	E	M	N	A	A	W	J	U	B	V	L	N
Q	E	W	U	E	T	S	H	I	R	T	S	E	H
E	V	I	J	S	I	Z	E	I	S	I	T	D	S
M	E	N	K	A	O	L	C	W	E	E	A	O	W
S	H	G	L	S	T	R	I	K	S	F	H	M	D

Solution on Page 312

AIR TRAVEL
BEACHES
CALIFORNIA
CHICAGO
CITIES
FAMILIES
FESTIVALS
FLORIDA
FOREIGN
GAMBLING
HAWAII
HIKING
HISTORY
HOTELS
INDUSTRY
LANDMARKS
MONUMENT
MOTEL
MOUNTAINS
MUSEUMS
NEW YORK
ORLANDO
RECREATION
RESORTS
STATES
SUMMER
TOURIST
TRAINS
TRIPS
VACATIONS
WATER
YOSEMITE

Touristy

T	D	H	S	S	F	L	O	R	I	D	A	S	R
S	G	I	N	L	N	E	W	Y	O	R	K	M	H
I	P	K	I	A	H	V	R	E	T	A	W	U	I
R	T	I	A	V	V	A	B	E	A	C	H	E	S
U	S	N	R	I	I	R	W	I	F	N	N	S	T
O	N	G	T	T	V	T	N	A	O	S	G	U	O
T	O	H	V	S	K	R	M	I	I	N	I	M	R
L	I	O	W	E	O	I	T	G	A	I	E	R	Y
J	T	T	H	F	L	A	N	D	M	A	R	K	S
C	A	E	I	I	E	I	S	L	E	T	O	M	A
H	C	L	E	R	L	T	J	O	F	N	F	K	V
I	A	S	C	B	A	Y	R	T	S	U	D	N	I
C	V	E	M	T	N	E	M	U	N	O	M	G	N
A	R	A	E	K	C	Y	O	S	E	M	I	T	E
G	G	S	T	R	O	S	E	R	E	M	M	U	S
O	R	L	A	N	D	O	S	E	I	T	I	C	W

Solution on Page 313

BIKES
BRAKES
CHOPPER
CHROME
CRUISING
CYCLE
ENGINE
FAST
FREEDOM
GANGS
GRIP
HARLEY
HELMET
HIGHWAY
HONDA
INDIAN
JACKET
KAWASAKI
LEATHER
MOPEDS
MOTORBIKE
PANNIERS
PARTS
PASSENGER
POWER
RACING
RIDERS
RIDING
ROAD
SAFETY
SCOOTERS
SEAT
SIDECAR
SPEED
SUZUKI
TRAFFIC
TRAVEL
WHEELIES
WIND
YAMAHA

Motorcycle Touring

D	E	E	P	S	G	A	H	A	M	A	Y	G	L
A	L	B	S	T	R	A	P	J	A	C	K	E	T
O	C	X	S	E	I	L	E	E	H	W	V	N	I
R	Y	C	S	S	K	A	W	A	S	A	K	I	K
V	C	R	U	I	S	I	N	G	R	S	F	G	U
P	V	S	E	K	A	R	B	T	U	E	R	N	Z
P	A	S	S	E	N	G	E	R	R	A	E	E	U
S	G	N	A	G	R	S	C	O	O	T	E	R	S
U	W	I	N	D	I	A	N	H	H	T	D	T	I
O	U	I	H	I	G	H	W	A	Y	R	O	E	D
C	H	O	P	P	E	R	S	R	B	A	M	M	E
L	E	A	T	H	E	R	A	L	Y	F	O	L	C
R	E	W	O	P	E	C	S	E	E	F	P	E	A
D	G	N	I	D	I	R	R	Y	S	I	E	H	R
Q	D	R	I	N	E	M	O	R	H	C	D	Y	T
A	G	R	G	F	R	Y	T	E	F	A	S	T	S

Solution on Page 313

BOATS
CATAMARAN
CATBOAT
CREW
CRUISING
CUTTER
DINGHY
FLOAT
FORE
FUN
GALLERY
HEADSAIL
HULLS
JIB
KEEL
KETCH
LAKE
MAINSAIL
MASTS
OAR
OCEAN
PORT
RACING
RECREATION
RIG
ROPE
RUDDER
SAILING
SCHOONER
SEA
SHIP
SLOOP
SPEED
SPINNAKER
STERN
VESSEL
WATERCRAFT
WIND
YACHTING
YAWL

Sails Up

L	P	R	K	S	P	E	E	D	D	T	L	D	O
G	O	R	F	Q	L	B	F	C	H	W	E	C	X
O	I	K	E	C	A	O	L	S	L	M	E	L	C
N	R	R	E	A	K	A	O	I	H	A	K	R	U
U	O	E	H	T	E	T	A	P	N	I	X	G	C
F	Y	I	P	B	C	S	T	E	N	N	P	N	G
P	O	R	T	O	D	H	R	A	O	S	V	I	A
E	R	T	F	A	R	C	R	E	T	A	W	C	L
P	G	E	E	T	E	A	W	D	E	I	D	A	L
W	N	H	K	R	M	R	G	S	X	L	I	R	E
J	I	B	U	A	E	S	C	H	O	O	N	E	R
N	T	N	T	L	N	D	T	E	B	Y	G	T	Y
K	H	A	D	G	L	N	D	E	R	E	H	T	A
Q	C	L	G	N	I	S	I	U	R	C	Y	U	W
Q	A	L	E	S	S	E	V	P	R	N	L	C	L
T	Y	T	G	N	I	L	I	A	S	T	S	A	M

Solution on Page 313

AKRON
AMERICAN
AVIATION
BASEBALL
BELLWETHER
BENGALS
CAMBRIDGE
CANTON
CARDINAL
CINCINNATI
COLUMBUS
CORN
DAYTON
FOOTBALL
GOVERNOR
INDIANS
KENT
LAKE ERIE
LOTTERY
OHIO RIVER
OHIO STATE
OHIOANS
PLAINS
POPULATION
PORTSMOUTH
SENECA
TOLEDO
UNIVERSITY
USA
YOUNGSTOWN

The Buckeye State

F	O	O	T	B	A	L	L	S	E	N	E	C	A
T	Z	H	L	E	G	D	I	R	B	M	A	C	V
O	B	E	L	L	W	E	T	H	E	R	B	W	I
L	N	T	A	A	P	N	A	C	I	R	E	M	A
E	O	A	B	N	O	U	N	Y	E	P	N	D	T
D	T	T	E	I	P	L	N	P	I	O	G	X	I
O	Y	S	S	D	U	Y	I	G	R	R	A	E	O
H	A	O	A	R	L	T	C	O	E	T	L	M	N
I	D	I	B	A	A	I	N	V	E	S	S	F	L
O	C	H	L	C	T	S	I	E	K	M	N	I	O
A	A	O	H	N	I	R	C	R	A	O	I	N	T
N	N	A	E	N	O	E	O	N	L	U	A	D	T
S	T	K	S	I	N	V	R	O	N	T	L	I	E
Z	O	R	H	U	C	I	N	R	T	H	P	A	R
G	N	O	Y	O	U	N	G	S	T	O	W	N	Y
H	Q	N	C	O	L	U	M	B	U	S	X	S	T

Solution on Page 313

AMTRAK
BUILD
BUSINESS
CARS
CIVIL WAR
COAL
CONDUCTOR
CONRAIL
DIESEL
ENGINEERS
EXPANSION
FREIGHT
GAUGE
INDUSTRY
IRON
JAY GOULD
LOCOMOTIVE
PACIFIC
PASSENGERS
PULLMAN
RAILROADS
REVOLUTION
SPEED
STATION
STEEL
STRIKES
TECHNOLOGY
TRACKS
TRAINS
TRAVEL
WESTERN

Railroad History

Y	N	O	I	T	U	L	O	V	E	R	E	A	Q
Z	Y	K	H	Q	E	O	D	K	M	K	X	M	L
L	E	S	E	I	D	C	S	E	Z	J	P	T	E
T	R	A	C	K	S	O	H	E	E	R	A	R	E
T	R	A	I	N	S	M	B	N	A	P	N	A	T
Q	G	W	F	L	A	O	C	W	O	P	S	K	S
F	R	E	I	G	H	T	L	L	A	L	I	R	J
P	A	N	C	C	T	I	E	S	B	D	O	E	J
U	I	G	A	R	V	V	S	U	S	T	N	G	A
L	L	I	P	I	A	E	S	T	C	W	L	U	Y
L	R	N	C	R	N	I	A	U	A	E	I	A	G
M	O	E	T	G	N	T	D	T	R	S	A	G	O
A	A	E	E	E	I	N	D	U	S	T	R	Y	U
N	D	R	S	O	O	N	O	R	I	E	N	S	L
E	S	S	N	C	D	L	I	U	B	R	O	D	D
Y	P	V	S	T	R	I	K	E	S	N	C	H	L

Solution on Page 314

ACCRA
ALGIERS
AMMAN
ANKARA
ATHENS
BAGHDAD
BANGKOK
BEIJING
BEIRUT
BELFAST
BERLIN
CAIRO
CARACAS
DUBLIN
HANOI
HAVANA
HELSINKI
JAKARTA
KIEV
LIMA
LISBON
LONDON
MADRID
MANILA
MONACO
MOSCOW
NASSAU
OSLO
OTTAWA
PARIS
PIERRE
PRAGUE
QUITO
RABAT
ROME
SEOUL
TOKYO
TRIPOLI
VIENNA
WARSAW

Capitals Around the World

G	M	A	D	R	I	D	B	S	A	M	M	A	N
Z	R	N	U	U	V	V	I	E	N	N	A	A	H
R	O	O	B	S	I	R	A	P	I	E	R	R	E
A	M	D	L	Q	U	I	T	O	T	R	H	Z	C
B	E	N	I	L	R	E	B	H	S	A	U	T	N
A	M	O	N	A	C	O	J	A	K	A	R	T	A
T	O	L	I	I	P	B	A	N	G	K	O	K	S
O	S	U	S	L	R	B	S	O	J	H	K	T	S
K	C	O	N	O	A	E	K	I	E	V	D	S	A
Y	O	E	O	P	G	I	V	L	A	H	A	A	U
O	W	S	B	I	U	J	S	H	R	C	L	F	D
L	A	P	S	R	E	I	G	L	A	L	I	L	A
S	S	T	I	T	N	N	A	R	K	V	N	E	R
O	R	O	L	K	A	G	A	D	N	J	A	B	C
I	A	L	I	M	A	C	R	H	A	V	M	N	C
U	W	Q	C	C	A	I	R	O	T	T	A	W	A

Solution on Page 314

ADDRESS
ALLEY
ASPHALT
AVENUE
BRICK
BUILDINGS
BUSY
CARS
CHILDREN
CIRCLE
CITY
CONCRETE
CURBS
DIRECTION
DRIVE
EASEMENT
GRAVEL
HIGHWAYS
LANES
LIGHTS
LINES
MOTORWAYS
NAME
ONE WAY
PARKING
PASS
PAVEMENT
PLACE
PUBLIC
ROADS
SIDEWALKS
SIGNS
TAR
TOWN
TRAFFIC
TRAVEL
TREES
URBAN
VEHICLES
VENDOR

On the Street

Y	C	U	R	B	S	O	N	E	W	A	Y	X	P
E	T	C	N	W	O	T	U	H	S	S	A	P	A
C	B	I	H	Q	P	N	H	K	H	P	L	S	V
A	C	R	C	I	E	S	L	G	A	H	Y	E	E
L	L	C	I	V	L	A	R	G	I	A	B	N	M
P	R	L	A	C	W	D	R	A	W	L	U	A	E
U	O	E	E	E	K	A	R	R	C	T	S	L	N
T	A	H	D	Y	V	R	O	E	O	G	Y	G	T
S	D	I	R	E	C	T	I	O	N	N	S	N	R
N	S	G	L	A	O	I	R	I	C	A	E	I	A
G	E	H	M	M	T	D	D	E	R	M	L	K	F
I	N	W	P	U	B	L	I	C	E	E	C	R	F
S	I	A	D	R	I	V	E	S	T	S	I	A	I
D	L	Y	F	U	T	R	A	V	E	L	H	P	C
X	Y	S	B	S	S	E	R	D	D	A	E	A	S
N	A	B	R	U	H	R	O	D	N	E	V	I	J

Solution on Page 314

BIG MAC
BREAKFAST
CHEESEBURGER
COFFEE
COKE
DOLLAR MENU
EGG MCMUFFIN
FAST FOOD
FISH FILET
FRENCH FRIES
GOLDEN ARCHES
HAMBURGERS
HAPPY MEALS
ICE CREAM
KETCHUP
MCCAFE
MCCHICKEN
MCDOUBLE
MCGRIDDLE
MCRIB
MILKSHAKES
PIES
QUARTER POUNDER
SANDWICHES
SNACK WRAP
SODA
SUNDAES
TASTY
TEA
WRAPS

Stop at McDonald's

M	C	R	I	B	F	A	S	T	F	O	O	D	S
R	H	M	C	G	R	I	D	D	L	E	O	G	P
S	E	K	A	H	S	K	L	I	M	L	O	U	A
E	E	L	B	U	O	D	C	M	L	L	H	T	R
I	S	E	A	D	N	U	S	A	D	C	U	J	W
R	E	D	N	U	O	P	R	E	T	R	A	U	Q
F	B	C	O	K	E	M	N	E	Y	T	S	A	T
H	U	O	B	R	E	A	K	F	A	S	T	W	E
C	R	F	K	N	R	B	I	G	M	A	C	T	L
N	G	F	U	C	H	M	A	E	R	C	E	C	I
E	E	E	H	A	P	P	Y	M	E	A	L	S	F
R	R	E	G	G	M	C	M	U	F	F	I	N	H
F	S	R	E	G	R	U	B	M	A	H	T	J	S
A	D	O	S	E	H	C	I	W	D	N	A	S	I
Y	S	N	A	C	K	W	R	A	P	I	E	S	F
N	E	K	C	I	H	C	C	M	C	C	A	F	E

Solution on Page 314

AIRCRAFT
AIRLINES
AIRPORTS
AIRSPACE
ALTITUDE
APPROACH
ARRIVAL
AVIATION
BROADCAST
CALL SIGN
CLEARANCE
COMPUTERS
CONTACT
CRASH
DEFENSE
DELAYS
DEPARTURE
DIRECTION
FAA
FLIGHTS
FLOW
GROUND
LANDING
LANGUAGE
MILITARY
PILOTS
RUNWAYS
SAFETY
SECURITY
TAKEOFF
TAXI
TECHNOLOGY
TERMINAL
TOWERS

Air Traffic Control

T	S	S	X	Z	T	C	A	T	N	O	C	O	P
A	E	T	D	R	C	A	F	P	I	L	O	T	S
K	N	R	H	I	F	A	S	R	E	W	O	T	L
E	I	O	S	D	R	E	C	A	P	S	R	I	A
O	L	P	A	C	T	E	R	M	I	N	A	L	N
F	R	R	R	T	S	A	C	D	A	O	R	B	G
F	I	I	C	E	N	O	I	T	A	I	V	A	U
D	A	A	D	C	A	L	L	S	I	G	N	L	A
E	P	S	E	H	R	Y	D	R	Y	O	D	A	G
F	P	Y	P	N	R	R	E	E	T	S	N	N	E
E	R	A	A	O	I	A	L	T	I	T	U	D	E
N	O	W	R	L	V	T	A	U	R	H	O	I	I
S	A	N	T	O	A	I	Y	P	U	G	R	N	X
E	C	U	U	G	L	L	S	M	C	I	G	G	A
F	H	R	R	Y	P	I	B	O	E	L	W	Z	T
S	A	F	E	T	Y	M	N	C	S	F	L	O	W

Solution on Page 315

ANACONDA
ANIMALS
ARGENTINA
BEACHES
BOLIVIA
BRAZIL
CHILE
COCAMA
COLOMBIA
CONTINENT
COUNTRY
CUISINE
CULTURE
ECUADOR
GOLD
GUYANA
HISTORY
INCAS
INDIANS
JAGUAR
LANDMASS
LATIN
LIMA
LLAMAS
PARAGUAY
PERU
PIRANHA
QUECHUA
RIO
SAMBA
SPANISH
SURINAME
TOURISM
TRAVEL
TRINIDAD
URUGUAY
VALDIVIA
VENEZUELA

Explore South America

E	L	A	T	I	N	O	T	R	A	V	E	L	I
R	O	D	A	U	C	E	L	I	H	C	I	L	D
U	C	L	B	R	A	Z	I	L	V	M	C	A	A
T	B	O	L	I	V	I	A	A	A	I	G	M	D
L	T	G	C	S	S	N	N	R	L	N	S	A	I
U	O	C	Y	A	D	A	A	G	D	D	V	S	N
C	U	U	Y	M	M	L	C	E	I	I	E	P	I
O	R	I	A	B	U	A	O	N	V	A	N	A	R
U	I	S	U	A	C	O	N	T	I	N	E	N	T
N	S	I	G	H	R	Y	D	I	A	S	Z	I	A
T	M	N	A	I	E	M	A	N	I	R	U	S	U
R	H	E	R	S	E	H	C	A	E	B	E	H	H
Y	K	V	A	T	B	A	I	B	M	O	L	O	C
U	R	E	P	O	S	L	A	M	I	N	A	I	E
A	H	N	A	R	I	P	Y	A	U	G	U	R	U
O	A	N	A	Y	U	G	R	A	U	G	A	J	Q

Solution on Page 315

AIR
BELL
BLACK
BOILER
BUFFERS
CARS
CHASSIS
COAL
CREW
DIESEL
DRIVER
ENGINEER
EXHAUST
FAST
FIREBOX
FREIGHT
FUEL
GEARS
HEAT
HISTORICAL
INVENTION
LOCOMOTIVE
PASSENGER
PISTON
POLLUTION
POWER
PRESSURE
RAILROAD
RAILWAYS
SPEED
STATION
STOKERS
TECHNOLOGY
TENDER
TRAVEL
VALVES
WHEELS
WHISTLES
WOOD

Steam Train

T	A	E	H	R	T	H	G	I	E	R	F	D	R
T	T	X	O	B	E	R	I	F	U	E	L	E	A
L	R	S	S	U	C	E	B	E	L	L	V	E	S
O	A	A	A	F	H	I	N	F	C	I	T	P	L
C	C	C	V	F	N	N	E	I	R	O	E	S	E
O	K	A	I	E	O	V	X	D	G	B	N	L	E
M	P	V	R	R	L	E	H	A	O	N	D	Q	H
O	O	A	Q	S	O	N	A	O	C	S	E	B	W
T	L	L	S	V	G	T	U	R	O	R	R	L	L
I	L	V	C	S	Y	I	S	L	A	E	U	A	U
V	U	E	H	R	E	O	T	I	L	K	S	C	P
E	T	S	A	A	E	N	L	A	H	O	S	K	I
D	I	E	S	E	L	W	G	R	N	T	E	D	S
O	O	W	S	G	A	K	O	E	I	S	R	Y	T
O	N	I	I	Y	Q	T	W	P	R	I	P	E	O
W	H	I	S	T	L	E	S	T	A	T	I	O	N

Solution on Page 315

ALGAE
BAIKAL
BASS
CLEAR
COOL
CRATER
DAM
DEEP
DEPTH
ECOSYSTEM
ERIE
FISH
FLOW
FUN
GLACIAL
GREAT
HURON
ICE
INLAND
LARGE
MICHIGAN
MOSS
MOUNTAIN
NATURAL
ONTARIO
PLANTS
PONDS
RECREATION
RESERVOIR
RIVERS
SALT WATER
SAND
SHORE
SKI
STREAMS
SUMMER
SUPERIOR
TURTLE
VALLEY
WET

At the Lake

K	D	N	A	L	N	I	J	D	Q	B	D	Q	F
K	S	A	M	O	U	N	T	A	I	N	A	U	E
P	U	T	E	A	G	L	A	M	B	M	R	S	A
O	M	U	S	A	N	D	N	G	A	K	G	S	S
N	M	R	E	S	E	R	V	O	I	R	L	K	T
D	E	A	E	E	Z	G	T	R	K	H	A	I	R
S	R	L	P	C	N	U	E	E	A	M	C	O	E
S	H	O	R	E	R	T	G	T	L	E	I	I	A
Z	M	U	I	T	A	E	R	A	E	T	A	R	M
F	G	D	L	R	G	I	A	W	D	S	L	A	S
S	K	E	C	I	E	R	L	T	C	Y	T	T	T
O	B	P	O	V	A	P	E	L	I	S	F	N	N
G	F	T	O	E	E	W	U	A	Y	O	U	O	A
U	A	H	L	R	M	O	S	S	T	C	N	R	L
L	F	C	I	S	A	V	A	L	L	E	Y	U	P
R	Z	E	E	C	H	W	O	L	F	I	S	H	K

Solution on Page 315

AGENT
AIRCRAFT
AIRPLANES
AIRPORT
AMERICAN
ARRIVAL
ATTENDANT
AVIATION
BAGGAGE
BOEING
CABIN
CAPTAIN
CREW
DEPARTURE
ECONOMY
FLIGHT
FREIGHT
FUEL
GATE
JETBLUE
LUGGAGE
NORTHWEST
PASSENGERS
PASSPORT
PILOTS
PRICES
RUNWAY
SAFETY
SCHEDULE
SECURITY
SERVICES
SKY
SOUTHWEST
TERMINAL
TICKETS
US AIRWAYS

Airlines

E	U	L	B	T	E	J	Y	T	E	F	A	S	F
C	N	A	G	E	N	T	H	G	I	E	R	F	U
R	O	V	V	N	R	G	S	E	C	I	R	P	E
E	I	I	Q	O	I	F	E	G	A	G	G	U	L
W	T	R	P	L	R	U	N	W	A	Y	K	S	A
N	A	R	F	A	T	T	E	N	D	A	N	T	N
I	I	A	Y	U	S	A	I	R	W	A	Y	S	I
A	V	Y	T	W	E	S	D	X	B	E	S	E	M
T	A	M	I	A	N	T	E	G	A	L	E	W	R
P	M	O	R	I	A	E	P	N	G	U	C	H	E
A	E	N	U	R	L	K	A	I	G	D	I	T	T
C	R	O	C	C	P	C	R	E	A	E	V	U	A
A	I	C	E	R	R	I	T	O	G	H	R	O	G
B	C	E	S	A	I	T	U	B	E	C	E	S	Y
I	A	I	K	F	A	T	R	O	P	S	S	A	P
N	N	O	R	T	H	W	E	S	T	O	L	I	P

Solution on Page 316

AUTO
BICYCLE
BMX
BOAT
CAMEL
CYCLING
DERBY
DRAG
FOOT
GREYHOUND
HORSE
KART
MARATHON
MOTOCROSS
MOTORCYCLE
MOTORSPORT
OFF ROAD
OLYMPICS
RALLY
RELAY
ROWING
RUNNING
SAILING
SKATING
SKIING
SLED DOG
SNOWMOBILE
SPEED
SPRINT
STOCK CAR
SWIMMING
TOUR
TRACK

At the Races

S	K	I	I	N	G	A	T	S	P	E	E	D	C
W	I	T	T	R	A	C	K	G	P	H	V	B	J
I	E	X	X	E	Y	G	Y	H	O	R	S	E	J
M	D	G	H	C	L	L	N	L	K	A	I	P	M
M	F	N	L	N	L	I	Y	I	M	U	Q	N	O
I	O	I	U	A	Q	M	B	A	W	T	C	D	T
N	N	T	R	O	P	S	R	O	T	O	M	Y	O
G	F	A	O	I	H	A	L	Y	M	Y	R	V	C
N	O	K	C	R	T	Y	D	E	A	W	N	L	R
I	O	S	Z	H	C	Y	E	L	D	U	O	A	O
N	T	A	O	B	B	Y	E	R	Q	D	C	N	S
N	R	N	M	R	D	R	C	B	G	K	O	M	S
U	A	X	E	C	A	M	E	L	C	A	E	G	A
R	K	D	A	O	R	F	F	O	E	V	R	S	P
C	K	V	B	R	U	O	T	B	I	R	X	D	V
G	N	I	L	I	A	S	B	I	C	Y	C	L	E

Solution on Page 316

ACTIVITIES
ADMISSION
ANCIENT
ANTIQUE
ARTIFACTS
ARTISTIC
CASES
CHILDREN
COLLECTION
CULTURE
CURATOR
DINOSAURS
DISPLAYS
EDUCATION
EXHIBITS
FAMOUS
GALLERY
HISTORICAL
LEARNING
MODERN
NATURAL
OBJECTS
OLD
PAINTINGS
PUBLIC
RARE
SCIENTIFIC
SCULPTURES
TOURS
TREASURES
VISITORS

Going to Museums

E	B	C	I	F	I	T	N	E	I	C	S	O	X
R	E	U	C	A	N	T	I	Q	U	E	R	A	R
U	N	T	A	P	A	I	N	T	I	N	G	S	J
T	A	B	S	C	U	L	P	T	U	R	E	S	G
L	T	A	E	E	X	H	I	B	I	T	S	U	A
U	U	R	S	S	H	V	C	U	R	A	T	O	R
C	R	T	N	O	I	T	C	E	L	L	O	C	T
D	A	I	D	T	S	R	O	T	I	S	I	V	I
V	L	F	C	L	T	R	E	A	S	U	R	E	S
N	E	A	D	N	O	I	S	S	I	M	D	A	T
N	A	C	E	S	R	U	A	S	O	N	I	D	I
R	R	T	N	O	I	T	A	C	U	D	E	A	C
E	N	S	A	N	C	I	E	N	T	O	U	R	S
D	I	S	P	L	A	Y	S	T	C	E	J	B	O
O	N	E	R	D	L	I	H	C	I	L	B	U	P
M	G	A	L	L	E	R	Y	F	A	M	O	U	S

Solution on Page 316

BACKSTROKE
CHEMICALS
CHILDREN
CHLORINE
CLEANING
CONCRETE
COOL
DECK
DEEP END
DEPTH
DIVING
EXERCISE
FILTER
FLOATING
FUN
HEATED
HOT TUB
INDOOR
KIDS
LADDERS
LANES
LAPS
LOUNGE
OUTDOOR
PUMP
RECREATION
RELAXING
SHALLOW
SKIMMER
SPLASH
SUMMER
SWIMMERS
SWIMSUIT
TILE
WADING
WATER POLO
WET

Motel Pool

G	F	L	J	G	N	I	T	A	O	L	F	L	E
N	G	A	K	N	R	C	S	R	E	D	D	A	L
I	N	P	M	I	E	H	K	O	X	L	E	N	I
D	I	S	D	N	M	E	S	L	E	I	P	E	T
A	X	S	E	A	M	M	W	O	R	E	T	S	R
W	A	B	T	E	U	I	I	P	C	N	H	E	Y
D	L	S	A	L	S	C	M	R	I	I	C	L	C
I	E	R	E	C	R	A	S	E	S	R	O	H	L
V	R	E	H	E	K	L	U	T	E	O	I	O	O
I	O	M	P	T	R	S	I	A	C	L	S	T	U
N	O	M	H	E	K	E	T	W	D	H	K	T	N
G	D	I	S	R	N	I	T	R	A	C	I	U	G
D	T	W	A	C	O	D	E	L	O	P	M	B	E
E	U	S	L	N	T	N	L	D	I	K	M	F	P
C	O	J	P	O	E	O	J	K	J	F	E	U	D
K	I	D	S	C	W	I	N	D	O	O	R	N	P

Solution on Page 316

ASPHALT
BRICKS
CARS
CEMENT
CINDERS
COMPOSITE
CONCRETE
CRACKS
GRANULAR
GRAVEL
HARD
HIGHWAY
HOT
ICY
LINES
MACADAM
MUD
PAVEMENT
PAVING
POTHOLE
RIDE
ROAD
ROCK
ROUGH
RUBBER
SALT
SAND
SLICK
SMOOTH
STONE
STREET
SURFACE
TARMAC
TRAFFIC
VEHICLES
WHITE
WOOD

Road Surface

Z	O	T	S	I	L	L	S	I	D	O	O	W	L
M	F	H	G	U	O	R	O	A	D	M	S	H	N
D	A	T	A	R	M	A	C	P	N	U	V	I	U
T	I	D	T	L	A	S	A	N	S	D	K	T	S
Z	N	Z	A	P	V	V	M	R	X	C	L	E	B
C	S	E	L	C	I	H	E	V	I	A	C	Y	G
R	T	L	M	N	A	D	V	L	H	C	O	A	O
A	R	O	G	E	N	M	S	P	C	D	N	W	M
C	E	H	B	I	V	U	S	B	A	R	C	H	S
K	E	T	C	W	R	A	L	U	N	A	R	G	K
S	T	O	C	F	Z	S	P	O	X	H	E	I	G
E	K	P	A	E	C	I	F	F	A	R	T	H	O
N	D	C	C	O	M	P	O	S	I	T	E	T	K
I	E	I	I	A	R	E	B	B	U	R	O	C	K
L	C	E	R	R	R	E	N	O	T	S	V	H	N
R	R	Y	B	W	B	S	H	T	O	O	M	S	Z

Solution on Page 317

ALPS
ARTISTS
BELGIUM
BONAPARTE
CHAMPAGNE
COUNTRY
CUISINE
CULTURE
ECONOMY
FOOD
FRANCISCA
GERMANY
GOVERNMENT
HISTORY
LANGUAGE
LITERATURE
LOIRE
LOUVRE
LOVE
LUXEMBOURG
LYON
MARIANNE
MUSEUM
NAPOLEON
PARLIAMENT
REVOLUTION
SEINE
SENATE
SPAIN
TOURISTS
TRAVEL
VERSAILLES
WINE

French Vacation

T	P	N	I	A	P	S	E	I	N	E	P	L	P
R	L	F	R	A	N	C	I	S	C	A	I	O	M
A	O	X	D	H	I	S	T	O	R	Y	N	U	U
V	I	R	G	N	A	P	O	L	E	O	N	V	E
E	R	A	O	R	X	M	I	U	I	J	W	R	S
L	E	R	V	A	U	A	A	T	T	E	I	E	U
Y	N	T	E	E	M	O	U	R	R	O	N	G	M
O	G	I	R	E	R	L	B	U	I	I	E	A	U
N	A	S	N	A	O	S	T	M	S	A	Y	U	I
G	P	T	M	V	P	A	A	I	E	R	N	G	G
E	M	S	E	X	R	A	U	I	T	X	Z	N	L
R	A	R	N	E	G	C	N	N	L	D	U	A	E
M	H	S	T	S	I	R	U	O	T	L	N	L	B
A	C	I	G	F	O	O	D	C	B	G	E	P	K
N	L	O	V	E	C	U	L	T	U	R	E	S	M
Y	M	O	N	O	C	E	T	A	N	E	S	L	T

Solution on Page 317

ADVENTURE
BACKPACK
CAJON PASS
CALIFORNIA
CANADA
CASCADE
DESERT
EQUESTRIAN
EXPLORE
FORESTS
HIKERS
HIKING
HISTORY
HORSES
LAKES
MAP
MEXICO
MOUNTAINS
OREGON
OUTDOORS
PARKS
PCT
RANGE
RECREATION
ROUTE
SCENIC
SEABOARD
SNOW
TERMINUS
TERRAIN
TRAILS
WASHINGTON
WEST
WILDERNESS
WILDLIFE
YOSEMITE

Pacific Crest Trail

Y	O	S	E	M	I	T	E	R	M	I	N	U	S
R	N	O	G	E	R	O	F	O	R	E	S	T	S
O	C	A	N	A	D	A	O	C	I	X	E	M	E
T	P	A	I	W	A	S	H	I	N	G	T	O	N
S	E	L	S	E	T	U	O	R	A	A	J	U	R
I	S	R	E	C	R	E	A	T	I	O	N	N	E
H	U	C	O	L	A	N	T	N	R	T	I	T	D
I	B	A	M	L	G	D	R	S	T	L	A	A	L
K	A	J	D	E	P	O	E	R	S	W	R	I	I
E	C	O	N	V	F	X	S	O	E	I	R	N	W
R	K	N	C	I	E	P	E	O	U	L	E	S	H
S	P	P	L	G	A	N	D	D	Q	D	T	C	I
B	A	A	A	R	P	C	T	T	E	L	S	E	K
Q	C	S	K	M	Z	A	O	U	K	I	E	N	I
Q	K	S	E	S	R	O	H	O	R	F	W	I	N
W	O	N	S	D	R	A	O	B	A	E	S	C	G

Solution on Page 317

ACCIDENTS
ALASKA
ARCTIC CAT
ATV
AVALANCHE
BOMBARDIER
COLD
DANGEROUS
DEEP SNOW
DRAG RACING
DRIVER
ENGINE
EXTREME
FAST
FOREST
FOUR STROKE
FUN
GASOLINE
ICE
JUMP
LAND
LOUD
MOTOR
MOUNTAIN
NOISE
PASSENGER
PATHS
POLARIS
RIDER
SKIS
SLED
SNOWCAT
SPEED
TRACKS
TRAILS
TRANSPORT
TRAVEL
VEHICLE
WINTER
YAMAHA

Snowmobile

P	G	Y	A	M	A	H	A	S	K	I	S	D	S
A	T	A	K	E	X	T	E	L	C	I	H	E	V
T	R	B	S	A	V	A	L	A	N	C	H	E	A
H	I	O	A	O	V	C	O	L	D	C	K	P	F
S	D	M	L	T	L	C	F	U	N	O	M	S	T
H	E	B	A	D	R	I	V	E	R	U	D	N	A
T	R	A	V	E	L	T	N	T	J	A	A	O	C
F	O	R	E	S	T	C	S	E	C	I	N	W	W
D	T	D	R	A	G	R	A	C	I	N	G	S	O
N	O	I	S	E	U	A	I	C	E	I	E	L	N
A	M	E	K	O	D	D	P	O	L	A	R	I	S
L	E	R	F	P	E	U	F	A	S	T	O	A	K
Y	T	R	A	N	S	P	O	R	T	N	U	R	C
W	I	N	T	E	R	D	E	L	S	U	S	T	A
P	A	S	S	E	N	G	E	R	A	O	M	Y	R
E	N	I	G	N	E	X	T	R	E	M	E	D	T

Solution on Page 317

ART
ATLANTIC
BASQUE
BEACH
CATHOLIC
CIVIL WAR
COAST
COUNTRY
CUISINE
CULTURE
DANCE
DEMOCRACY
EUROPE
EXPLORERS
FLAMENCO
FOOTBALL
FRANCO
GAZPACHO
HISTORY
IBIZA
KINGDOM
LATIN
MONARCHY
MUSIC
PAELLA
PENINSULA
PORTUGAL
PYRENEES
RICE
ROMANCE
SEVILLE
SPANIARDS
TAPAS
TRADITION
VALENCIA
WARM
WINE

Going to Spain

K	I	N	G	D	O	M	C	U	L	T	U	R	E
S	Y	R	T	N	U	O	C	U	I	A	D	L	U
R	D	A	N	C	E	C	H	O	I	P	R	A	Q
E	A	T	L	A	N	T	I	C	C	S	X	T	S
R	H	W	E	J	I	S	N	L	A	N	I	I	A
O	N	C	L	Q	W	E	D	P	O	P	A	N	B
L	F	O	L	I	L	B	E	A	C	H	Z	R	E
P	O	B	I	A	V	N	M	E	M	S	T	A	F
X	O	L	V	T	I	I	O	L	U	E	F	A	G
E	T	A	E	N	I	M	C	L	S	E	L	E	C
C	B	G	S	L	S	D	R	A	I	N	A	P	S
I	A	U	U	R	O	M	A	N	C	E	M	O	I
R	L	T	T	S	A	O	C	R	X	R	E	R	B
A	L	R	W	A	R	M	Y	L	T	Y	N	U	I
Y	R	O	T	S	I	H	U	K	C	P	C	E	Z
S	A	P	A	T	Y	H	C	R	A	N	O	M	A

Solution on Page 318

AIR SPORTS
AIRCRAFT
AIRPLANE
AVIATION
CONTROLS
DRAG
ENGINE
FIBERGLASS
FLIGHT
FLYING
GLIDING
HANG
HOBBY
LAND
LAUNCH
LIFT
MILITARY
MODELS
PAPER
PARACHUTE
PARAGLIDER
PILOT
RECREATION
RISING AIR
SAILPLANE
SOAR
TAIL
TOW
TRAINING
ULTRALIGHT
UNPOWERED
WEIGHT
WINGS

Glider Aircraft

R	T	F	A	R	C	R	I	A	X	A	J	Y	J
B	M	I	L	I	T	A	R	Y	Q	Y	F	B	S
S	W	B	E	T	R	G	N	I	Y	L	F	B	H
Z	T	E	V	N	O	I	T	A	I	V	A	O	Q
P	X	R	I	T	A	W	A	G	G	T	L	H	E
L	R	G	O	G	G	L	H	G	G	H	I	A	T
I	P	L	N	P	H	T	P	D	N	G	A	N	U
M	I	A	S	I	S	T	E	L	O	I	T	G	H
P	S	S	R	L	D	R	T	F	I	L	S	A	C
V	L	S	G	A	E	I	I	H	T	A	X	I	A
K	O	A	S	W	G	D	L	A	A	R	S	R	R
L	R	A	O	S	R	L	O	G	E	T	G	P	A
D	T	P	A	P	E	R	I	M	R	L	N	L	P
G	N	I	N	I	A	R	T	D	C	U	I	A	N
U	O	W	F	E	N	G	I	N	E	Q	W	N	J
H	C	N	U	A	L	A	N	D	R	R	V	E	T

Solution on Page 318

BOROUGH
CARS
CITIES
COMMUNITY
COMMUTING
DISTRICT
FAMILIES
FENCES
GRASS
HIGHWAYS
HOMES
HOUSEWIFE
HOUSING
LAND
LAWNS
MALLS
OPEN
OUTLYING
OUTSIDE
OUTSKIRTS
PARK
PEOPLE
PERFECT
POPULATION
QUIET
RICH
RURAL
SCHOOLS
SPRAWL
STREETS
STRIP MALL
SUBURBIA
TOWN
TRAFFIC
TREES
YARDS
ZONING

Suburbs

X	H	O	L	S	C	H	O	O	L	S	P	S	K
B	C	U	W	F	S	D	R	A	Y	O	A	S	G
P	I	T	A	A	S	R	R	A	U	I	E	P	F
E	R	S	R	M	A	U	W	T	B	M	O	Q	E
R	F	K	P	I	R	H	S	R	O	P	U	L	N
F	S	I	S	L	G	I	U	H	U	I	H	E	C
E	T	R	W	I	D	B	O	L	E	Y	P	O	E
C	E	T	H	E	U	U	A	T	T	O	M	P	S
T	E	S	C	S	S	T	R	I	P	M	A	L	L
R	R	D	C	I	I	U	N	X	U	R	A	B	W
A	T	B	N	O	R	U	O	T	K	W	N	O	E
F	S	G	N	A	M	T	I	H	N	M	W	R	L
F	R	W	B	M	L	N	S	S	P	A	O	O	P
I	A	D	O	B	G	G	N	I	Y	L	T	U	O
C	C	C	I	T	I	E	S	V	D	L	C	G	E
Z	O	N	I	N	G	T	R	E	E	S	I	H	P

Solution on Page 318

ACTIVITIES
AMENITIES
ATTRACTION
BARS
BEACHES
CARIBBEAN
CASINO
CLUB MED
DINING
EXPENSIVE
FOOD
FOREIGN
FRONT DESK
GOLF
GUESTS
HEALTH
HOLIDAYS
HOTELS
INCLUSIVE
ISLAND
MOUNTAIN
PARADISE
POOL
RECREATION
RELAXATION
RESTAURANT
SERVICE
SHOPPING
SKI RESORT
SKIING
SPA
SUN
SWIMMING
VACATION

Resort

C	A	S	I	N	O	I	T	A	C	A	V	I	G
F	L	O	G	O	A	G	N	I	I	K	S	C	U
G	N	I	N	I	D	M	P	O	O	L	L	A	E
S	C	B	T	T	H	F	E	N	A	U	C	V	S
Y	O	E	R	A	E	K	U	N	B	T	I	L	T
A	N	A	O	X	A	S	D	M	I	S	E	N	S
D	C	C	S	A	L	E	E	V	U	T	O	G	E
I	A	H	E	L	T	D	I	L	O	I	I	I	V
L	R	E	R	E	H	T	C	H	T	S	S	E	I
O	I	S	I	R	I	N	R	A	P	G	H	R	S
H	B	I	K	E	I	O	E	A	Z	F	O	O	N
I	B	D	S	S	E	R	V	I	C	E	P	F	E
S	E	A	X	S	C	F	O	O	D	T	P	P	P
V	A	R	R	E	M	O	U	N	T	A	I	N	X
T	N	A	R	U	A	T	S	E	R	L	N	O	E
I	B	P	N	S	W	I	M	M	I	N	G	L	N

Solution on Page 318

ALAMO
AMUSEMENT
BEACHES
BOARDWALK
BUILDING
CALIFORNIA
CANYON
CAPE COD
CASINOS
CHICAGO
DISNEYLAND
EVERGLADES
FLORIDA
GAMBLING
HISTORY
HOLLYWOOD
LANDMARKS
LAS VEGAS
MONUMENTS
MOUNTAINS
MUSEUMS
NAVY PIER
NEW YORK
NIAGARA
ORLANDO
PARKS
PLAINS
VACATION
YOSEMITE
ZOOS

Tourist Attractions

R	A	I	N	R	O	F	I	L	A	C	N	H	A
S	M	U	E	S	U	M	Z	O	O	S	L	O	R
B	U	I	L	D	I	N	G	O	O	N	A	L	A
A	S	N	I	A	T	N	U	O	M	I	S	L	G
D	E	E	J	N	O	I	T	A	C	A	V	Y	A
I	M	W	C	A	S	I	N	O	S	L	E	W	I
R	E	Y	O	S	E	M	I	T	E	P	G	O	N
O	N	O	U	K	K	L	A	W	D	R	A	O	B
L	T	R	G	N	I	L	B	M	A	G	S	D	E
F	H	K	D	I	S	N	E	Y	L	A	N	D	A
C	I	S	A	C	H	I	C	A	G	O	C	D	C
A	S	K	L	A	N	D	M	A	R	K	S	D	H
N	T	R	A	M	O	N	U	M	E	N	T	S	E
Y	O	A	M	R	E	I	P	Y	V	A	N	K	S
O	R	P	O	T	H	C	A	P	E	C	O	D	Q
N	Y	O	R	L	A	N	D	O	D	D	Q	B	S

Solution on Page 319

ADVENTURE
AIRPLANES
ATTRACTION
AUTOMOBILE
BEACH
BUSINESS
CAMP
COMMUTING
COUNTRIES
DISCOVERY
EUROPE
GEOGRAPHY
HIKING
HOLIDAY
HOTEL
LOCATIONS
MAPS
MOTEL
MOVEMENT
PACKING
PASSPORT
RECREATION
RELAXATION
ROUNDTRIP
SHIPS
STAY
TOURIST
TRAINS
TRANSPORT
VACATION
VISIT
WALKING

Let's Go!

P	V	A	C	A	T	I	O	N	K	S	T	C	P
A	E	U	R	O	P	E	R	C	N	R	W	A	I
C	I	T	M	A	P	S	O	O	O	A	S	E	R
K	H	O	T	E	L	M	I	P	L	S	R	S	T
I	P	M	A	C	M	T	S	K	P	U	H	A	D
N	C	O	J	U	A	N	I	O	T	I	S	I	N
G	O	B	T	C	A	N	R	N	P	N	S	R	U
E	U	I	O	R	G	T	E	S	I	C	E	P	O
O	N	L	T	H	T	V	C	A	O	L	S	L	R
G	T	E	O	C	D	N	R	V	A	G	G	A	Y
R	R	I	U	A	A	T	E	X	I	N	U	N	A
A	I	M	R	E	D	R	A	M	I	S	D	E	D
P	E	M	I	B	Y	T	T	K	E	M	I	S	I
H	S	T	S	A	I	J	I	T	E	V	M	T	L
Y	L	E	T	O	M	H	O	H	A	I	O	A	O
A	B	S	N	S	S	E	N	I	S	U	B	M	H

Solution on Page 319

ACTIVITIES
ADVENTURER
BOLD
BOOKS
CLIMBING
DANGER
DARING
ENCOUNTER
EXCITEMENT
EXCITING
EXOTIC
EXPERIENCE
EXPLORING
EXTREME
FEAR
HIKING
JOURNEY
KNOWLEDGE
LAND
LEARNING
LIFE
NEW
PHYSICAL
RACING
RECREATION
RISKY
SKYDIVING
TRAVEL
UNUSUAL

Adventure Travel

N	W	Q	A	N	E	X	C	I	T	I	N	G	X
Y	K	S	I	R	W	Y	E	N	R	U	O	J	S
D	L	O	B	E	X	P	E	R	I	E	N	C	E
N	A	O	K	R	O	M	J	F	Q	W	G	X	G
A	L	R	V	U	E	O	D	A	N	G	E	R	N
L	S	E	I	T	I	V	I	T	C	A	N	N	I
I	I	B	I	N	O	I	T	A	E	R	C	E	R
F	R	C	E	E	G	O	L	G	P	A	O	X	O
E	X	W	A	V	L	E	D	C	F	C	U	O	L
E	N	U	A	D	V	E	L	E	N	I	N	T	P
M	Z	N	W	A	L	I	A	A	W	N	T	I	X
E	H	V	R	W	M	R	G	R	U	G	E	C	E
R	X	T	O	B	O	O	K	S	N	S	R	R	X
T	G	N	I	V	I	D	Y	K	S	I	U	G	L
X	K	N	P	H	Y	S	I	C	A	L	N	N	B
E	G	N	I	K	I	H	Q	Y	L	Q	R	G	U

Solution on Page 319

BICYCLES
BIKE
CANOEING
CART
CLIMBING
CRAWLING
CYCLING
ENERGY
EXERCISE
GONDOLA
HANDCAR
ICE SKATE
KAYAKING
LEISURE
MUSCLES
PEDAL
PUSHING
RICKSHAW
ROW BOAT
ROWING
RUNNING
SCOOTER
SKATEBOARD
SPRINTING
SWIMMING
TECHNOLOGY
TRANSPORT
TRICYCLE
UNICYCLE
WALKING
WHEELCHAIR

Human Powered

S	E	L	C	S	U	M	K	E	N	E	R	G	Y
W	G	N	I	K	L	A	W	R	O	W	I	N	G
I	S	R	V	H	Y	A	L	O	D	N	O	G	Z
M	R	E	Y	A	H	A	N	D	C	A	R	C	F
M	U	S	K	S	B	I	C	Y	C	L	E	S	U
I	N	I	K	R	E	T	O	O	C	S	K	N	N
N	N	C	W	H	E	E	L	C	H	A	I	R	I
G	I	R	L	S	P	R	I	N	T	I	N	G	C
R	N	E	E	T	A	K	S	E	C	I	Z	N	Y
O	G	X	F	G	N	I	B	M	I	L	C	I	C
W	T	E	C	H	N	O	L	O	G	Y	W	L	L
B	I	K	E	C	A	N	O	E	I	N	G	W	E
O	D	P	T	R	O	P	S	N	A	R	T	A	T
A	L	A	D	E	P	K	L	E	I	S	U	R	E
T	R	I	C	Y	C	L	E	T	S	W	A	C	A
P	U	S	H	I	N	G	N	I	L	C	Y	C	D

Solution on Page 319

ALEXANDRIA
AMERICA
ARLINGTON
ATTRACTION
COLONIAL
DISTILLERY
ESTATE
FAIRFAX
FAMILY
FARM
GARDENS
GEORGE
GIFT SHOP
GROUNDS
HISTORICAL
HOME
HOUSE
LANDMARK
MANSION
MARTHA
MONUMENT
NATIONAL
PADDOCK
PARK
PLANTATION
PRESIDENT
PROPERTY
RESIDENCE
STABLE
TOMB
VIRGINIA
WASHINGTON
WOOD

Mount Vernon

T	H	P	A	R	K	R	A	M	D	N	A	L	P
G	E	O	R	G	E	C	N	E	D	I	S	E	R
H	D	I	S	T	I	L	L	E	R	Y	B	S	O
V	I	R	G	I	N	I	A	D	N	M	Q	U	P
A	Y	S	S	O	F	W	N	H	O	M	T	O	E
C	H	A	T	T	R	A	C	T	I	O	N	H	R
I	B	H	A	O	X	S	O	B	T	N	E	L	T
R	L	T	B	E	R	H	G	M	A	U	D	A	Y
E	A	R	L	O	F	I	A	M	T	M	I	N	F
M	I	A	E	A	F	N	C	R	N	E	S	O	A
A	N	M	M	T	S	G	E	A	A	N	E	I	I
J	O	I	S	I	E	T	L	F	L	T	R	T	R
V	L	H	O	M	A	O	I	W	P	W	P	A	F
Y	O	N	O	T	G	N	I	L	R	A	O	N	A
P	C	H	S	K	K	C	O	D	D	A	P	O	X
S	N	E	D	R	A	G	R	O	U	N	D	S	D

Solution on Page 320

ARCTIC OCEAN
ATLANTIC OCEAN
BLUE
BOAT
CORAL
CRABS
CURRENTS
DEEP
DEPTH
DOLPHINS
EXPLORATION
FLOOR
GULF
HURRICANE
HYDROSPHERE
INDIAN OCEAN
ISLANDS
LARGE
MARINE
OCEANOGRAPHY
PACIFIC OCEAN
PLANKTON
PORT
SALINE
SALT WATER
SEA LIFE
SHIP
SHORE
SOUTHERN OCEAN
SURFACE
TRAVEL
TRENCHES
VAST
WHALES

Ocean Voyage

T	E	G	I	I	S	L	A	N	D	S	X	N	E
R	R	T	U	N	L	E	V	A	R	T	A	T	X
D	E	O	R	L	D	P	E	E	D	E	S	R	P
E	H	N	P	E	F	I	F	C	C	A	U	E	L
P	P	T	I	L	N	I	A	O	V	M	R	T	O
T	S	A	O	L	L	C	C	N	A	F	F	A	R
H	O	O	C	A	A	I	H	R	O	P	A	W	A
U	R	B	E	I	T	S	I	E	I	C	C	T	T
R	D	S	D	N	F	N	W	H	S	B	E	L	I
R	Y	X	A	Q	E	I	S	T	G	L	S	A	O
I	H	L	A	R	G	E	C	U	W	U	B	S	N
C	T	A	R	C	T	I	C	O	C	E	A	N	N
A	C	U	R	R	E	N	T	S	C	O	R	A	L
N	Y	H	P	A	R	G	O	N	A	E	C	O	F
E	R	O	H	S	L	N	O	T	K	N	A	L	P
W	H	A	L	E	S	D	O	L	P	H	I	N	S

Solution on Page 320

ANIMALS
ATTRACTIONS
BISON
BOATING
BUFFALO
CABIN
CALDERA
CAMPING
DEER
DESTINATION
ECOSYSTEMS
ELK
FAMOUS
FLORA
GEOTHERMAL
HIKING
HOT SPRINGS
IDAHO
LAKES
MOOSE
MOUNTAINS
NATURE
OLD FAITHFUL
PROTECTED
RIVERS
TOURISTS
TRAILS
VISITORS
WATERFALLS
WILDERNESS
WILDLIFE
WOLVES

Yellowstone National Park

T	G	Z	S	S	E	N	R	E	D	L	I	W	M
R	R	C	H	L	G	L	A	K	E	S	O	O	M
A	E	A	W	U	N	N	Z	T	N	R	U	L	C
I	S	M	M	F	I	O	I	O	U	N	E	V	A
L	L	P	S	H	B	I	I	R	T	R	G	E	L
S	L	I	T	T	A	T	V	A	P	V	E	S	D
L	A	N	S	I	C	A	I	B	L	S	O	E	E
A	F	G	I	A	S	N	C	O	L	D	T	C	R
M	R	S	R	F	S	I	N	A	E	E	H	O	A
I	E	T	U	D	M	T	H	T	F	B	E	S	H
N	T	L	O	L	N	S	C	I	A	U	R	Y	I
A	A	Y	T	O	R	E	L	N	M	F	M	S	K
R	W	Q	S	E	T	D	L	G	O	F	A	T	I
O	U	I	V	O	L	M	M	K	U	A	L	E	N
L	B	I	R	I	D	A	H	O	S	L	E	M	G
F	R	P	W	R	V	I	S	I	T	O	R	S	B

Solution on Page 320

APPETIZER
BANQUET
BREAKFAST
BRUNCH
BUFFET
CAFETERIAS
COOKING
COURSE
CUISINE
DESSERT
DINNER
DRINK
EATING
FAST FOOD
FRUIT
FULL
HOLIDAYS
HOMES
KITCHEN
LEFTOVERS
LIGHT
LUNCH
MEAT
NUTRITION
PICNIC
PREPARE
RESTAURANT
SALAD
SHARE
SIDE DISH
SNACK
SOUP
SUPPER
VEGETABLE
WINE

Stop for a Bite

P	C	P	B	C	D	E	T	D	I	N	N	E	R
I	S	U	A	G	S	R	E	V	O	T	F	E	L
C	Y	O	N	D	E	A	F	S	Y	H	Z	L	F
N	A	S	Q	O	M	P	F	I	U	I	J	B	W
I	D	F	U	O	O	E	U	D	T	P	F	A	K
C	I	K	E	F	H	R	B	E	N	D	P	T	N
K	L	I	T	T	B	P	P	D	A	X	H	E	I
C	O	T	N	S	E	P	E	I	R	D	C	G	R
A	H	C	U	A	A	R	N	S	U	E	N	E	D
N	P	H	T	F	X	I	I	H	A	S	U	V	X
S	D	E	R	A	H	S	W	A	T	S	L	G	H
J	G	N	I	K	O	O	C	D	S	E	L	D	F
M	E	A	T	S	A	F	K	A	E	R	B	R	U
K	E	N	I	S	I	U	C	L	R	T	U	W	L
K	T	C	O	U	R	S	E	A	T	I	N	G	L
J	H	C	N	U	R	B	Y	S	T	H	G	I	L

Solution on Page 320

ATHLETICS
CARDIO
DISTANCE
ENDURANCE
ENERGY
EVENTS
EXERCISE
FAST
FEET
FITNESS
FOOT
HEALTH
HURDLES
JOGGING
KNEE
LAPS
LEGS
LOCOMOTION
MARATHONS
MILE
MUSCLE
OLYMPICS
PACE
QUADRICEPS
RACING
RUN
SHOES
SOCKS
SPEED
SPORTS
SPRINTING
STREET
STRIDE
SWEAT
TIME
TRAINING
TREADMILL
WALKING

Run Away

S	G	E	L	T	I	M	E	D	X	Y	B	V	X
O	N	R	S	T	R	O	P	S	T	N	E	V	E
C	I	P	A	C	E	N	D	U	R	A	N	C	E
K	G	D	B	Q	E	E	H	V	O	O	N	E	S
S	G	F	R	U	S	U	R	L	I	A	N	A	I
W	O	I	U	A	R	N	Y	T	T	K	T	G	C
E	J	T	N	D	C	M	O	S	S	H	N	L	R
A	F	N	L	R	P	M	I	H	L	I	A	L	E
T	A	E	E	I	O	D	D	E	T	P	I	I	X
E	S	S	C	C	S	E	T	N	S	A	U	M	E
E	T	S	O	E	E	I	I	Y	E	Q	R	D	B
F	D	L	O	P	C	R	G	N	I	K	L	A	W
C	J	H	S	S	P	R	M	U	S	C	L	E	M
O	S	U	Q	S	E	G	N	I	N	I	A	R	T
R	A	C	I	N	G	S	S	H	E	A	L	T	H
M	I	L	E	D	I	R	T	S	F	O	O	T	I

Solution on Page 321

AIRPLANE
ALCOHOL
BEEF
BEVERAGE
BLAND
BOX
BREAKFAST
CART
CATERING
CHICKEN
CHOICE
COFFEE
CUTLERY
DESSERT
DRINK
ECONOMY
FISH
FOOD
FREE
FROZEN
HOT
IN-FLIGHT
KITCHENS
KOSHER
LUNCH
MEAT
NAPKIN
PEPPER
PLASTIC
PRETZELS
QUALITY
ROLL
SALT
SERVICE
SMALL
SNACK
SPORK
STEAK
TRAVEL
WATER

Airline Meals

Q	V	E	K	G	G	T	O	H	C	O	I	R	Q
R	F	R	O	Z	E	N	C	H	O	I	C	E	S
R	F	I	S	H	U	N	I	E	X	N	J	P	J
X	O	B	H	E	U	C	G	R	I	Y	O	P	E
K	O	D	E	L	K	A	N	K	E	R	T	E	C
A	D	E	R	E	R	R	P	O	K	T	S	P	I
E	S	S	N	E	N	A	L	P	R	I	A	N	V
T	B	S	V	M	N	V	C	N	A	D	F	C	R
S	P	E	C	O	N	O	M	Y	N	L	K	A	E
A	B	R	E	R	F	A	T	A	I	I	A	R	S
L	M	T	E	F	I	I	L	G	T	K	E	T	N
T	E	T	E	T	L	B	H	C	N	W	R	R	A
O	A	E	W	A	Z	T	H	I	O	F	B	A	C
W	T	C	U	T	L	E	R	Y	B	H	R	V	K
K	F	Q	Q	J	N	D	L	L	O	R	O	E	W
L	L	A	M	S	P	L	A	S	T	I	C	L	E

Solution on Page 321

ASHEVILLE
BARBECUE
BASKETBALL
BEACHES
BOBCATS
CARDINAL
CAROLINA
CHAPEL HILL
COLONY
CONFEDERATE
COTTON
DOGWOOD
EAST COAST
FLIGHT
FORT BRAGG
FURNITURE
GOLF
GREENSBORO
HISTORIC
HURRICANES
KITTY HAWK
MT. MITCHELL
OUTER BANKS
PANTHERS
PINE
RALEIGH
SAND
SOUTHERN
WILMINGTON

North Carolina

S	K	J	N	O	T	G	N	I	M	L	I	W	Q
E	I	O	E	F	R	S	O	U	T	H	E	R	N
N	T	T	U	E	Q	O	A	F	L	I	G	H	T
A	T	W	S	T	A	C	B	O	B	M	S	G	P
C	Y	G	T	A	E	P	I	S	C	B	D	I	E
I	H	G	E	R	F	R	A	R	N	T	N	E	L
R	A	A	H	E	H	S	B	N	O	E	S	L	B
R	W	R	P	D	E	E	E	A	T	T	E	A	H
U	K	B	C	E	F	R	U	H	N	H	S	R	E
H	D	T	A	F	L	J	U	C	C	K	E	I	G
C	O	R	R	N	O	H	C	T	E	A	S	R	H
O	O	O	D	O	G	K	I	T	I	B	E	J	S
T	W	F	I	C	Y	M	B	L	G	N	R	B	X
T	G	F	N	F	T	A	N	I	L	O	R	A	C
O	O	D	A	M	L	C	O	L	O	N	Y	U	B
N	D	E	L	L	I	V	E	H	S	A	N	D	F

Solution on Page 321

BALLAST
BOILER
BOOSTER
BOXCAR
BUFFER
CABOOSE
CARS
COAL
COUPLER
DIESEL
EXPRESS
FIREBOX
FIREMAN
FLATCAR
FREIGHT
GAUGE
GONDOLA
HANDCAR
LANTERN
LINE
LOOP
PISTON
RAILCAR
RAILROAD
RAILWAY
ROUTE
SIGNAL
SLEEPER
SPIKES
STATIONS
STEEL
SUBWAY
SWITCH
TICKETS
TIES
TOKEN
TRACKS
TRAINS
WHEELS
WHISTLE

Railroad Words

D	I	E	S	E	L	A	N	G	I	S	E	I	T
A	A	B	T	O	K	E	N	K	V	C	F	F	M
O	P	O	O	L	R	A	C	X	O	B	I	T	J
R	E	O	D	R	E	F	F	U	B	R	R	S	W
L	G	S	S	S	E	R	P	X	E	A	E	E	H
I	U	T	S	A	L	L	A	B	I	I	M	K	E
A	A	E	N	A	E	L	O	N	T	L	A	I	E
R	G	R	O	R	E	X	S	C	Y	W	N	P	L
E	O	C	I	E	C	F	A	N	T	A	O	S	S
P	N	C	T	R	L	B	R	R	B	Y	T	T	B
E	D	S	A	A	O	A	A	E	O	G	S	E	G
E	O	E	T	O	C	C	I	T	I	B	I	K	L
L	L	C	S	D	K	A	L	N	L	G	P	C	I
S	A	E	N	S	T	R	C	A	E	B	H	I	N
R	Y	A	W	B	U	S	A	L	R	O	U	T	E
W	H	I	S	T	L	E	R	S	W	I	T	C	H

Solution on Page 321

AIRCRAFT
AIRPLANE
BICYCLES
BOATS
BRIDGES
BUSES
CARS
DEPOT
DRIVER
FARE
FERRY
FREIGHT
FUEL
GAS
GOODS
HIGHWAYS
HORSE
JET
METRO
MONORAIL
MOVEMENT
PEOPLE
PUBLIC
RAILROAD
ROADS
ROCKET
SAILBOAT
SHIPS
SPEED
TERMINALS
TRACKS
TRAFFIC
TRAINS
TRAVEL
TRUCKS
VAN
VEHICLES
WALKING
WATER
WHEELS

Getting Around

K	T	Z	X	M	P	F	U	E	L	A	S	E	G
W	H	E	E	L	S	E	E	V	T	D	B	N	T
S	S	T	J	N	M	D	O	R	E	V	I	R	D
F	R	E	I	G	H	T	A	P	R	K	C	H	T
O	E	A	G	Q	W	C	O	O	L	Y	Y	U	E
G	R	R	C	D	K	T	S	A	R	E	C	S	K
T	T	B	A	S	I	Y	W	P	U	B	L	I	C
M	A	R	T	F	A	R	C	R	I	A	E	S	O
E	O	L	A	W	Q	L	B	T	N	I	S	H	R
S	B	V	H	I	B	I	R	I	S	R	E	I	E
R	L	G	E	U	L	A	M	L	A	P	L	P	T
O	I	N	S	M	F	R	B	E	G	L	C	S	A
H	A	E	Y	F	E	O	O	V	O	A	I	V	W
V	S	C	I	T	C	N	A	A	O	N	H	M	Q
S	K	C	U	R	T	O	T	R	D	E	E	P	S
L	Z	Q	J	R	Q	M	S	T	S	E	V	G	J

Solution on Page 322

AIRPORT
AMUSEMENT PARK
ANIMAL KINGDOM
ATTRACTIONS
BEACH
CITY
DESTINATION
DISNEY WORLD
DOWNTOWN
ENTERTAINMENT
FAMILY
FUN
HEAT
HOTELS
HUMID
HURRICANE
MAGIC KINGDOM
METROPOLITAN
OCEAN
ORANGE COUNTY
ORLANDO MAGIC
RESORT
ROLLER COASTER
SENTINEL
SUN BELT
THEME PARKS
TRAVEL
WALT DISNEY

Orlando

H	U	R	R	I	C	A	N	E	T	A	E	H	D
M	N	W	O	T	N	W	O	D	H	T	D	V	E
O	O	S	U	N	B	E	L	T	E	T	L	K	S
R	Y	D	B	E	A	C	H	S	M	R	R	N	T
L	E	C	G	M	F	U	N	L	E	A	O	A	I
A	N	T	D	N	M	B	M	E	P	C	W	T	N
N	S	R	S	I	I	C	L	T	A	T	Y	I	A
D	I	O	D	A	I	K	N	O	R	I	E	L	T
O	D	P	Q	T	O	E	C	H	K	O	N	O	I
M	T	R	Y	R	M	C	G	I	S	N	S	P	O
A	L	I	L	E	V	A	R	T	G	S	I	O	N
G	A	A	S	T	R	O	S	E	R	A	D	R	A
I	W	U	Q	N	F	A	M	I	L	Y	M	T	E
C	M	Q	S	E	N	T	I	N	E	L	Q	E	C
A	N	I	M	A	L	K	I	N	G	D	O	M	O
G	P	Y	T	N	U	O	C	E	G	N	A	R	O

Solution on Page 322

AMERICAS
ATLANTIC
CAPTAIN
COLONIZER
DISCOVERY
ENGLAND
EUROPE
EXPEDITION
EXPLORER
FERDINAND
FLAT
GENOA
HISPANIOLA
HISTORY
HOLIDAY
INDIANS
ISABELLA
ITALIAN
NAVIGATOR
NEW WORLD
NINA
OCEAN
OCTOBER
PORTUGAL
QUEEN
SAILING
SEA
SHIPS
SPAIN
SPICES
TRADING
TRAVEL
VOYAGES

Christopher Columbus

C	Y	D	E	X	P	E	D	I	T	I	O	N	T
E	F	I	N	I	A	P	S	H	D	T	R	A	F
Z	L	S	D	A	G	R	K	I	L	A	S	V	A
E	A	C	N	I	N	A	O	S	R	L	N	I	E
U	T	O	A	V	I	I	A	T	O	I	A	G	S
R	H	V	L	C	L	C	D	O	W	A	I	A	P
O	O	E	G	G	I	E	S	R	W	N	D	T	I
P	L	R	N	R	A	T	V	Y	E	A	N	O	H
E	I	Y	E	I	S	O	N	A	N	F	I	R	S
F	D	M	K	Z	S	P	N	A	R	C	A	E	E
N	A	E	C	O	I	A	I	E	L	T	T	R	G
J	Y	Q	U	E	E	N	B	C	G	T	P	O	A
T	R	E	B	O	T	C	O	E	E	X	A	L	Y
Y	P	O	R	T	U	G	A	L	L	S	C	P	O
D	U	H	I	S	P	A	N	I	O	L	A	X	V
L	K	T	R	A	D	I	N	G	C	C	A	E	Y

Solution on Page 322

BANJO
BEBOP
BIG BAND
BOB DYLAN
BROADWAY
CHRISTIAN
CLASSICAL
CONCERTS
DANCE
DRUMS
FOLK
FUSION
GENRE
GOSPEL
GRUNGE
GUITAR
HARD ROCK
HAWAIIAN
HIP HOP
INDIE
JAZZ
MEMPHIS
MOTOWN
MTV
NASHVILLE
ORCHESTRA
PATRIOTIC
POP
PUNK ROCK
RADIO
RAGTIME
RECORD
REGGAE
RHYTHM
SINGERS
SOUL
SWING
SYMPHONY
TECHNO

Car Radio Music

R	E	S	I	H	P	M	E	M	E	D	K	L	V
M	A	M	O	T	O	W	N	F	C	N	C	B	G
H	G	U	T	F	H	R	U	O	N	A	O	Z	B
T	G	R	O	V	P	S	T	L	A	B	R	Z	E
Y	E	D	G	N	I	W	S	K	D	G	K	A	B
H	R	Y	N	O	H	P	M	Y	S	I	N	J	O
R	E	P	N	N	N	C	L	Q	C	B	U	N	P
A	C	M	B	A	A	A	E	S	L	E	P	A	A
T	O	W	I	R	N	S	I	T	A	I	O	I	T
I	R	H	P	T	O	N	H	T	S	D	I	I	R
U	D	R	O	S	G	A	N	V	S	N	D	A	I
G	O	S	P	E	L	A	D	J	I	I	A	W	O
E	J	S	R	H	C	B	R	W	C	L	R	A	T
N	N	S	K	C	O	R	D	R	A	H	L	H	I
R	A	L	G	R	U	N	G	E	L	Y	U	E	C
E	B	I	C	O	N	C	E	R	T	S	O	U	L

Solution on Page 322

APPETIZER
BALANCE
BANQUET
BREAKFAST
BRUNCH
BUFFET
CALORIE
CHEESE
CHEWING
COOK
CUISINE
DESSERT
DIET
DIGESTION
DINING
DINNER
DRINK
ENERGY
FRUIT
GROWTH
HEALTHY
HERBIVORE
HUNGER
INGESTION
INTAKE
LUNCH
NUTRITION
OBESITY
OMNIVORES
PASTA
PLATE
SNACKING
SWALLOWING
VEGETABLES

Eating on the Road

P	H	E	A	L	T	H	Y	U	M	E	F	P	Y
L	G	N	O	I	T	I	R	T	U	N	N	G	T
A	R	I	T	R	E	S	S	E	D	R	R	R	I
T	O	S	E	L	B	A	T	E	G	E	V	E	U
E	W	I	I	S	F	R	L	N	N	Z	L	G	R
U	T	U	D	K	E	D	I	E	D	I	N	N	F
Q	H	C	A	N	S	W	J	I	R	T	O	U	T
N	Z	E	N	M	O	E	N	B	I	E	I	H	A
A	R	I	R	L	G	I	R	N	N	P	T	C	Y
B	D	B	L	B	N	G	T	O	K	P	S	N	T
P	Q	A	E	G	I	A	N	S	V	A	E	U	I
A	W	L	S	W	K	V	V	I	E	I	G	L	S
S	W	A	E	E	C	O	O	K	W	G	N	Z	E
T	L	N	E	C	A	L	O	R	I	E	I	M	B
A	G	C	H	C	N	U	R	B	E	Y	H	D	O
U	F	E	C	F	S	B	U	F	F	E	T	C	Z

Solution on Page 323

AIR FORCE
APOLLO
ASTRONAUTS
BASE
CHALLENGER
COLUMBIA
COUNTDOWN
DISCOVERY
EXPLORE
FLIGHTS
FLORIDA
GEMINI
GOVERNMENT
HISTORY
KENNEDY
LAUNCH PAD
LIFTOFF
MARS
MERCURY
MISSIONS
MOON
NASA
ORBITER
ORLANDO
ROCKETS
SATELLITE
SATURN
SCIENCE
SHUTTLES
SKY
SPACE
TECHNOLOGY
TOURS
TRAINING

Kennedy Space Center

E	C	A	P	S	C	I	E	N	C	E	S	A	B
F	L	I	G	H	T	S	H	U	T	T	L	E	S
S	R	A	M	I	S	S	I	O	N	S	I	R	T
F	L	O	R	I	D	A	K	E	A	Y	F	O	E
A	P	O	L	L	O	A	M	Y	S	G	T	L	K
S	A	T	U	R	N	N	P	L	A	O	O	P	C
T	Y	R	U	C	R	E	M	H	C	L	F	X	O
R	E	G	N	E	L	L	A	H	C	O	F	E	R
O	G	C	V	O	N	W	O	D	T	N	U	O	C
N	O	O	M	Y	R	O	T	S	I	H	U	O	O
A	G	L	V	A	I	R	F	O	R	C	E	A	R
U	E	U	T	D	I	S	C	O	V	E	R	Y	L
T	M	M	T	E	T	I	L	L	E	T	A	S	A
S	I	B	K	E	N	N	E	D	Y	A	W	E	N
G	N	I	N	I	A	R	T	O	U	R	S	I	D
F	I	A	O	R	B	I	T	E	R	O	W	R	O

Solution on Page 323

AUGUSTA
BIRDIE
BOGEY
CADDIES
CART
CHIP
CLUBS
COURSES
DRIVER
EAGLE
EIGHTEEN
FAIRWAY
FLAGS
GAME
GRASS
GREENS
HANDICAP
HAZARD
HOLES
IRONS
LEISURE
MASTERS
MATCH
PAR
PGA
PIN
PLAYERS
PUTTER
ROUGH
SAND TRAP
SCOTLAND
SHOES
SPORT
STROKE
SWING
TEES
WALK
WATER
WEDGE
WOODS

Golf Vacation

E	G	D	E	W	O	O	D	S	Q	K	C	T	R
L	R	M	G	R	R	O	U	G	H	S	N	R	W
M	A	G	R	S	E	I	D	D	A	C	C	A	A
G	S	T	R	O	K	E	S	T	Y	O	T	C	L
A	S	H	O	E	S	C	S	D	U	E	S	A	K
Y	E	M	A	C	E	U	L	R	R	U	G	H	M
K	W	A	S	N	G	N	S	U	U	I	D	O	N
F	K	S	G	U	D	E	S	M	B	D	V	L	B
P	F	T	A	L	S	I	F	C	N	S	Z	E	D
X	V	E	L	N	E	G	C	A	H	B	N	S	R
H	P	R	F	L	D	H	L	A	I	I	I	R	A
Y	P	S	P	U	T	T	E	R	P	R	P	E	Z
B	Y	N	Z	G	O	E	R	U	U	D	W	Y	A
B	O	O	Z	C	A	E	E	A	U	I	G	A	H
E	Z	R	S	W	I	N	G	S	P	E	K	L	Y
F	W	I	O	O	E	R	O	G	T	R	O	P	S

Solution on Page 323

BICYCLE
BIKE
BOX
BUSINESS
CARRIER
CITY
COMPANY
DELIVERY
DHL
DISTANCE
DOCUMENTS
EXPENSIVE
EXPRESS
FAST
FEDEX
IMPORTANT
MAIL
MESSAGES
MESSENGER
OFFICE
OVERNIGHT
PACKAGES
PARCEL
PERSON
PIGEON
ROUTE
RUNNER
SCALES
SECURITY
SEND
SERVICES
SIGNATURE
SPEED
TRACKING
TRANSPORT
TRAVEL
TYPEFACE
UPS
VAN

Courier

F	E	D	E	X	B	U	S	I	N	E	S	S	R
A	B	K	I	M	P	O	R	T	A	N	T	I	E
S	E	L	A	C	S	P	U	D	X	N	H	G	N
T	E	X	P	E	N	S	I	V	E	C	G	N	N
R	E	G	N	E	S	S	E	M	N	O	I	A	U
A	D	H	L	S	T	S	U	O	F	W	N	T	R
C	N	P	Y	A	E	C	E	F	T	X	R	U	Y
K	E	A	N	J	O	G	I	R	T	O	E	R	Q
I	S	C	A	D	I	C	A	L	P	B	V	E	N
N	E	K	P	P	E	V	G	S	E	X	O	I	O
G	R	A	M	W	E	L	N	D	S	C	E	R	S
V	V	G	O	L	R	A	I	U	P	E	R	R	R
G	I	E	C	O	R	O	N	V	E	L	M	A	E
Q	C	S	Y	T	I	R	U	C	E	S	I	C	P
N	E	L	C	Y	C	I	B	T	D	R	N	A	V
B	S	B	I	K	E	C	A	F	E	P	Y	T	M

Solution on Page 323

ACTION
BACCARAT
BETTING
BLACKJACK
BROKE
CHANCE
CONCERTS
CRAPS
FUN
GAMBLING
GAMING
HAND
HOTELS
INDIAN
LAS VEGAS
MACHINES
MIRAGE
MONACO
NEVADA
ODDS
PEOPLE
PIT
PLAYER
POKER
RENO
RESORT
RESTAURANT
REVENUE
ROULETTE
SECURITY
SHOPPING
SLOT
SPORTS
TABLES
TOURIST
WIN

Casino

O	C	A	N	O	M	N	E	V	A	D	A	O	T
D	P	Q	S	S	E	G	A	R	I	M	E	I	T
D	E	R	H	E	R	E	N	O	T	U	F	O	R
S	O	E	O	C	W	Z	J	I	N	N	U	K	O
W	P	Y	P	U	B	S	P	E	M	R	C	S	S
M	L	A	P	R	L	R	V	F	I	A	O	P	E
I	E	L	I	I	Z	E	O	S	J	B	G	O	R
N	C	P	N	T	R	S	T	K	N	E	Q	R	E
D	N	B	G	Y	S	T	C	T	E	T	S	T	K
I	A	M	A	D	N	A	H	Y	E	T	E	S	O
A	H	H	M	C	L	U	G	Z	R	I	N	E	P
N	C	O	B	B	C	R	A	E	W	N	I	L	N
I	R	T	L	Y	F	A	C	G	V	G	H	B	H
W	A	E	I	U	M	N	R	X	C	S	C	A	A
G	P	L	N	O	O	T	T	A	N	C	A	T	D
H	S	S	G	C	N	S	L	O	T	J	M	L	E

Solution on Page 324

AIR FILTER
BEARINGS
BODY WORK
BUGGY
CABRIOLET
COMPACTS
CORVAIR
CV JOINT
DEFROSTER
FUEL PUMP
GAS GAUGE
GASKETS
HEADLIGHTS
HOT ROD
HUB CAPS
ODOMETER
OIL CHANGE
PONY CAR
RAGTOP
REST STOPS
ROAD SIGNS
STRUTS
STUDEBAKER
TACHOMETER
THROTTLE
TRANS AM
TRANSAXLE
TUNE UP
V ENGINE
VW BUS
WOODIE

Passenger Vehicle

I	V	W	B	U	S	T	C	A	P	M	O	C	E
G	A	S	K	E	T	S	P	O	N	Y	C	A	R
R	I	A	V	R	O	C	Y	Y	G	G	U	B	V
E	I	D	O	O	W	B	O	D	Y	W	O	R	K
A	T	A	C	H	O	M	E	T	E	R	I	I	S
R	S	T	U	D	E	B	A	K	E	R	L	O	T
E	E	J	O	D	O	M	E	T	E	R	C	L	R
T	L	S	T	H	G	I	L	D	A	E	H	E	U
S	X	G	T	E	N	I	G	N	E	V	A	T	T
O	A	A	T	S	F	B	E	A	R	I	N	G	S
R	S	S	N	R	T	U	N	E	U	P	G	H	P
F	N	G	I	I	P	O	T	G	A	R	E	O	A
E	A	A	O	P	M	U	P	L	E	U	F	T	C
D	R	U	J	S	N	G	I	S	D	A	O	R	B
Q	T	G	V	E	L	T	T	O	R	H	T	O	U
M	R	E	C	T	R	A	N	S	A	M	D	D	H

Solution on Page 324

ANIMALS
BEARS
BIKING
CANYONS
EL CAPITAN
FIRE
FOREST
FUN
GEOLOGY
HABITAT
HALF DOME
HISTORY
JOHN MUIR
LAKES
MADERA
MOUNTAINS
NATURE
PLANTS
PROTECTED
RANGERS
RECREATION
SEQUOIAS
STREAMS
SUBALPINE
TOURISTS
TRAILS
TUOLUMNE
USA
VALLEY
VEGETATION
VISITORS
VOLCANO
WATERFALLS
WILDERNESS
WILDLIFE

Scenic Yosemite

L	C	M	G	E	O	L	O	G	Y	S	K	U	U
A	F	O	R	E	S	T	A	T	I	B	A	H	N
K	B	I	S	E	Q	U	O	I	A	S	U	A	M
E	F	T	U	O	L	U	M	N	E	J	Q	L	O
S	R	U	D	E	T	C	E	T	O	R	P	F	U
W	R	E	N	I	P	L	A	B	U	S	N	D	N
V	I	S	I	T	O	R	S	P	E	O	U	O	T
Y	U	L	T	R	A	I	L	S	I	A	I	M	A
R	M	A	D	R	A	V	L	T	R	T	R	E	I
O	N	M	D	E	O	A	A	R	A	O	A	S	N
T	H	I	Y	L	R	T	F	E	N	U	G	N	S
S	O	N	C	E	E	N	R	A	G	R	N	O	T
I	J	A	D	G	L	C	E	M	E	I	I	Y	N
H	N	A	E	R	E	L	T	S	R	S	K	N	A
O	M	V	E	R	U	T	A	N	S	T	I	A	L
E	F	I	L	D	L	I	W	V	P	S	B	C	P

Solution on Page 324

ATLANTIC
BANK
BEACHES
BOAT
BORDER
CALIFORNIA
CLIFFS
CORAL
COVE
DOCK
EAST COAST
EROSION
FISHING
GULF
HARBOR
INLET
LAND
LEVEE
MAP
OCEANS
PACIFIC
PORT
RIVER
ROCKY
SAND
SEAGULLS
SEAWEED
SHORE
SUNBATHING
SURFING
SWIMMING
TIDES
TOURISTS
VIEW
WATER
WAVES
WEST
ZONE

Coastline

W	D	P	O	R	T	Q	G	C	S	A	N	D	S
E	O	D	O	F	B	Q	O	W	W	A	V	E	S
S	C	C	T	O	U	R	I	S	T	S	D	F	S
T	K	U	R	A	A	M	F	D	R	I	X	E	H
Y	E	D	S	L	M	A	P	N	T	I	H	Q	S
K	E	L	U	I	N	N	U	A	S	C	V	N	H
R	A	I	N	R	O	F	I	L	A	C	A	E	O
G	Y	G	B	I	I	V	Y	E	O	E	X	B	R
N	F	C	A	R	S	A	B	D	C	H	R	O	E
I	L	I	T	O	O	S	T	O	T	O	B	A	E
F	E	F	H	G	R	F	I	L	S	R	V	T	C
R	V	I	I	K	E	F	S	E	A	W	E	E	D
U	E	C	N	G	K	I	W	H	E	N	O	Z	C
S	E	A	G	U	L	L	S	E	W	A	T	E	R
L	B	P	K	L	H	C	G	N	I	H	S	I	F
K	H	Z	G	F	E	M	J	R	D	V	X	D	C

Solution on Page 324

ARCHITECTURE
BASKETBALL
BEN FRANKLIN
BETSY ROSS
BROTHERLY LOVE
CITY
CONSTITUTION
DELAWARE RIVER
EAGLES
FAIRMOUNT PARK
FRESH PRINCE
GREEN
HISTORY
INDEPENDENCE
INQUIRER
LIBERTY BELL
MARKET STREET
MINT
NORTH
PARKS
POPULATION
ROCKY
SOCIETY HILL
UNITED STATES
UNIVERSITY
URBAN

Philadelphia

E	B	N	I	L	K	N	A	R	F	N	E	B	F
R	R	B	B	C	R	I	G	P	T	S	V	S	D
U	F	A	E	O	O	V	H	O	N	K	O	E	I
T	R	S	T	N	C	X	I	P	I	R	L	T	N
C	E	K	S	S	K	S	S	U	M	A	Y	A	D
E	S	E	Y	T	Y	O	T	L	W	P	L	T	E
T	H	T	R	I	T	C	O	A	M	T	R	S	P
I	P	B	O	T	I	I	R	T	I	N	E	D	E
H	R	A	S	U	S	E	Y	I	N	U	H	E	N
C	I	L	S	T	R	T	S	O	Q	O	T	T	D
R	N	L	G	I	E	Y	E	N	U	M	O	I	E
A	C	A	V	O	V	H	L	K	I	R	R	N	N
O	E	E	B	N	I	I	G	C	R	I	B	U	C
G	R	E	E	N	N	L	A	I	E	A	C	A	E
N	O	R	T	H	U	L	E	T	R	F	M	Z	N
W	E	L	I	B	E	R	T	Y	B	E	L	L	M

Solution on Page 325

ACROPOLIS
AEGEAN SEA
ALEXANDER
ANCIENT
ARISTOTLE
ATHENS
CLASSICAL
CRETE
CUISINE
CYPRUS
DEMOCRACY
DRAMA
EUROPEAN
GODS
HELLENIC
HOMER
LANGUAGE
LITERATURE
MACEDONIA
MOUNTAINS
MYTHOLOGY
OLIVE OIL
ORTHODOX
PARTHENON
PENINSULA
PHILOSOPHY
REPUBLIC
SPARTA
TRAVEL
TURKEY
WINE
ZEUS

Greece

S	M	O	E	L	T	O	T	S	I	R	A	M	W
U	Y	D	N	A	L	E	X	A	N	D	E	R	S
R	T	R	E	P	U	B	L	I	C	R	S	E	N
P	H	A	N	M	Y	E	K	R	U	T	N	G	I
Y	O	M	I	G	O	D	S	T	W	S	A	A	A
C	L	A	S	S	I	C	A	L	I	T	E	U	T
O	O	H	I	O	R	R	R	L	R	N	G	G	N
R	G	H	U	Z	E	H	O	A	I	T	E	N	U
T	Y	Y	C	T	M	P	P	W	C	X	A	A	O
H	P	H	I	L	O	S	O	P	H	Y	S	L	M
O	O	L	Q	R	H	E	L	L	E	N	I	C	S
D	M	A	C	E	D	O	N	I	A	V	H	G	N
O	H	A	T	P	A	R	T	H	E	N	O	N	E
X	Z	E	U	S	E	U	R	O	P	E	A	N	H
I	R	A	L	U	S	N	I	N	E	P	R	V	T
C	T	R	A	V	E	L	T	N	E	I	C	N	A

Solution on Page 325

AXLE
BIG RIG
BOX TRUCK
BROKER
CARRIER
CONSIGNOR
CONTAINER
CONVOY
DEMURRAGE
DIESEL
DOCK
DRIVER
ENGINE
FLATBED
FREIGHT
FUEL
GAS
INDUSTRY
KINGPIN
LOG BOOK
MANIFEST
OVERSIZE
PALLET
RADIO
RECEIVER
ROAD
ROUTE
SEMI
SHIPMENT
SHIPPER
SLEEPER
TANDEM
TERMINAL
TRACTOR
TRAILER
TRANSPORT
TRUCK STOP
TRUCKLOAD

Trucking Words

R	E	L	I	A	R	T	A	T	T	L	B	T	E
P	T	H	G	I	E	R	F	R	R	E	R	A	S
T	S	E	F	I	N	A	M	U	A	U	O	N	H
K	H	N	L	Y	S	N	K	C	C	F	K	D	I
I	I	G	A	R	A	S	B	K	T	O	E	E	P
N	P	I	T	T	G	P	L	S	O	L	R	M	P
G	M	N	B	S	B	O	X	T	R	U	C	K	E
P	E	E	E	U	A	R	R	O	A	D	O	K	R
I	N	O	D	D	X	T	U	P	E	R	N	O	E
N	T	V	B	N	L	T	D	M	E	Y	S	O	V
D	P	E	I	I	E	O	U	P	O	E	I	B	I
R	A	R	G	M	C	R	E	V	M	A	G	G	E
I	L	S	R	K	R	E	N	I	A	T	N	O	C
V	L	I	I	A	L	O	I	D	A	R	O	L	E
E	E	Z	G	S	C	A	R	R	I	E	R	U	R
R	T	E	R	M	I	N	A	L	E	S	E	I	D

Solution on Page 325

AIRPORTS
ART
BANKS
BEIJING
BUSINESS
CENTER
CHICAGO
CULTURAL
DIVERSE
ECONOMY
FINANCE
GEOGRAPHY
HISTORY
HONG KONG
IMPORTANT
INFLUENCE
LARGE
LONDON
MEGACITY
METROPOLIS
MOSCOW
NEW YORK
OPERA
PARIS
POLITICAL
POPULATION
ROME
SEOUL
SHANGHAI
SINGAPORE
SYDNEY
TORONTO
TRAFFIC
URBAN
WORLD CITY

Global Cities

S	E	O	U	L	T	O	R	O	N	T	O	F	J
H	I	S	T	O	R	Y	P	K	N	F	I	M	S
A	M	H	O	P	E	R	A	O	G	N	E	Y	I
N	E	W	Y	O	R	K	D	E	A	T	Y	A	N
G	G	O	S	P	U	N	O	N	R	T	E	I	G
H	A	C	I	U	O	G	C	O	I	H	G	R	A
A	C	S	R	L	R	E	P	C	O	B	R	P	P
I	I	O	A	A	P	O	D	N	D	U	A	O	O
O	T	M	P	T	L	L	G	I	R	S	L	R	R
G	Y	H	P	I	R	K	V	B	E	I	A	T	E
A	Y	E	S	O	O	E	A	E	T	N	R	S	C
C	R	M	W	N	R	N	U	I	N	E	U	Y	O
I	O	O	G	S	K	T	C	J	E	S	T	D	N
H	T	R	E	S	A	A	A	I	C	S	L	N	O
C	E	I	N	F	L	U	E	N	C	E	U	E	M
S	C	I	F	F	A	R	T	G	T	I	C	Y	Y

Solution on Page 325

AMERICAN
BARRACUDA
BOYS
BRAND
CARS
CHEVY
CHILDREN
CLASSICS
COLORS
CRASH
DESIGN
DIE CAST
DRIVE
FAST
FLAME
FORD
FUN
HOBBY
HOT RODS
KIDS
MATCHBOX
MATTEL
METAL
MODELS
MUSTANG
NASCAR
PLASTIC
RACING
RED LINE
REPLICA
SERIES
SMALL
SPEED
TOYS
TRACKS
TRUCKS
VAN
VEHICLES
VOLKSWAGEN
WHEELS

Hot Wheels

G	V	O	W	M	S	E	I	R	E	S	R	V	S
D	E	W	H	U	M	S	K	C	A	R	T	M	P
E	H	D	E	S	I	G	N	A	S	C	A	R	Y
E	I	Y	E	T	D	N	A	R	B	L	I	B	T
P	C	V	L	A	M	O	D	E	L	S	B	N	F
S	L	E	S	N	K	S	R	O	L	O	C	O	G
E	E	H	M	G	E	B	P	T	H	X	R	T	E
S	S	C	I	S	S	A	L	C	O	D	N	S	N
Y	D	F	U	N	E	R	D	L	I	H	C	A	I
A	C	I	L	P	E	R	S	Y	O	T	C	C	L
V	O	L	K	S	W	A	G	E	N	I	N	E	D
P	L	A	S	T	I	C	C	S	R	A	C	I	E
F	L	A	M	E	R	U	Y	E	V	I	R	D	R
P	M	E	T	A	L	D	M	A	T	T	E	L	R
B	O	Y	S	O	M	A	T	C	H	B	O	X	U
O	O	H	H	S	K	C	U	R	T	S	A	F	A

Solution on Page 326

ADVENTURE
BALANCE
BICYCLES
BIKES
BMX
BRAKES
CLIMB
CYCLING
DANGEROUS
DOWNHILL
ENDURANCE
EQUIPMENT
EXTREME
FIRE ROADS
FITNESS
FREERIDE
GEARS
GLOVES
HELMETS
INJURY
MOUNTAINS
OFF ROAD
PEDALS
PROTECTION
RACING
RUGGED
SHOES
SINGLETRACK
SKILL
SPEED
SPORTS
STEEP
STRENGTH
SUSPENSION
TREK
TRIALS

Mountain Biking

B	I	K	E	S	N	I	A	T	N	U	O	M	K
G	P	G	Y	R	U	J	N	I	S	A	T	B	E
D	E	E	S	T	R	O	P	S	R	R	R	F	X
A	D	V	E	N	T	U	R	E	A	A	I	R	T
O	A	G	N	T	X	W	O	E	E	C	A	E	R
R	L	E	O	K	S	F	T	N	G	I	L	E	E
F	S	Q	I	H	E	I	E	D	B	N	S	R	M
F	S	U	S	T	L	R	C	U	R	G	A	I	E
O	S	I	N	G	L	E	T	R	A	C	K	D	C
S	E	P	E	N	I	R	I	A	K	C	G	E	N
H	N	M	P	E	H	O	O	N	E	O	N	K	A
O	T	E	S	R	N	A	N	C	S	K	I	L	L
E	I	N	U	T	W	D	S	E	V	O	L	G	A
S	F	T	S	S	O	S	E	L	C	Y	C	I	B
R	U	G	G	E	D	E	E	P	S	L	Y	H	M
H	E	L	M	E	T	S	B	M	I	L	C	E	X

Solution on Page 326

BIG MAC
BREAKFAST
BURGER KING
CALORIES
CHAINS
CHEAP
CONVENIENCE
DINNER
DRIVE THRU
FISH
FRANCHISE
FRENCH FRIES
FRIED CHICKEN
GREASE
HAMBURGERS
HOT DOGS
KFC
LUNCH
MCDONALD'S
MEALS
MENU
ORDER
PITAS
PIZZA HUT
PREPARED
RESTAURANTS
SANDWICHES
SERVICE
SUPER SIZE
TACO BELL
TRANS FAT
WHITE CASTLE

Road Food

A	F	I	S	H	T	R	A	N	S	F	A	T	A
N	R	E	S	T	A	U	R	A	N	T	S	A	I
S	E	H	C	I	W	D	N	A	S	P	L	C	T
E	N	K	M	E	A	L	S	G	O	D	T	O	H
I	C	H	C	N	U	L	C	A	M	G	I	B	L
R	H	W	H	I	T	E	C	A	S	T	L	E	J
O	F	E	S	I	H	C	N	A	R	F	O	L	B
L	R	P	I	D	E	C	I	V	R	E	S	L	M
A	I	R	E	D	R	O	D	I	N	N	E	R	C
C	E	E	C	N	E	I	N	E	V	N	O	C	D
H	S	P	A	E	H	C	V	P	I	T	A	S	O
A	P	A	G	N	I	K	R	E	G	R	U	B	N
I	B	R	E	A	K	F	A	S	T	K	F	C	A
N	M	E	N	U	P	I	Z	Z	A	H	U	T	L
S	M	D	H	A	M	B	U	R	G	E	R	S	D
G	R	E	A	S	E	Z	I	S	R	E	P	U	S

Solution on Page 326

ANCIENT
ANTIQUITY
AURORA
CHICHEN ITZA
CN TOWER
COLOSSUS
EARTH
EGYPT
GREAT PYRAMID
GREAT WALL
HAGIA SOPHIA
HANGING GARDENS
HOOVER DAM
LEANING TOWER
MANMADE
MAUSOLEUM
MEDIEVAL WORLD
MOUNT EVEREST
PANAMA CANAL
PETRA
PYRAMID OF GIZA
SEVEN
SPECTACULAR
STATUE OF ZEUS
VICTORIA FALLS

Wonders of the World

F	P	G	S	P	E	C	T	A	C	U	L	A	R
J	T	R	Z	Y	E	A	R	T	H	W	C	D	G
S	N	E	D	R	A	G	G	N	I	G	N	A	H
C	E	A	L	A	I	Y	T	S	C	M	T	M	T
O	I	T	R	M	H	T	D	M	H	L	O	A	S
L	C	W	O	I	P	I	I	A	E	A	W	D	E
O	N	A	W	D	O	U	M	U	N	N	E	R	R
S	A	L	L	O	S	Q	A	S	I	A	R	E	E
S	L	L	A	F	A	I	R	O	T	C	I	V	V
U	N	A	V	G	I	T	Y	L	Z	A	E	O	E
S	E	R	E	I	G	N	P	E	A	M	G	O	T
A	V	O	I	Z	A	A	T	U	A	A	Y	H	N
R	E	R	D	A	H	K	A	M	Q	N	P	D	U
T	S	U	E	Z	F	O	E	U	T	A	T	S	O
E	D	A	M	N	A	M	R	L	M	P	M	D	M
P	L	E	A	N	I	N	G	T	O	W	E	R	F

Solution on Page 326

AMENITIES
ANCHOR
BAR
CABINS
COMFORT
CREW
CRUISING
DECK
ENGINE
EXPENSIVE
FAST
FISHING
FUEL
GALLEY
HARBOR
HUGE
HULL TYPE
LARGE
LEISURE
LUXURIOUS
MAST
MOTOR
OCEAN
PRIVATE
PROPULSION
RACING
RECREATION
RICH
SAILBOAT
SAILING
SEA
SHIP
SHORE
SPORT
STEAMBOAT
VESSEL
WATERCRAFT
WEALTHY
WEEKENDER

Yachting

H	E	R	U	S	I	E	L	S	H	O	R	E	Z
U	N	E	T	Q	F	Y	E	L	L	A	G	W	F
G	I	D	S	U	O	I	R	U	X	U	L	A	W
E	G	N	A	R	T	O	P	R	I	V	A	T	E
H	N	E	F	I	O	B	L	T	C	P	G	E	A
C	E	K	N	O	I	T	A	E	R	C	E	R	L
I	V	E	W	I	O	O	O	O	U	V	P	C	T
R	M	E	T	S	B	C	P	M	I	F	Y	R	H
A	R	W	S	M	G	U	E	S	S	F	T	A	Y
C	P	A	A	S	L	N	N	A	I	D	L	F	H
A	O	E	M	S	E	E	I	S	N	E	L	T	A
E	T	M	I	K	P	L	H	L	G	C	U	S	R
S	G	O	F	X	B	I	T	V	I	K	H	P	B
H	N	R	E	O	N	S	N	I	B	A	C	O	O
I	W	H	A	G	R	A	C	I	N	G	S	R	R
P	V	T	R	L	C	T	B	A	R	I	X	T	D

Solution on Page 327

AIR HOST
AIRCREW
AIRLINES
AIRPLANE
AIRPORT
AISLE
AVIATION
BOARDING
CABIN CREW
COCKPIT
COMFORT
COMMERCIAL
DELTA
DOMESTIC
DRINKS
EMERGENCY
EVACUATION
FLIGHTS
FLYING
FOOD
GALLEY
HAT
HELP
JET
JOB
LUGGAGE
PASSENGERS
PILOTS
PLANES
PURSER
SEAT BELT
SERVICE
SINGLE
TRAINING
UNIFORMS
WINGS
WORK

Flight Attendants

W	P	Z	D	C	A	B	I	N	C	R	E	W	G
E	V	A	C	U	A	T	I	O	N	D	O	I	K
R	W	D	S	Y	C	O	M	F	O	R	T	J	E
C	I	S	R	S	T	M	J	H	K	J	O	M	A
R	N	T	Z	I	E	S	E	A	T	B	E	L	T
I	G	H	S	R	N	N	O	T	D	R	A	T	L
A	S	G	C	E	J	K	G	H	G	I	S	A	E
U	N	I	F	O	R	M	S	E	R	A	E	I	D
G	A	L	L	E	Y	V	N	L	R	I	N	R	G
L	C	F	V	W	U	C	I	P	S	S	A	P	N
U	O	S	S	K	Y	N	D	C	K	L	L	O	I
G	C	I	T	S	E	M	O	D	E	E	P	R	D
G	K	N	O	S	G	N	I	N	I	A	R	T	R
A	P	G	L	V	S	N	O	I	T	A	I	V	A
G	I	L	I	R	E	S	R	U	P	C	A	R	O
E	T	E	P	D	O	O	F	L	Y	I	N	G	B

Solution on Page 327

BARISTA
BEANS
BISCOTTI
BOOKS
CAFFEINE
CAPPUCCINO
COFFEE
COLLEGE
COUNTER
CUSTOMERS
DECAF
DRINKS
ESPRESSO
FOOD
HIP
INTERNET
JAVA
LATTE
MILK
MOCHA
MUFFINS
MUSIC
ORDER
PASTRY
PEOPLE
READ
RELAXED
RESTAURANT
SCONES
SEATTLE
SNACKS
SOCIAL
SPOON
STARBUCKS
TABLES
TALK
TEAS
WARM
WIFI

Coffee Stop

N	O	O	P	S	E	N	O	C	S	G	M	Z	B
F	E	C	W	L	A	T	T	E	O	G	U	F	Y
T	A	L	K	R	L	S	A	D	F	F	F	A	O
O	O	D	P	H	E	T	K	M	R	O	F	C	R
S	R	E	M	O	T	S	U	C	O	I	I	E	D
S	J	X	Y	L	E	S	T	D	A	I	N	D	E
E	K	A	E	L	I	P	R	A	T	N	S	K	R
R	Q	L	V	C	A	E	H	T	U	K	S	Z	S
P	S	E	M	A	T	I	O	I	C	R	C	B	U
S	I	R	O	N	I	C	C	U	P	P	A	C	Y
E	A	W	U	J	S	A	B	O	D	T	F	N	R
W	S	O	D	I	H	R	Y	Y	S	A	F	W	T
I	C	K	B	C	A	K	L	I	M	T	E	A	S
F	Q	X	O	T	E	N	R	E	T	N	I	R	A
I	C	M	S	O	T	A	B	L	E	S	N	J	P
R	S	N	A	E	B	S	C	O	L	L	E	G	E

Solution on Page 327

APARTMENTS
BAGELS
BIG APPLE
BOROUGHS
BROADWAY
BUILDINGS
BUSINESS
CABS
CHEESECAKE
CITY
CONCERTS
CRIME
CROWDED
CULTURE
FASHION
FERRY
FINANCE
FOOD
GOTHAM
HARLEM
JETS
LIGHTS
MANHATTAN
MONEY
MUSEUMS
NEW YORK
RANGERS
SHOPPING
SUBWAYS
TAXIS
THE BRONX
THEATRE
TOURISTS
TRAFFIC
URBAN
WALKING

Gotham

C	R	I	M	E	K	A	C	E	S	E	E	H	C
T	R	A	F	F	I	C	Y	T	G	L	C	B	O
G	O	T	H	A	M	A	N	Y	N	P	N	W	N
P	K	R	O	Y	W	E	N	E	I	P	A	A	C
Y	F	O	O	D	M	Z	T	N	D	A	N	L	E
T	H	E	A	T	R	E	S	O	L	G	I	K	R
X	N	O	R	B	E	H	T	M	I	I	F	I	T
Z	R	A	B	A	G	E	L	S	U	B	H	N	S
B	P	H	T	U	R	B	A	N	B	E	M	G	T
A	C	A	O	T	O	U	R	I	S	T	S	A	F
C	R	R	F	R	A	N	G	E	R	S	X	U	X
A	O	L	X	Y	S	H	O	P	P	I	N	G	M
B	W	E	B	U	S	I	N	E	S	S	T	E	J
S	D	M	N	O	I	H	S	A	F	E	R	R	Y
A	E	R	U	T	L	U	C	Y	M	C	I	T	Y
I	D	S	U	B	W	A	Y	S	T	H	G	I	L

Solution on Page 327

ASPHALT
BICYCLE
BIKE
BRIDGE
BUS
CARRIAGE
DELIVERY
DRIVER
ENGINE
FOOD
FREIGHT
GOODS
HAULING
HIGHWAYS
LANE
LICENSE
LOAD
LOGS
PAVEMENT
RICKSHAW
ROADS
ROUTE
SCOOTER
SEMI
SIGNS
SPEED
TAXI
TIRES
TOLL ROAD
TRACTOR
TRAFFIC
TRAILER
TRANSPORT
TRAVEL
TRUCKERS
TRUCKING
TURNPIKE
VAN
VEHICLES
WHEELS

Back on the Road

C	W	S	E	L	C	I	H	E	V	D	V	L	I
V	Z	P	I	B	B	I	K	E	N	A	L	M	K
E	L	E	X	U	L	I	C	E	N	S	E	T	T
T	E	E	A	S	P	H	A	L	T	S	T	R	H
U	V	D	T	N	E	M	E	V	A	P	R	A	G
O	A	W	R	R	O	T	C	A	R	T	U	I	I
R	R	U	S	I	O	D	B	I	C	Y	C	L	E
L	T	T	C	D	V	P	O	B	I	F	K	E	R
O	W	R	O	S	M	E	S	O	F	M	E	R	F
G	A	U	O	D	E	B	R	N	F	G	R	D	H
S	H	C	T	O	L	L	R	O	A	D	S	A	E
L	S	K	E	O	M	N	R	I	R	R	U	O	N
E	K	I	R	G	S	E	R	I	T	L	T	L	G
E	C	N	S	O	Y	R	E	V	I	L	E	D	I
H	I	G	H	W	A	Y	S	N	G	I	S	K	N
W	R	I	L	C	M	E	G	D	I	R	B	J	E

Solution on Page 328

ADVENTURE
AMERICA
ANCIENT
ANTARCTICA
ASTRONAUT
CAVE
DE SOTO
DISCOVERY
EXPEDITION
EXPLORERS
FIND
GEOGRAPHY
INFORMATION
JOURNEY
KIRA SALAK
MARCO POLO
MOON
NAVIGATION
NEW WORLD
OCEAN
PORTUGAL
RESEARCH
RESOURCES
SCIENTIFIC
SEARCHING
SHIP
SPAIN
SPECIES
TERRAIN
TRAVELING
UNCOVER
UNKNOWN

Journey of Discovery

N	T	K	D	P	P	O	T	N	H	N	U	K	A
A	E	J	E	A	O	L	U	W	C	A	N	N	O
E	R	O	S	C	R	O	A	O	R	V	C	O	L
C	R	U	O	I	T	P	N	N	A	I	O	O	S
O	A	R	T	R	U	O	O	K	E	G	V	M	E
T	I	N	O	E	G	C	R	N	S	A	E	N	C
R	N	E	T	M	A	R	T	U	E	T	R	E	R
A	O	Y	K	A	L	A	S	A	R	I	K	W	U
V	I	N	F	O	R	M	A	T	I	O	N	W	O
E	T	J	S	E	I	C	E	P	S	N	S	O	S
L	I	S	C	I	E	N	T	I	F	I	C	R	E
I	D	S	E	A	R	C	H	I	N	G	N	L	R
N	E	A	P	Y	R	E	V	O	C	S	I	D	E
G	P	E	R	U	T	N	E	V	D	A	A	N	V
E	X	P	L	O	R	E	R	S	H	I	P	I	A
G	E	O	G	R	A	P	H	Y	Y	Q	S	F	C

Solution on Page 328

AUTOMOBILE
BATTERY
CAR
CHARGING
CLEAN
COMPACT
COST
DRIVING
ECONOMICAL
EFFICIENT
ELECTRIC
EMISSIONS
ENERGY
ENGINE
EXPENSIVE
FRIENDLY
FUTURE
GAS
GREEN
HYBRID
LEAF
LITHIUM
MILEAGE
MOTOR
PLUG IN
POLLUTION
POWER
PRIUS
QUIET
RANGE
RECHARGE
RENEWABLE
SAVINGS
SLOW
SMALL
TECHNOLOGY
VEHICLE
VOLT
WHEELS

Electric Cars

X	G	B	G	N	I	V	I	R	D	C	O	S	T
L	C	N	M	D	Y	V	E	H	I	C	L	E	E
P	L	F	I	G	C	C	G	R	E	E	N	J	V
E	E	A	R	G	H	J	T	S	U	I	R	P	I
G	A	E	M	A	R	C	O	M	P	A	C	T	S
A	N	L	R	S	E	A	D	I	R	B	Y	H	N
E	Y	G	O	L	O	N	H	C	E	T	I	K	E
L	E	P	E	E	F	F	I	C	I	E	N	T	P
I	E	L	I	B	O	M	O	T	U	A	O	A	X
M	P	U	B	Q	S	N	O	I	S	S	I	M	E
U	O	G	U	A	O	A	Y	R	E	T	T	A	B
I	W	I	Q	M	W	Q	G	F	U	T	U	R	E
H	E	N	I	G	N	E	G	N	A	R	L	O	T
T	R	C	S	A	V	I	N	G	S	O	L	T	L
I	A	W	O	L	S	L	E	E	H	W	O	O	O
L	C	A	Y	L	D	N	E	I	R	F	P	M	V

Solution on Page 328

ABU DHABI
BEACHES
BUILDINGS
BURJ
BUSINESS
CAPITAL
CITY
DIVERSE
EXPENSIVE
FAMOUS
FINANCIAL
GOLD
HEAT
HOTELS
KUWAIT
MONARCHY
MUSLIM
NEW
OIL
QATAR
RICH
SAND DUNES
SHEIK
SHOPPING
SULTAN
TOURISTS
TRADE
WATER
WEALTHY

Dubai

F	F	H	H	Y	O	I	K	N	P	G	O	T	F
F	M	K	S	S	Q	L	B	E	A	C	H	E	S
P	I	I	U	S	K	Y	L	A	T	I	P	A	C
W	L	Y	L	E	Z	K	R	A	H	O	X	L	E
E	S	E	T	N	X	O	K	C	S	D	A	Y	Z
K	U	W	A	I	T	P	I	H	Y	I	U	Z	L
W	M	Z	N	S	C	R	E	H	C	P	V	B	S
F	A	M	O	U	S	I	T	N	D	L	O	G	A
U	M	R	V	B	K	L	A	R	S	D	N	H	N
B	Y	H	C	R	A	N	O	M	I	I	S	O	D
U	P	O	F	E	I	G	E	L	D	V	V	T	D
R	Z	R	W	F	O	N	L	L	T	E	H	E	U
J	A	S	H	O	P	P	I	N	G	R	E	L	N
O	S	T	S	I	R	U	O	T	N	S	A	S	E
R	E	T	A	W	B	X	R	H	A	E	T	D	S
Y	R	Y	V	Q	I	V	W	H	O	J	W	T	E

Solution on Page 328

ACCENT
BBC
BEATLES
CAMBRIDGE
CASTLES
CHIPS
CHURCH
COUNTRY
CRICKET
CROWN
DIANA
EDWARD
ELTON JOHN
EMPIRE
EUROPE
FISH
FOOTBALL
GUARD
HISTORY
IRELAND
ISLAND
KINGS
LIVERPOOL
MONARCHY
OXFORD
PALACE
PARLIAMENT
PINT
POUND
PUB
RAIN
RUGBY
SCOTLAND
SOCCER
STONEHENGE
TEA
THAMES
TOURISM
UNION JACK
WALES

English Holiday

G	I	S	L	A	N	D	R	A	W	D	E	C	E
D	V	E	Y	T	N	E	M	A	I	L	R	A	P
D	R	M	C	R	I	C	K	E	T	I	N	M	O
D	I	A	N	A	O	L	C	O	E	V	K	B	R
N	T	H	U	U	S	T	N	H	F	E	I	R	U
U	O	T	N	G	T	J	S	M	I	R	N	I	E
O	U	T	I	Y	O	C	I	I	S	P	G	D	P
P	R	E	O	H	N	I	A	R	H	O	S	G	I
Y	I	C	N	C	E	H	A	S	E	O	L	E	N
B	S	A	J	R	H	B	E	A	T	L	E	S	T
G	M	L	A	A	E	S	C	G	A	L	A	N	G
U	C	A	C	N	N	A	O	B	U	P	E	N	W
R	I	P	K	O	G	T	T	C	B	C	H	S	D
E	R	I	P	M	E	O	E	H	C	R	U	H	C
D	N	A	L	T	O	C	S	A	S	E	L	A	W
J	A	O	X	F	O	R	D	N	W	O	R	C	T

Solution on Page 329

ASTROS
AUSTIN
BIG
BORDER
CATTLE
COLLEGE
COTTON
COWGIRL
DESERT
EL PASO
FARMING
FOOTBALL
FORT WORTH
GALVESTON
GULF COAST
HEAT
HOUSTON
LARGE
LIVESTOCK
LONE STAR
LONGHORNS
LUBBOCK
MEXICO
OIL
PANHANDLE
PETROLEUM
RANCHES
REFINERIES
RIO GRANDE
RODEO
SOUTH
SPURS
THE ALAMO
UNIVERSITY

The Lone Star State

H	L	R	I	G	W	O	C	A	T	T	L	E	C
H	T	G	I	B	L	U	B	B	O	C	K	H	S
N	S	R	G	O	E	G	E	L	L	O	C	N	D
O	A	D	O	A	G	L	L	A	B	T	O	O	F
T	O	M	Y	W	L	R	I	S	O	R	T	S	A
T	C	O	U	T	T	V	A	O	J	D	S	H	R
O	F	E	S	E	I	R	E	N	I	F	E	R	M
C	L	G	L	A	L	S	O	S	D	A	V	A	I
H	U	O	O	D	P	O	R	F	T	E	I	N	N
K	G	M	N	R	N	L	R	E	V	O	L	C	G
A	M	A	G	E	O	A	E	T	V	C	N	H	H
U	E	L	H	D	S	D	H	G	E	I	I	E	T
S	X	A	O	R	A	T	E	N	R	P	N	S	U
T	I	E	R	O	I	J	A	O	A	A	C	U	O
I	C	H	N	B	S	P	U	R	S	P	L	A	S
N	O	T	S	U	O	H	D	E	S	E	R	T	W

Solution on Page 329

ALPS
ART
BOOT
CATHOLIC
CHEESE
COUNTRY
CUISINE
CULTURE
DA VINCI
DANTE
EUROPE
FAMILY
FASHION
FERRARI
FLAG
FLORENCE
FOOD
GALILEO
GELATO
HISTORY
ITALIANS
LANGUAGE
LASAGNA
LATIN
MAFIA
MILAN
MUSEUMS
NAPLES
PASTA
PISA
PIZZA
POPE
ROMANTIC
RUINS
SICILY
TOURISM
TRAVEL
TUSCANY
VENICE
WINE

Italian Tour

J	I	R	A	R	R	E	F	A	M	I	L	Y	V
F	O	O	D	Q	Y	R	O	T	S	I	H	P	E
R	S	M	U	E	S	U	M	O	L	A	T	I	N
M	L	E	V	A	R	T	O	E	F	L	A	G	I
E	I	W	I	N	E	L	J	E	S	E	E	H	C
P	B	L	E	G	A	U	G	N	A	L	X	C	E
O	O	F	A	S	X	C	A	A	A	W	A	M	E
R	O	M	A	N	T	I	C	T	T	T	S	F	T
U	T	G	D	S	L	C	O	C	H	I	L	U	N
E	N	A	R	A	H	J	U	O	R	O	S	O	A
A	R	S	T	B	V	I	L	U	R	C	I	K	D
Y	L	I	C	I	S	I	O	E	A	I	F	A	M
P	O	P	E	I	C	T	N	N	A	P	L	E	S
Y	R	T	N	U	O	C	Y	C	A	T	S	A	P
W	N	E	H	B	E	O	E	L	I	L	A	G	L
K	N	A	Z	Z	I	P	R	U	I	N	S	S	A

Solution on Page 329

ALBUM
APERTURE
ART
BEAUTY
CAMERA
CAPTURE
COLORS
COMPUTER
DARKROOM
DEVELOP
DIGITAL
DOCUMENT
EVENT
EXPOSURE
FACE
FILM
FLASH
FOCUS
FRAME
HISTORY
IMAGES
LENS
LIGHT
MODEL
NATURE
NEGATIVE
PANORAMIC
PAPER
PEOPLE
PHOTO
PICTURES
PORTRAIT
POSING
PRINTING
RECORD
SCENE
SENSOR
SHARE
SLIDE
STILL

Take Pictures

S	H	A	R	E	M	A	R	F	D	J	D	F	V
L	C	O	L	O	R	S	K	I	O	E	A	R	T
I	R	A	C	B	M	E	G	K	V	C	P	P	S
D	R	E	P	B	U	I	T	E	E	T	U	O	T
E	E	V	P	E	T	M	L	U	I	N	Z	S	I
L	C	I	M	A	R	O	N	A	P	E	M	I	L
E	O	T	L	U	P	T	R	G	S	M	O	N	L
N	R	A	I	T	K	T	U	E	C	U	O	G	E
S	D	G	F	Y	R	J	R	R	U	C	R	C	D
O	I	E	Q	O	R	U	Y	U	E	O	K	A	O
P	M	N	P	O	T	R	U	S	N	D	R	P	M
F	A	I	S	C	O	T	L	O	A	Y	A	T	E
L	G	N	I	T	N	I	R	P	T	R	D	U	N
A	E	P	S	E	G	V	A	X	U	O	B	R	E
S	S	I	V	H	C	A	M	E	R	A	H	E	C
H	H	E	T	Q	E	L	P	O	E	P	L	P	S

Solution on Page 329

ADVENTURES
BAMBOO
BEACH
BOAT
BOB DENVER
CAPTAIN
CASTAWAYS
CLASSIC
COCONUT
COMEDY
CRUISE
GILLIGAN
GINGER
HAMMOCK
HOWELLS
ISLAND
LAGOON
LOST
LOVEY
MARY ANN
MOVIE STAR
MR. HOWELL
OCEAN
PROFESSOR
RADIO
RESCUE
SHIPWRECK
SITCOM
SKIPPER
STORM
STRANDED
TELEVISION
THE MINNOW
THEME SONG
TOUR
TROPICAL
TV SHOW

Stuck on Gilligan's Island

O	C	E	A	N	I	A	T	P	A	C	V	S	E
L	A	C	I	P	O	R	T	A	O	B	H	K	U
C	M	Q	Q	S	H	I	P	W	R	E	C	K	C
Y	A	G	C	S	C	A	S	T	A	W	A	Y	S
D	R	D	I	L	T	R	M	I	O	B	E	P	E
E	Y	H	V	L	A	H	U	M	V	U	B	R	R
M	A	E	Q	E	L	S	E	I	O	E	R	O	M
O	N	Y	V	W	N	I	S	M	S	C	L	F	R
C	N	S	M	O	W	T	G	I	I	E	K	E	O
O	O	T	O	H	L	O	U	A	C	N	V	S	T
C	O	R	C	R	O	R	H	R	N	N	N	S	S
O	G	A	T	M	R	A	T	S	E	I	V	O	M
N	A	N	I	S	L	A	N	D	V	S	T	R	W
U	L	D	S	B	A	M	B	O	O	T	S	O	L
T	H	E	M	E	S	O	N	G	I	N	G	E	R
O	I	D	A	R	B	S	K	I	P	P	E	R	F

Solution on Page 330

ALCOHOL
ALTBIER
AMBER ALE
AMERICAN
AROMA
ASSYRIAN
BELGIAN
BOCK
BREWED
BROWN ALE
CHAMPAGNE
CIDER
COLOR
CREAM ALE
DARK
DUNKEL
FRUIT
GERMAN
GRAINS
GRAVITY
HEAD
HOPS
IPA
LAGERS
LAMBIC
LIGHT
MALT
MOUTHFEEL
OLD ALE
PALE ALE
PILSNER
PORTER
RED ALE
RYE BEER
SPICED
STRENGTH
SWEETNESS
VISCOSITY
WATER
YEAST

Beers Around the World

S	P	O	H	F	I	N	A	M	R	E	G	J	M
P	K	W	G	R	A	I	N	S	V	N	A	E	A
I	T	C	I	B	M	A	L	I	S	G	L	E	L
C	I	D	E	R	I	P	S	R	R	A	T	L	T
E	U	S	E	G	I	C	E	A	N	P	B	A	S
D	R	S	L	L	O	G	V	W	C	M	I	D	A
E	F	E	S	S	A	I	O	A	O	A	E	E	E
W	B	N	I	L	T	R	W	P	L	H	R	R	Y
E	E	T	A	Y	B	A	E	V	O	C	B	E	R
R	Y	E	M	I	K	C	O	B	R	R	R	E	A
B	L	E	E	F	H	T	U	O	M	E	T	B	M
T	H	W	R	K	I	P	A	L	E	A	L	E	O
H	N	S	I	R	D	A	E	H	W	M	W	Y	R
G	T	R	C	A	S	S	Y	R	I	A	N	R	A
I	E	L	A	D	L	O	H	O	C	L	A	Q	D
L	E	K	N	U	D	H	T	G	N	E	R	T	S

Solution on Page 330

AEROSTAT
AIRCRAFT
AIRPLANE
AIRPORT
AKRON
AVIATION
BALLOON
BLIMPS
BUOYANT
CRASH
DIRIGIBLES
ENGINE
FLIGHT
FLOAT
FUEL
GAS
GERMANY
GONDOLA
HINDENBURG
HISTORY
HOT AIR
HYDROGEN
LANDING
LIFT
PASSENGERS
PILOT
PROPELLERS
RESEARCH
SKY
TECHNOLOGY
THRUST
TURBULENCE
UNPOWERED
WINGS
ZEPPELINS

Airships

G	O	N	D	O	L	A	E	N	I	G	N	E	Z
E	L	I	F	T	H	I	S	T	O	R	Y	Q	E
R	N	S	Y	G	O	L	O	N	H	C	E	T	P
M	E	A	P	M	R	A	I	R	P	O	R	T	P
A	G	M	L	M	F	U	H	S	A	R	C	R	E
N	O	V	N	P	I	U	B	B	S	F	O	E	L
Y	R	A	O	O	R	L	E	N	S	P	K	W	I
U	D	I	R	I	G	I	B	L	E	S	G	D	N
T	Y	R	K	E	C	E	A	L	N	D	E	A	S
A	H	C	A	W	S	F	L	O	G	R	N	V	S
T	U	R	B	U	L	E	N	C	E	I	O	I	T
S	W	A	U	O	R	T	A	W	R	A	O	A	H
O	I	F	A	S	O	T	O	R	S	T	L	T	G
R	N	T	U	L	T	P	N	S	C	O	L	I	I
E	G	N	I	D	N	A	L	K	N	H	A	O	L
A	S	P	T	U	T	N	A	Y	O	U	B	N	F

Solution on Page 330

AIR
AXLE
BICYCLE
BIKE
BMX
BOLTS
BRAKES
DIAMETER
DROPOUTS
FAST
FORK
FRAME
GEARS
INFLATE
LACING
LOCK
METAL
MOUNTAIN
NUT
PARTS
PATCH
PEDAL
PRESSURE
RACING
RIDING
RIMS
ROAD
ROLLING
ROTATING
ROUND
RUBBER
SEAT
SPEED
SPOKES
SPROCKET
SUPPORT
TRACTION
TREAD
VALVE
WRENCH

Bicycle Wheels

B	I	K	E	L	Q	S	V	D	D	G	F	R	N
K	C	O	L	J	T	H	L	G	B	R	P	I	T
B	U	S	X	R	C	A	N	R	A	R	A	A	D
V	I	U	A	T	D	I	A	M	E	T	E	R	F
X	X	P	A	E	L	K	E	S	N	S	O	A	R
B	M	P	P	L	E	D	S	U	S	P	S	C	Z
Q	B	O	O	S	A	U	O	G	O	T	T	I	R
C	O	R	T	O	R	M	K	U	N	V	U	N	U
A	L	T	R	E	R	O	T	A	T	I	N	G	B
A	T	A	A	C	K	S	R	O	U	N	D	L	B
H	S	F	C	E	L	C	Y	C	I	B	A	I	E
W	D	O	T	I	I	D	O	G	B	T	N	G	R
Z	A	R	I	K	N	J	W	R	E	N	C	H	I
S	E	K	O	P	S	G	I	M	P	A	R	O	M
H	R	I	N	F	L	A	T	E	A	S	R	S	S
M	T	V	A	L	V	E	M	D	E	E	P	S	M

Solution on Page 330

ANTEATER
BANANAS
BANYAN
BASILISK
BINTURONG
CASSOWARY
CLEARING
COATI
COBRA
COCKATOO
CROCODILES
FERNS
FLYING FOX
GIBBON
JAGUARS
KAKAPO
KINKAJOU
LEMUR
MACHETE
MANIOC
MONSOON
OKAPIS
PHARMACY
PIRANHA
PORCUPINES
PROTECTED
RHINOCEROS
SLOTH
TAPIRS
TEMPERATE
TERMITES
VINES

Jungle Journey

A	H	T	O	L	S	B	S	R	A	U	G	A	J
H	O	R	U	O	J	A	K	N	I	K	S	R	M
N	Q	T	C	O	I	N	A	M	R	S	I	B	P
A	W	E	O	T	B	A	N	Y	A	N	P	O	H
R	K	R	A	A	V	N	R	S	R	R	A	C	A
I	S	M	T	K	M	A	S	E	E	E	K	H	R
P	I	I	I	C	W	S	E	L	W	F	O	B	M
R	L	T	X	O	F	G	N	I	Y	L	F	I	A
O	I	E	S	C	I	A	I	D	P	T	M	N	C
T	S	S	E	B	G	N	P	O	S	A	A	T	Y
E	A	Z	B	B	O	T	U	C	E	P	C	U	O
C	B	O	S	O	R	E	C	O	N	I	H	R	P
T	N	P	S	U	C	A	R	R	I	R	E	O	A
E	L	N	M	M	F	T	O	C	V	S	T	N	K
D	O	E	T	A	R	E	P	M	E	T	E	G	A
M	L	X	G	N	I	R	A	E	L	C	A	K	K

Solution on Page 331

ACURA
AUDI
BENTLEY
BMW
BRAND
CADILLAC
CLASS
COMFORT
DESIRABLE
EXPENSIVE
FAST
FEATURES
FERRARI
INFINITI
JAGUAR
LARGE
LEATHER
LEXUS
LIMOUSINE
LINCOLN
LUXURY
MERCEDES
MONEY
PLEASANT
PORSCHE
PREMIUM
PRESTIGE
RICH
RIDE
RIMS
SEDAN
SMOOTH
SPACE
STATUS
STYLE
SUNROOF
SUPERIOR
TOWN CAR
VALUE
WEALTHY

Luxury Vehicles

E	C	L	S	I	S	T	A	T	U	S	M	I	R
D	F	A	E	N	V	E	R	E	H	T	A	E	L
I	W	C	D	F	J	A	G	U	A	R	S	J	S
R	Q	O	A	I	C	R	O	I	R	E	P	U	S
F	F	M	N	N	L	E	L	Y	T	S	A	F	A
M	O	F	W	I	Z	L	E	X	U	S	C	E	L
W	E	O	O	T	N	B	A	S	F	R	E	R	C
E	T	R	R	I	L	A	E	C	L	V	S	R	I
A	W	T	C	N	P	R	E	M	I	U	M	A	P
L	A	R	G	E	U	I	A	S	M	N	O	R	O
T	U	D	V	T	D	S	N	R	O	L	O	I	R
H	D	N	A	R	B	E	T	I	U	O	T	M	S
Y	I	E	L	I	P	D	S	C	S	C	H	O	C
H	F	L	U	X	U	R	Y	H	I	N	A	N	H
W	M	B	E	N	T	L	E	Y	N	I	F	E	E
B	F	A	S	T	N	A	S	A	E	L	P	Y	X

Solution on Page 331

AIR
BATHROOM
BREAK
CAMP
CARS
COFFEE
DIRECTIONS
DRIVER
EAT
EXPRESSWAY
FOOD
FREEWAY
GAS
HIGHWAY
INTERSTATE
MAPS
PARKING
PASSENGER
PICNIC
PLAZA
PUBLIC
REFUEL
REST STOP
RESTAURANT
RESTROOMS
ROAD
SCENIC
SERVICE
STRETCH
TABLES
TOILETS
TOURIST
TRAVELERS
TRUCKERS
TURNPIKE
VENDING
WATER

Rest Areas

T	O	I	L	E	T	S	K	Y	I	D	O	O	F
O	G	A	S	E	L	B	A	T	H	R	O	O	M
U	N	R	E	T	A	W	O	R	M	I	D	H	S
R	I	O	P	A	E	S	E	A	X	V	I	C	P
I	D	A	A	E	T	S	T	V	C	E	R	T	U
S	N	D	R	C	N	M	A	E	A	R	E	E	B
T	E	F	K	I	A	O	T	L	M	X	C	R	L
R	V	G	I	V	R	O	S	E	P	T	T	T	I
E	S	H	N	R	U	R	R	R	C	P	I	S	C
F	C	I	G	E	A	T	E	S	O	O	O	P	I
U	E	G	B	S	T	S	T	P	F	T	N	L	N
E	N	H	R	Y	S	E	N	A	F	S	S	A	C
L	I	W	E	W	E	R	I	M	E	T	R	Z	I
I	C	A	A	I	R	E	G	N	E	S	S	A	P
I	J	Y	K	Z	T	R	U	C	K	E	R	S	C
F	F	L	N	F	E	K	I	P	N	R	U	T	L

Solution on Page 331

BARGE
BOATS
CANALS
CARRIER
COMMERCE
CONTAINERS
CREW
CRUISE
DECK
DOCKS
DREDGER
EXPORT
FERRIES
FREIGHT
GOODS
HARBOR
HOLD
HULL
IMPORT
INVENTORY
LINER
LOAD
MARINERS
MERCHANT
MILITARY
OCEAN
PACIFIC
PASSENGERS
PORTS
RECREATION
RIVERS
ROPE
SAILBOAT
SEA
SHIPPING
TANKERS
TRAVEL
TUGBOAT
WATERCRAFT

On a Ship

T	H	N	D	H	O	L	D	Y	R	O	P	E	S
J	M	A	R	E	I	R	R	A	C	S	G	S	D
X	E	P	R	N	C	O	T	M	V	R	C	C	O
G	R	S	E	B	T	K	A	H	A	E	O	E	O
N	C	R	S	N	O	S	O	B	G	N	M	X	G
I	H	E	E	O	R	R	B	W	T	I	M	P	A
P	A	V	I	I	E	E	L	A	A	R	E	O	G
P	N	I	R	T	G	G	I	T	N	A	R	R	C
I	T	R	R	A	D	N	A	E	K	M	C	T	F
H	U	L	E	E	E	E	S	R	E	W	E	R	C
S	G	E	F	R	R	S	C	C	R	U	I	S	E
L	B	V	S	C	D	S	D	R	S	K	C	O	D
A	O	A	T	E	T	A	P	A	C	I	F	I	C
N	A	R	A	R	O	P	R	F	O	C	E	A	N
A	T	T	O	L	Y	R	A	T	I	L	I	M	U
C	L	P	B	I	M	P	O	R	T	H	U	L	L

Solution on Page 331

ASIAN
BANGKOK
BHUTAN
BUDDHISM
BURMA
CAMBODIA
CHINA
COUNTRY
CUISINE
CULTURE
EASTERN
ECONOMY
EURASIA
GEOGRAPHY
HINDUISM
HONG KONG
INDONESIA
ISLAM
JAPAN
LANGUAGES
LAOS
LARGE
MALAYSIA
MONGOLIA
MYANMAR
NEPAL
ORIENTAL
PAKISTAN
PEOPLE
POPULOUS
RUSSIA
SINGAPORE
SRI LANKA
TAIWAN
TEA
THAILAND
VIETNAM

Around Asia

A	M	R	U	B	B	E	A	S	T	E	R	N	I
N	A	T	U	H	B	C	U	L	T	U	R	E	S
Z	N	Y	M	O	N	O	C	E	G	R	A	L	L
T	T	A	E	T	L	S	R	I	L	A	N	K	A
B	E	I	I	U	H	O	N	G	K	O	N	G	M
U	I	L	P	S	P	P	E	O	P	L	E	X	A
D	V	O	Y	A	A	I	S	E	N	O	D	N	I
D	P	G	G	S	E	G	A	U	G	N	A	L	S
H	I	N	D	U	I	S	M	R	N	A	I	A	Y
I	I	O	Z	N	N	Y	A	A	E	T	D	T	A
S	U	M	A	A	A	P	C	S	P	S	O	N	L
M	S	P	W	N	H	L	H	I	A	I	B	E	A
R	A	I	M	Y	A	M	I	A	L	K	M	I	M
J	A	A	K	O	K	G	N	A	B	A	A	R	V
T	R	U	S	S	I	A	A	U	H	P	C	O	K
E	N	I	S	I	U	C	O	U	N	T	R	Y	J

Solution on Page 332

ACTIVITIES
ADVENTURE
BACKPACK
BALLOONING
BEACH
BICYCLING
BIKING
CAMPING
CANOEING
CAVING
CLIMBING
FISHING
FITNESS
GLIDING
HUNTING
JOGGING
KAYAKING
LEISURE
MOUNTAINS
NATURE
PARK
RACING
RAFTING
RUNNING
SAFARI
SAILING
SKIING
SPORTS
SURFING
SWIMMING
TENTS
TREKKING
WALKING

Outdoor Recreation

G	R	A	Z	G	N	I	C	A	R	A	S	O	R
G	U	S	C	P	C	R	A	F	T	I	N	G	S
N	N	K	S	T	L	G	N	I	M	M	I	W	S
I	N	I	G	N	I	N	O	O	L	L	A	B	G
T	I	I	H	T	M	V	E	E	R	U	T	A	N
N	N	N	W	S	B	F	I	T	G	A	N	C	I
U	G	G	T	Z	I	G	N	T	N	D	U	K	K
H	D	N	N	T	N	F	G	G	I	V	O	P	L
G	E	L	N	I	G	P	N	N	L	E	M	A	A
T	N	E	D	F	P	I	I	I	C	N	S	C	W
G	S	I	X	S	K	M	K	V	Y	T	A	K	G
S	L	S	G	K	A	R	A	A	C	U	I	H	N
G	V	U	E	G	A	F	Y	C	I	R	L	C	I
S	P	R	X	P	O	Q	A	T	B	E	I	A	K
F	T	E	M	K	B	J	K	R	Y	X	N	E	I
S	P	O	R	T	S	U	R	F	I	N	G	B	B

Solution on Page 332

AIRPORT
CHATTAHOOCHEE
CITY
CIVIL WAR
CNN
COCA-COLA
ENTERTAINMENT
FULTON COUNTY
HARTSFIELD
HISTORICAL
HOME DEPOT
HUB
LARGE
METROPOLITAN
MODERN
PEACHTREE
PHILIPS ARENA
PIEDMONT PARK
SKYSCRAPERS
SPORTS
TED TURNER
THRASHERS
TOURISM
TRAVEL
TURNER FIELD
UNDERGROUND
UNITED STATES
URBAN
USA

Atlanta

D	N	U	O	R	G	R	E	D	N	U	G	Y	L
Y	A	A	N	S	R	E	H	S	A	R	H	T	S
H	T	P	L	I	M	O	D	E	R	N	O	N	K
T	I	N	H	O	T	O	U	R	I	S	M	E	Y
E	L	S	U	I	C	E	L	A	R	G	E	M	S
D	O	C	T	O	L	A	D	B	U	H	D	N	C
T	P	I	A	O	C	I	C	S	C	P	E	I	R
U	O	V	I	S	R	N	P	O	T	N	P	A	A
R	R	I	R	P	N	I	O	S	C	A	O	T	P
N	T	L	P	O	A	H	C	T	A	B	T	R	E
E	E	W	O	R	A	U	S	A	L	R	X	E	R
R	M	A	R	T	R	A	V	E	L	U	E	T	S
H	A	R	T	S	F	I	E	L	D	O	F	N	D
K	R	A	P	T	N	O	M	D	E	I	P	E	A
R	H	D	L	E	I	F	R	E	N	R	U	T	I
C	I	T	Y	P	E	A	C	H	T	R	E	E	G

Solution on Page 332

BARGE
BOW
CABIN
CANOE
CREW
CRUISE
DECKS
ENGINE
FERRYBOAT
FIBERGLASS
FISHING
FLOAT
HULL
KAYAK
KEEL
LAKE
LIFEBOAT
MOTOR
NAUTICAL
OCEAN
PADDLES
PORT
RAFT
RECREATION
RIVER
ROW
SAILBOAT
SAILING
SEA
SHIP
SKI
STARBOARD
STERN
SUN
TRAVEL
TRIP
WATER
WHEEL
WOODEN
YACHT

Watercraft

O	E	G	T	M	C	F	S	I	A	Q	I	N	Z
W	G	N	D	E	C	K	S	O	P	E	K	H	M
T	N	T	I	R	G	N	I	L	I	A	S	D	W
R	I	R	U	G	P	L	A	C	I	T	U	A	N
A	H	I	E	I	N	E	O	N	A	C	W	N	O
V	S	P	H	T	F	E	R	R	Y	B	O	A	T
E	I	S	R	L	S	K	B	R	O	I	S	U	A
L	F	O	A	M	I	O	V	D	T	E	A	R	O
N	P	H	O	L	A	F	D	A	L	T	I	D	L
W	A	T	E	R	G	O	E	D	S	F	L	A	F
W	O	O	D	E	N	R	D	B	C	A	B	I	N
R	E	L	B	N	C	A	E	L	O	R	O	K	U
O	H	E	A	E	P	M	C	B	O	A	A	L	S
W	G	E	R	E	V	I	R	W	I	Y	T	L	R
P	C	H	G	L	A	K	E	N	A	F	Y	U	Q
O	M	W	E	R	B	O	W	K	Y	A	C	H	T

Solution on Page 332

ALPS
AMSTERDAM
ANCIENT
AUSTRIA
BELGIUM
BERLIN
BLACK SEA
BORDERS
CITIES
CONTINENT
COUNTRIES
CURRENCY
DENMARK
ENGLAND
EURASIA
FINLAND
FRANCE
GERMANY
HISTORY
ICELAND
IRELAND
ITALY
KINGS
LANGUAGES
LONDON
LUXEMBOURG
MONARCHY
NATO
PARIS
POLAND
PORTUGAL
SCOTLAND
SERBIA
SPAIN
VATICAN

Around Europe

Z	S	E	I	T	I	C	E	L	A	N	D	M	V
S	N	A	C	I	T	A	V	C	K	I	N	G	S
G	E	R	M	A	N	Y	B	O	R	D	E	R	S
Y	H	U	S	C	O	T	L	A	N	D	S	U	D
H	Q	N	R	S	D	N	A	L	N	I	F	O	N
C	R	I	P	A	A	E	S	K	C	A	L	B	A
R	U	L	C	T	S	N	I	A	P	S	L	M	L
A	A	R	O	O	A	I	R	T	S	U	A	E	E
N	E	E	R	I	U	T	A	Y	I	D	G	X	R
O	N	B	T	E	N	N	R	S	R	P	U	U	I
M	G	A	E	E	N	O	T	E	A	T	T	L	E
B	L	Y	I	L	T	C	T	R	P	H	R	O	C
Y	A	C	B	S	G	S	Y	B	I	N	O	N	N
H	N	J	I	E	M	I	C	I	K	E	P	D	A
A	D	H	L	A	N	G	U	A	G	E	S	O	R
P	O	L	A	N	D	E	N	M	A	R	K	N	F

Solution on Page 333

AMERICA
BASKETBALL
BLACKHAWKS
BLUES
BUILDINGS
BULLS
BUSINESS
CARS
COLD
CRIME
DALEY
FIRE
FOOTBALL
HOT DOG
ILLINOIS
INDUSTRY
JAZZ
JORDAN
LAKEFRONT
LIGHTS
MIDWEST
MUSICAL
NAVY PIER
PIZZA
POLITICS
SNOW
THE LOOP
TOURISM
TRAFFIC
TRIBUNE
UNIVERSITY
URBAN
WHITE SOX
WINDY CITY

The Windy City

M	I	D	W	E	S	T	O	U	R	I	S	M	W
L	I	G	H	T	S	R	A	C	Y	J	A	Z	Z
W	O	N	S	Q	E	W	H	I	T	E	S	O	X
Z	S	S	S	G	N	I	D	L	I	U	B	L	C
L	E	N	U	B	I	R	T	I	S	E	A	L	I
L	U	A	C	E	S	B	Y	K	R	K	N	A	F
A	L	M	R	L	U	M	W	D	E	A	F	B	F
B	B	E	I	A	B	A	P	F	V	W	G	T	A
T	U	R	M	L	H	O	R	Y	I	G	O	O	R
E	L	I	E	K	L	O	P	N	N	F	D	O	T
K	L	C	C	I	N	I	D	L	U	I	T	F	D
S	S	A	T	T	E	Y	N	A	D	R	O	J	A
A	L	I	C	R	C	P	O	O	L	E	H	T	L
B	C	O	E	I	K	L	A	C	I	S	U	M	E
S	L	E	T	D	R	I	N	D	U	S	T	R	Y
D	J	Y	A	Z	Z	I	P	N	A	B	R	U	Z

Solution on Page 333

ALOHA
AMERICA
CLIMATE
COCONUT
COFFEE
CULTURE
HISTORY
HONOLULU
HOTEL
HUMID
ISLANDS
KAUAI
LAVA
LUAU
MAUI
MOUNTAIN
OAHU
OBAMA
PINEAPPLE
POLYNESIAN
RAINBOW
RESORTS
SAND
SEA
SUGARCANE
SUNSET
SURFING
TOURISTS
TRAVEL
TROPICS
USA
VOLCANOES
WATER
WAVES

Visit Hawaii

A	V	L	E	T	O	H	M	Z	A	P	G	R	U
M	W	A	V	E	S	O	Z	L	U	I	U	A	M
A	W	A	L	S	U	C	O	C	O	N	U	T	R
B	O	E	S	N	Q	L	W	A	T	E	R	H	I
O	B	T	T	U	E	N	A	C	R	A	G	U	S
G	N	A	I	S	E	N	Y	L	O	P	M	A	L
J	I	M	Q	E	U	T	K	U	S	P	A	A	A
N	A	I	W	O	I	A	O	A	J	L	M	S	N
H	R	L	L	N	U	W	N	U	O	E	C	I	D
U	I	C	K	A	L	D	L	H	R	I	I	C	S
M	T	S	I	C	V	U	A	I	P	I	W	U	E
I	N	R	T	L	L	A	C	O	N	H	S	L	Q
D	U	H	A	O	I	A	R	E	S	O	R	T	S
N	S	E	N	V	R	T	G	N	I	F	R	U	S
A	S	O	Z	S	E	Y	R	O	U	U	Z	R	J
R	H	Y	H	Y	I	L	C	O	F	F	E	E	N

Solution on Page 333

BOSTON
BRITAIN
BRITISH
COLONIES
CONGRESS
COTTON
DELAWARE
DEMOCRACY
DUTCH
ENGLAND
FRANKLIN
FREEDOM
GOVERNMENT
JAMESTOWN
KING
MARYLAND
MAYFLOWER
NEW YORK
PILGRIMS
PLYMOUTH
PURITANS
RELIGION
REVOLUTION
SALEM
SETTLEMENT
SPAIN
TAXATION
TEA
THIRTEEN
TRADE
VIRGINIA
WASHINGTON

Colonial Tour

K	Y	S	D	O	N	I	L	K	N	A	R	F	B
A	R	C	N	U	S	W	Z	C	E	M	G	C	R
I	E	O	A	A	T	N	O	T	S	O	B	O	I
N	N	N	Y	R	T	C	E	T	V	D	G	T	T
I	G	G	I	W	C	I	H	E	S	E	N	T	I
G	L	R	N	A	E	O	R	X	T	E	O	O	S
R	A	E	O	V	P	N	M	U	M	R	M	N	H
I	N	S	T	A	M	S	G	E	P	F	I	A	T
V	D	S	G	E	E	N	L	L	D	K	S	H	J
B	E	V	N	O	I	T	U	L	O	V	E	R	T
R	L	T	I	K	T	R	E	L	I	G	I	O	N
I	A	R	H	E	M	A	R	Y	L	A	N	D	M
T	W	A	S	M	I	R	G	L	I	P	O	B	E
A	A	D	A	G	H	T	U	O	M	Y	L	P	L
I	R	E	W	O	L	F	Y	A	M	Q	O	F	A
N	E	T	A	X	A	T	I	O	N	Y	C	M	S

Solution on Page 333

ANIMALS
AREA
BEEF
BISON
BRANDING
BULLS
CALF
CATTLE
CORRAL
COUNTRY
COWBOYS
COWHAND
CROPS
DUDE
EMU
FARMERS
FARMING
FENCES
FIELD
GRAZING
HAY
HERD
HOMESTEAD
HORSES
LANDSCAPE
LIVESTOCK
MEAT
PASTURE
PRAIRIE
RANCHING
RIDE
RODEO
ROPE
SADDLE
SHEEP
SOUTH
STEER
TEXAS
WESTERN
WOOL

Dude Ranch

R	E	E	T	S	L	O	E	L	D	D	A	S	K
C	C	R	O	P	S	O	C	A	T	T	L	E	E
S	A	X	E	T	R	C	O	O	Z	E	E	S	U
A	L	N	A	A	E	O	W	W	U	G	P	R	Q
G	F	G	I	E	M	R	B	E	B	N	L	O	T
H	N	N	O	M	R	R	O	S	J	I	T	H	R
O	J	I	E	L	A	A	Y	T	V	H	G	R	T
B	I	Z	D	A	F	L	S	E	K	C	G	D	Y
E	E	A	O	N	E	P	S	R	I	N	N	L	A
E	I	R	R	D	A	T	K	N	N	A	I	E	X
F	R	G	U	S	O	R	Y	A	H	R	M	I	V
E	I	D	T	C	S	I	B	W	B	P	R	F	X
N	A	U	K	A	O	J	O	U	I	E	A	A	R
C	R	S	M	P	U	C	D	X	S	E	F	L	I
E	P	D	A	E	T	S	E	M	O	H	E	R	D
S	L	L	U	B	H	N	G	E	N	S	X	B	E

Solution on Page 334

ARCH
ATOLL
BASIN
BAYOU
BEACH
BUTTE
CANYON
CAPE
CAVE
CLIFF
COVE
CRATER
DELTA
DESERT
DUNE
FIELD
FJORD
FLUVIAL
GLACIER
GULLY
HILL
ISLAND
ISTHMUS
MARSH
MESA
OASIS
PLATEAU
RANGE
RAVINE
REEF
RIDGE
RIVER
ROCK
SEA
SLOPE
SOIL
SOUND
SWAMP
VALLEY
VOLCANO

Landforms along the Way

Y	G	P	U	C	C	B	E	P	O	L	S	U	X
S	A	Q	T	R	A	X	D	H	E	I	D	A	F
O	M	H	O	K	P	M	A	W	S	G	Z	D	H
U	K	C	J	J	E	M	E	A	H	R	D	C	N
N	K	R	B	N	Y	C	O	G	K	U	A	I	S
D	K	A	I	I	O	L	D	F	N	E	S	M	R
R	C	C	G	V	S	M	L	E	B	A	Y	O	U
O	B	D	E	L	E	T	T	U	B	T	R	X	F
J	D	U	N	S	A	R	H	O	G	O	G	F	E
F	S	E	A	A	U	C	N	M	X	L	I	T	E
F	I	O	L	J	L	A	I	V	U	L	F	R	R
K	X	E	I	T	C	S	E	E	C	S	E	E	V
C	Y	E	L	L	A	V	I	T	R	T	V	S	I
R	A	L	O	D	N	O	Y	N	A	C	A	E	S
M	I	V	E	N	I	V	A	R	U	L	C	D	S
H	W	T	U	M	O	H	C	Z	C	P	P	W	E

Solution on Page 334

BALANCE
BRISK
COMMUTE
DISTANCE
DOG
EXERCISE
FEET
FITNESS
FOOTPATH
FUN
GAIT
GROUND
HEALTHY
HIKING
JOGGING
KNEES
LEGS
LEISURE
MALL
MARCHING
MILES
MOVEMENT
MUSCLES
NATURE
PACE
POWER
ROAD
RUNNING
SIDEWALK
SLOW
SPEED
STEPS
STICK
STRENGTH
STRIDE
TRAILS
TRAVEL
WATER
WELLNESS
WORKOUT

Walking

E	T	U	M	M	O	C	S	T	I	C	K	S	I
R	I	S	O	L	L	A	M	T	O	K	G	F	H
U	A	T	V	G	R	O	U	N	D	E	N	E	S
S	G	R	E	P	E	C	N	A	L	A	B	E	H
I	E	E	M	G	E	C	A	P	T	T	L	T	R
E	C	N	E	N	F	U	N	U	R	I	A	K	O
L	C	G	N	I	H	C	R	A	M	P	S	L	A
G	F	T	T	G	E	E	V	S	T	I	E	A	D
N	S	H	U	G	A	E	P	O	R	S	I	W	W
I	L	I	O	O	L	E	O	B	I	D	I	E	A
N	O	K	K	J	T	F	R	C	E	P	L	D	T
N	W	I	R	S	H	J	R	E	Q	L	G	I	E
U	F	N	O	A	Y	E	P	K	N	E	E	S	R
R	J	G	W	V	X	S	S	E	N	T	I	F	S
N	P	O	W	E	R	C	S	E	L	C	S	U	M
X	E	D	I	R	T	S	L	I	A	R	T	A	F

Solution on Page 334

AGRICULTURE
BADGER STATE
BEER
BREWERS
BUCKS
CHEESEHEADS
CHIPPEWA
COLD
CORN
DAIRYLAND
DOOR COUNTY
FARMING
FOOTBALL
GREAT LAKES
ICE FISHING
KENOSHA
LAKE MICHIGAN
LAKE SUPERIOR
LAMBEAU FIELD
NORTHERN
PAPER MILLS
RIVERS
ROBIN
SKIING
SNOW
SPORTS
SUGAR MAPLE
SUMMERFEST
UNIVERSITY

Wisconsin

U	N	I	V	E	R	S	I	T	Y	G	L	Y	S
D	B	R	E	W	E	R	S	T	R	A	N	U	P
N	O	R	T	H	E	R	N	E	K	I	M	F	O
A	D	L	E	I	F	U	A	E	B	M	A	L	R
L	C	Y	H	I	O	T	M	O	E	R	Y	E	T
Y	O	U	B	C	L	I	R	R	M	E	E	S	S
R	L	B	R	A	C	O	F	I	R	B	D	L	U
I	D	O	K	H	D	E	N	U	A	A	L	S	G
A	O	E	I	K	S	G	T	W	E	I	K	R	A
D	S	G	Y	T	S	L	E	H	M	I	N	E	R
L	A	K	E	S	U	P	E	R	I	O	R	V	M
N	W	A	K	C	P	S	E	N	S	M	O	I	A
I	P	C	I	I	E	P	G	V	W	T	C	R	P
U	U	R	H	E	A	F	O	O	T	B	A	L	L
B	G	C	H	P	K	E	N	O	S	H	A	T	E
A	I	C	E	F	I	S	H	I	N	G	X	G	E

Solution on Page 334

AFRICA
AMERICAS
ANTARCTICA
AREAS
ATLAS
AUSTRALIA
BORDERS
BOUNDARY
CITIES
CONTINUOUS
CONVENTION
COUNTRY
DIVISIONS
DRIFT
EURASIA
GEOGRAPHY
GEOLOGICAL
GREENLAND
INDIA
ISLAND
LANDMASSES
MAINLAND
MOUNTAINS
NORTH AMERICA
OCEANS
POPULATION
REGIONS
SEPARATION
SHELF
SOUTH AMERICA
WORLD

Continents

A	Q	V	B	O	U	N	D	A	R	Y	B	F	D
T	T	F	I	R	D	N	A	L	N	I	A	M	N
L	T	E	F	C	R	E	G	I	O	N	S	J	A
A	G	E	O	L	O	G	I	C	A	L	N	N	L
S	C	L	N	C	O	N	T	I	N	U	O	U	S
M	Y	I	A	O	S	J	V	O	C	R	I	S	I
O	H	A	R	N	I	Y	I	E	T	A	S	N	L
U	P	I	I	F	D	T	R	H	N	H	I	A	G
N	A	D	A	S	A	M	A	T	E	T	V	E	R
T	R	N	B	R	A	M	A	L	N	T	I	C	E
A	G	I	A	D	E	R	F	S	U	U	D	O	E
I	O	P	N	R	C	A	U	D	S	P	O	T	N
N	E	C	I	T	I	E	S	E	L	E	O	C	L
S	G	C	I	J	B	O	R	D	E	R	S	P	A
X	A	C	I	R	E	M	A	H	T	U	O	S	N
S	A	U	S	T	R	A	L	I	A	B	F	W	D

Solution on Page 335

BOXCAR
CARS
COAL
CONTAINER
CONVEYANCE
CROSSINGS
DIESEL
DINING CAR
ELECTRICAL
ENGINES
FREIGHT
GOODS
HAUL
LINE
LOCOMOTIVE
MONORAIL
MOVEMENT
PASSENGERS
PEOPLE
PLATFORM
RAILROADS
RAILWAY
ROUTE
SHIPPING
SLEEPERS
STATION
STEEL
STOPS
SWITCHES
TICKET
TIES
TRACKS
TRAINS
TRANSPORT
TRAVEL
WHISTLE

By Rail

T	W	S	T	A	T	I	O	N	C	T	R	E	L	
I	H	Y	A	W	L	I	A	R	R	E	T	S	U	
C	I	G	O	O	D	S	O	A	N	U	R	T	A	
K	S	L	I	N	E	S	I	I	O	T	A	E	H	
E	T	T	I	E	S	L	A	R	N	H	N	E	T	
T	L	A	C	I	R	T	C	E	L	E	S	L	R	
R	E	I	N	O	N	F	M	R	S	R	P	O	A	
A	A	G	A	O	N	E	U	E	L	A	O	C	V	
C	S	D	C	R	V	V	H	Y	S	C	R	O	E	
K	S	S	D	O	O	C	E	S	S	G	T	M	L	
S	E	P	M	I	T	N	E	Y	R	N	B	O	P	
N	N	O	H	I	E	N	O	D	A	I	O	T	O	
I	I	T	W	N	G	S	U	M	C	N	X	I	E	
A	G	S	L	E	E	P	E	R	S	I	C	V	P	
R	N	M	R	O	F	T	A	L	P	D	A	E	K	
T	E	S	H	I	P	P	I	N	G	N	R	X	R	

Solution on Page 335

ACADIAN
AMERICAN
APPLES
BAKED BEANS
BARBECUE
BEER
CAJUN
CLAMBAKE
COLONIAL
COOKING
CORN
CREOLE
EMERIL
ETHNIC
FAST FOOD
FATS
FRUITS
GRILLING
HAMBURGERS
HOT DOGS
LOBSTER
LOUISIANA
NEW ENGLAND
PAULA DEEN
PIZZA
POTATOES
REGIONAL
RESTAURANTS
SANDWICH
SEAFOOD
SOUL FOOD
SOUTHERN
TEX MEX
TURKEY
WINE

Cuisine Across the U.S.

D	O	O	F	A	E	S	T	I	U	R	F	P	A
S	N	A	E	B	D	E	K	A	B	M	A	L	C
A	U	A	M	N	N	R	E	H	T	U	O	S	A
N	T	D	L	E	I	S	O	U	L	F	O	O	D
D	H	E	O	G	R	W	G	A	Z	Z	I	P	I
W	A	B	X	O	N	I	D	O	R	E	E	B	A
I	M	A	R	M	F	E	C	N	D	L	C	L	N
C	B	R	E	L	E	T	W	A	O	T	A	J	S
H	U	B	T	N	O	X	S	E	N	I	O	J	N
C	R	E	S	T	A	U	R	A	N	T	S	H	U
I	G	C	B	U	N	C	I	O	F	A	T	S	J
N	E	U	O	R	R	A	L	S	E	L	P	P	A
H	R	E	L	K	C	O	O	K	I	N	G	R	C
T	S	O	G	E	C	S	E	O	T	A	T	O	P
E	R	C	C	Y	G	R	I	L	L	I	N	G	U
L	I	R	E	M	E	R	E	G	I	O	N	A	L

Solution on Page 335

ARABS
ARCHITECTURE
ARID CLIMATE
BEACHES
BUILDINGS
CAPITAL
CITY
CONSTRUCTION
COSMOPOLITAN
CUISINE
CULTURE
DESERT
DIVERSE
DUBAI
EMIRATES PALACE
ETIHAD AIRWAYS
ETISALAT
GOVERNMENT
METROPOLIS
MIDDLE EAST
OIL
PERSIAN GULF
PORT
REAL ESTATE
REEM ISLAND
RICH
SALAM STREET
SAND
SKYSCRAPERS
UAE
WEALTHY

Abu Dhabi

A	Y	S	K	Y	S	C	R	A	P	E	R	S	S
M	R	C	S	I	L	O	P	O	R	T	E	M	B
I	Z	C	I	E	T	I	S	A	L	A	T	N	A
D	C	Y	H	T	L	A	E	W	I	T	U	O	R
D	O	A	L	I	Y	T	M	C	O	S	T	I	A
L	S	R	T	H	T	E	M	A	U	E	S	T	P
E	M	I	R	A	T	E	S	P	A	L	A	C	E
E	O	D	E	D	N	R	C	I	E	A	N	U	R
A	P	C	E	A	E	T	U	T	R	E	D	R	S
S	O	L	M	I	M	S	I	A	U	R	I	T	I
T	L	I	I	R	N	M	S	L	T	R	V	S	A
R	I	M	S	W	R	A	I	R	L	D	E	N	N
E	T	A	L	A	E	L	N	I	U	U	R	O	G
S	A	T	A	Y	V	A	E	C	C	B	S	C	U
E	N	E	N	S	O	S	E	H	C	A	E	B	L
D	L	Q	D	S	G	N	I	D	L	I	U	B	F

Solution on Page 335

BUS STOP
CHARTER
CITY BUS
COACH
COMMUTE
DIESEL
DOORS
DRIVER
ENGINE
FARE
LONG
METRO
MINI
PASSENGERS
PEOPLE
PRIVATE
RAIL
RIDE
ROUTES
SCHOOL BUS
SEATS
SERVICE
SIT
STATION
STOPS
TICKET
TOUR
TRANSFER
TRAVEL
TROLLEY
VEHICLE
WINDOW
YELLOW

Bus Trip

L	E	V	A	R	T	G	E	K	S	B	U	H	P
V	D	S	T	A	E	S	S	E	R	V	I	C	E
O	I	G	E	P	G	V	E	W	S	S	O	A	L
E	R	S	U	B	Y	T	I	C	E	M	C	O	C
L	F	A	R	E	P	N	H	R	M	E	T	C	I
M	D	N	L	X	D	O	E	U	D	I	C	K	H
H	O	L	P	O	O	T	T	A	S	H	N	T	E
Y	O	K	W	L	A	E	E	S	A	M	R	I	V
W	R	Z	B	V	Y	N	H	R	S	E	A	C	D
E	S	U	I	D	I	Y	T	L	F	U	S	K	I
K	S	R	E	G	N	E	S	S	A	P	B	E	E
V	P	K	N	M	R	S	N	O	I	T	A	T	S
K	W	E	R	W	E	A	X	P	E	O	P	L	E
Y	E	L	L	O	R	T	I	I	Q	U	U	O	L
J	R	O	U	T	E	S	R	L	X	R	E	N	P
A	J	O	Z	C	R	S	P	O	T	S	H	G	O

Solution on Page 336

AIR
ANIMALS
BEAUTY
BIOLOGY
CLIMATE
CLOUDS
DESERT
EARTH
ECOLOGY
FAUNA
FIELD
FISH
FLORA
FORESTS
GEOLOGY
GRASS
GREEN
HUMAN
LAKES
LAND
LEAVES
MOTHER
NATURAL
OCEANS
OUTSIDE
PLANTS
POND
RAIN
RIVERS
ROCKS
SKY
SNOW
SOIL
STREAMS
SUN
TREES
WATER
WEATHER
WILDLIFE
WIND

See Nature

U	V	H	I	S	S	N	U	S	N	A	E	C	O
A	R	T	K	E	Y	Z	D	C	J	K	A	A	W
I	I	R	V	K	G	U	B	L	P	W	N	R	Q
R	V	A	V	A	O	K	Y	I	O	I	U	O	H
P	E	E	J	L	L	G	G	M	M	L	A	L	S
L	R	H	C	D	O	J	O	A	B	D	F	F	I
Y	S	I	T	L	E	G	L	T	D	L	E	I	F
W	O	G	O	A	G	S	O	E	L	I	O	S	T
S	M	C	S	R	E	B	I	S	Q	F	U	Z	R
N	E	P	I	U	R	W	B	T	O	E	H	Q	E
O	D	V	L	T	A	W	D	R	D	B	U	S	E
W	I	D	A	A	I	A	E	E	E	Q	M	G	S
A	S	Z	N	N	N	S	M	A	S	S	A	R	G
T	T	Y	D	O	T	T	U	M	E	W	N	E	L
E	U	J	K	S	P	T	S	S	R	N	R	E	Q
R	O	C	K	S	Y	R	E	H	T	O	M	N	X

Solution on Page 336

AIRCRAFT
AUTOMOBILE
BICYCLES
BIKE
BOATS
BUS
CART
DRIVE
ELECTRIC
ENGINE
FORD
GAS
HELICOPTER
HOVERCRAFT
LAND
LICENSE
MECHANIC
MOTORCYCLE
OIL
PASSENGER
PEOPLE
PLANE
POWER
ROAD
ROCKET
SCOOTER
SEDAN
SHIPS
SPACECRAFT
STEERING
TRAINS
TRANSPORT
TRAVEL
TRUCK
VAN
WATER
WHEELED
YACHT

Vehicles

E	T	G	A	S	P	Q	S	A	D	R	I	V	E
N	T	E	T	U	S	E	I	E	O	N	C	A	N
I	R	C	L	N	T	R	O	C	D	I	E	N	A
G	V	B	I	C	C	O	K	P	N	A	S	T	L
N	N	A	C	R	Y	E	M	A	L	H	N	F	P
E	R	I	A	P	T	C	H	O	T	E	E	A	Y
T	D	F	R	S	O	C	R	K	B	L	C	R	A
Z	T	L	T	E	E	W	E	O	B	I	I	C	C
S	R	A	I	M	E	M	E	L	T	C	L	R	H
U	O	S	C	O	O	T	E	R	E	O	I	E	T
B	P	R	E	G	N	E	S	S	A	P	M	V	S
I	S	P	A	C	E	C	R	A	F	T	R	O	S
K	N	W	F	B	I	C	Y	C	L	E	S	H	L
E	A	W	H	E	E	L	E	D	T	R	I	A	M
T	R	A	V	E	L	R	O	A	D	P	N	Z	C
V	T	R	U	C	K	Z	W	S	S	D	R	O	F

Solution on Page 336

AIRFARE
AIRLINES
ATTENDANTS
CARRYON
COACH
CONCOURSE
CUSTOMS
ELEVATORS
ESCALATORS
FUSELAGE
GATE
GIFT SHOP
JET
KITTY HAWK
LAX
MECHANICS
NAVIGATORS
NYC
OVERHEAD
PILOTS
PROPELLER
RESTAURANT
RUDDER
RUNWAY
SKYCAPS
TAKEOFF
TAXI
WALKWAY
WINGS

Around the Airport

U	H	T	E	Y	A	W	N	U	R	V	K	E	K
E	C	W	X	B	P	O	X	T	P	L	T	A	N
I	Y	E	A	S	F	F	O	E	K	A	T	A	H
A	I	R	L	I	N	E	S	J	G	T	V	C	F
P	R	O	P	E	L	L	E	R	E	I	A	O	M
N	D	Q	M	K	V	A	F	N	G	O	C	N	A
O	S	G	N	I	W	A	D	A	C	K	U	C	G
Y	E	S	C	A	L	A	T	O	R	S	S	O	D
R	W	C	F	P	N	O	H	O	K	Q	T	U	A
R	A	I	U	T	R	O	S	Y	R	X	O	R	E
A	L	N	S	S	P	I	L	O	T	S	M	S	H
C	K	A	E	T	N	A	R	U	A	T	S	E	R
Y	W	H	L	X	P	O	H	S	T	F	I	G	E
N	A	C	A	I	R	F	A	R	E	A	W	K	V
T	Y	E	G	S	P	A	C	Y	K	S	X	C	O
X	M	M	E	R	E	D	D	U	R	K	T	I	R

Solution on Page 336

ALPS
BANKING
BERN
CANTONS
CHEESE
CHOCOLATE
COLD
COUNTRY
EUROPEAN
FONDUE
FRANC
FRENCH
FUN
GENEVA
GERMANY
GLACIERS
HEIDI
ITALIAN
LANDLOCKED
LUCERNE
MATTERHORN
MOUNTAINS
NATION
NEUTRALITY
PARLIAMENT
RED CROSS
REPUBLIC
SKIING
SNOW
SWISS
TOURISTS
TRAVEL
VALLEYS
WATCHES
WEALTH
WINE
YODELING

Switzerland

X	S	S	Y	N	A	L	P	S	Q	F	W	D	N
M	E	S	N	R	L	U	C	E	R	N	E	W	S
C	H	O	C	O	L	A	T	E	O	K	U	E	S
I	C	R	N	H	W	C	N	R	C	R	R	A	K
L	T	C	E	R	E	C	O	O	A	T	O	L	I
B	A	D	U	E	H	E	L	L	P	V	P	T	I
U	W	E	T	T	Y	D	S	I	D	I	E	H	N
P	Y	R	R	T	N	S	R	E	I	C	A	L	G
E	K	I	A	A	Y	Y	J	S	W	I	N	E	N
R	S	T	L	M	O	U	N	T	A	I	N	S	I
F	Y	A	I	S	D	B	S	S	I	W	S	P	K
R	E	L	T	N	E	M	A	I	L	R	A	P	N
A	L	I	Y	R	L	G	E	R	M	A	N	Y	A
N	L	A	N	N	I	C	O	U	N	T	R	Y	B
C	A	N	T	O	N	S	F	O	N	D	U	E	S
A	V	E	N	E	G	N	A	T	I	O	N	U	F

Solution on Page 337

ANCIENT
ASIAN
BAHT
BANGKOK
BEACH
BOXING
BUDDHIST
BURMA
CAMBODIA
CHINESE
COUNTRY
CUISINE
CULTURE
CURRY
DANCE
EXPORTS
FOOD
FOREIGN
FRIENDLY
GULF
HISTORY
HOT
ISLANDS
KINGDOM
LAOS
MALAYSIA
MEKONG
MONARCHY
MONSOONS
PACIFIC
POLITICS
RICE
SIAM
SOUTHEAST
TEMPLES
TOURISM
TRAVEL
TROPICAL
VIETNAM
WATER

Thailand

P	O	L	I	T	I	C	S	A	M	R	U	B	G
Y	G	C	U	I	S	I	N	E	F	O	O	D	H
R	N	Y	Q	U	Q	A	I	D	O	B	M	A	C
R	I	N	H	F	R	I	E	N	D	L	Y	U	A
U	X	R	I	C	E	S	R	H	A	W	L	Y	E
C	O	U	N	T	R	Y	I	O	T	T	U	R	B
K	B	C	F	E	B	A	S	A	U	U	R	O	C
D	I	T	L	C	A	L	N	R	M	W	O	T	I
S	L	N	U	N	N	A	E	O	A	S	N	S	F
S	E	E	G	A	G	M	N	T	M	D	G	I	I
E	V	I	Y	D	K	S	E	S	E	N	I	H	C
L	A	C	I	P	O	R	T	J	K	A	E	D	A
P	R	N	B	O	K	M	F	U	O	L	R	D	P
M	T	A	N	Z	A	S	I	A	N	S	O	U	T
E	H	S	T	R	O	P	X	E	G	I	F	B	O
T	O	U	R	I	S	M	A	N	T	E	I	V	H

Solution on Page 337

ADVANCED
APPLE
BAY AREA
BUSINESS
CALIFORNIA
CHIP
CISCO
COMPANY
COMPUTER
EBAY
ENGINEERS
EXPERIMENT
FACEBOOK
GOOGLE
HIGH TECH
INDUSTRY
INNOVATORS
INTERNET
INVENTION
MICROSOFT
MONEY
PALO ALTO
PROCESSOR
RADIO
RESEARCH
SAN JOSE
SOFTWARE
STANFORD
STEVE JOBS
TECHNOLOGY
TRANSISTOR
YAHOO

Silicon Valley

S	B	I	N	T	E	R	N	E	T	X	F	T	Y
T	Y	G	O	L	O	N	H	C	E	T	H	F	Y
A	E	G	C	A	L	I	F	O	R	N	I	A	N
N	R	B	U	S	I	N	E	S	S	E	G	C	A
F	A	I	I	M	O	N	E	Y	A	M	H	E	P
O	W	N	Y	T	B	O	N	H	N	I	T	B	M
R	T	D	A	A	R	V	G	O	J	R	E	O	O
D	F	U	H	P	S	A	I	B	O	E	C	O	C
H	O	S	O	P	M	T	N	A	S	P	H	K	O
C	S	T	O	L	N	O	E	S	E	X	I	R	M
R	O	R	L	E	E	R	E	V	I	E	P	A	P
A	R	Y	V	A	A	S	R	E	E	S	H	D	U
E	C	N	Z	Y	O	C	S	I	C	J	T	I	T
S	I	Y	A	B	E	L	G	O	O	G	O	O	E
E	M	B	N	A	D	V	A	N	C	E	D	B	R
R	O	S	S	E	C	O	R	P	T	A	Q	V	S

Solution on Page 337

AMERICAN
ASSEMBLY
BRONCO
CARS
DEARBORN
DETROIT
DRIVING
EDSEL
ENGINE
ESCAPE
ESCORT
EXPLORER
FACTORY
FAIRLANE
FIESTA
FOCUS
FUSION
HISTORY
HYBRIDS
INDUSTRY
JOBS
LINCOLN
MAZDA
MERCURY
MICHIGAN
MODEL T
MOTORS
MUSTANG
NASCAR
QUALITY
TAURUS
TEMPO
TRACTORS
TRADITION
VEHICLES
WINDSTAR

Drive a Ford

N	A	S	C	A	R	A	T	S	D	N	I	W	J
M	D	S	E	L	C	I	H	E	V	M	B	P	O
O	Z	M	O	S	Q	U	A	L	I	T	Y	D	B
T	A	U	C	U	T	R	A	C	T	O	R	S	S
O	M	S	N	C	B	F	H	M	M	R	O	Y	E
R	O	T	O	O	C	I	S	V	E	E	T	L	P
S	D	A	R	F	G	H	U	E	R	R	S	B	A
M	E	N	B	A	Y	F	R	N	C	O	I	M	C
E	L	G	N	B	D	V	U	A	U	L	H	E	S
L	T	S	R	A	C	I	A	L	R	P	O	S	E
A	I	I	N	D	U	S	T	R	Y	X	P	S	S
T	D	N	O	U	N	A	C	I	R	E	M	A	C
S	X	U	C	R	V	M	G	A	O	N	E	F	O
E	E	Y	R	O	T	C	A	F	Z	N	T	W	R
I	E	D	S	E	L	E	N	G	I	N	E	R	T
F	U	S	I	O	N	N	D	R	I	V	I	N	G

Solution on Page 337

AERIAL
BRITISH
BUS
CABLE CAR
CARRIAGE
CITIES
COACH
COMMUTE
CONDUCTOR
DIESEL
DRIVER
ELECTRIC
FARE
FAST
LIGHT RAIL
LINE
LONDON
PANTOGRAPH
PASSENGERS
PUBLIC
RAILWAY
RIDE
ROUTE
STATION
STEAM
STOP
STREETS
SUBWAY
TICKET
TOUR
TRACKS
TRAFFIC
TRAINS
TRAMWAY
TRANSPORT
TRAVEL
TROLLEY
VEHICLE
WHEELS
WIRE

Trams

S	T	O	P	A	T	E	K	C	I	T	T	K	I
R	R	L	S	E	S	U	B	W	A	Y	O	C	V
E	A	C	I	R	T	C	E	L	E	N	U	O	E
V	V	I	D	I	E	S	E	L	P	O	R	N	H
I	E	F	L	A	A	G	L	A	E	I	Y	D	I
R	L	F	I	L	M	O	N	G	D	T	A	U	C
D	C	A	G	U	R	T	A	E	S	A	W	C	L
W	I	R	H	T	O	I	L	N	S	T	L	T	E
S	L	T	T	G	R	O	I	I	B	S	I	O	N
L	B	O	R	R	C	A	B	L	E	C	A	R	C
E	U	A	A	W	R	R	N	T	S	F	R	P	I
E	P	C	I	T	I	H	U	S	K	C	A	R	T
H	T	R	L	T	C	M	J	Z	P	R	B	R	I
W	E	U	I	A	M	N	O	D	N	O	L	U	E
K	A	S	O	O	F	A	S	T	E	E	R	T	S
J	H	C	C	R	N	Y	A	W	M	A	R	T	A

Solution on Page 338

AIRCRAFT
AIRPLANES
AIRPORT
APPROACH
ARRIVAL
ASPHALT
AVIATION
CEMENT
CONCRETE
DEPARTURE
DIRECTION
DISTANCE
FAA
FLAT
FLIGHTS
FLYING
GATE
GEAR
GRAVEL
JETS
LANDING
LIGHTING
LONG
MARKINGS
OVERRUN
PARALLEL
PATH
PAVEMENT
PILOTS
SAFETY
SECURITY
SKY
STRAIGHT
TAKEOFF
TARMAC
TAXIWAY
TERMINAL
TOUCHDOWN
TOWER

Runway

E	L	F	L	I	G	H	T	S	T	O	L	I	P
T	A	K	E	O	F	F	T	L	A	H	P	S	A
A	N	O	V	E	R	R	U	N	S	T	E	J	R
X	I	P	Y	T	A	V	I	A	T	I	O	N	A
I	M	A	L	I	G	H	T	I	N	G	A	T	E
W	R	T	G	J	A	P	P	R	O	A	C	H	G
A	E	H	N	D	I	R	E	C	T	I	O	N	L
Y	T	S	I	E	R	U	T	R	A	P	E	D	E
G	R	A	D	G	P	U	O	A	R	M	S	T	L
G	O	F	N	R	L	L	U	F	M	A	E	N	L
N	P	E	A	A	A	T	C	T	A	R	C	E	A
I	R	T	L	V	N	A	H	G	C	K	U	M	R
Y	I	Y	I	E	E	L	D	N	Y	I	R	E	A
L	A	R	M	L	S	F	O	O	K	N	I	V	P
F	R	E	W	O	T	C	W	L	S	G	T	A	R
A	C	D	I	S	T	A	N	C	E	S	Y	P	K

Solution on Page 338

ARTISTS
ARTWORK
BOOKS
CERAMICS
CITY
CLASSICAL
COLLECTION
CULTURE
CURATOR
DISPLAY
DRAWINGS
EDUCATION
EXHIBITS
GALLERY
HISTORY
LIGHTING
LOUVRE
MODERN ART
MOMA
MONA LISA
PAINTINGS
PARIS
PASTELS
PEOPLE
PHOTOGRAPH
PICASSO
PICTURES
PRINTS
SCULPTURES
STYLE
VOLUNTEER

Art Museum Tour

P	G	N	I	T	H	G	I	L	S	I	R	A	P
E	B	C	N	O	I	T	A	C	U	D	E	T	G
L	S	H	O	P	S	C	I	M	A	R	E	C	A
P	M	T	I	L	I	A	R	T	I	S	T	S	L
O	O	B	I	S	L	E	T	S	A	P	N	C	L
E	N	P	S	B	T	E	C	U	L	T	U	R	E
P	A	A	E	H	I	O	C	A	X	S	L	X	R
I	L	I	R	I	P	H	R	T	M	K	O	V	Y
C	I	N	U	E	M	A	X	Y	I	O	V	U	S
A	S	T	T	R	A	N	R	E	D	O	M	G	E
S	A	I	P	V	N	V	S	G	W	B	N	L	R
S	S	N	L	U	Y	E	R	N	O	I	Y	D	U
O	M	G	U	O	T	K	R	O	W	T	R	A	T
K	E	S	C	L	I	L	C	A	S	W	O	K	C
Z	Q	N	S	J	C	U	R	A	T	O	R	H	I
S	T	N	I	R	P	D	I	S	P	L	A	Y	P

Solution on Page 338

ATM
BEVERAGE
BREAD
CHIPS
CIRCLE K
CLERKS
COFFEE
CONVENIENT
CORNER
CUSTOMERS
DOUGHNUTS
DRINKS
EASY
FAST
FOOD
FUEL
GASOLINE
GROCERIES
GUM
HOT DOGS
ICE CREAM
LOTTERY
MAGAZINES
MAPS
MILK
MONEY
NEWSPAPERS
POP
PUMP
PURCHASE
QUICK
SANDWICH
SHOPPING
SLURPEES
SMALL
SNACKS
STOP
TOBACCO
TOILETRIES
WATER

Convenience Store Stop

A	T	S	P	I	H	C	R	S	M	A	L	L	B
H	C	E	N	I	L	O	S	A	G	X	E	O	G
R	L	Z	E	A	S	E	E	P	R	U	L	S	U
P	E	S	A	H	C	R	U	P	F	P	O	A	M
M	R	T	O	N	C	K	M	S	O	S	T	N	I
U	K	G	A	E	F	A	S	T	P	K	T	D	L
P	S	N	C	W	P	P	S	U	T	N	E	W	K
Y	E	I	E	S	O	S	R	N	O	I	R	I	C
S	I	P	G	P	R	E	E	H	B	R	Y	C	I
A	R	P	A	A	E	I	M	G	A	D	E	H	U
E	T	O	R	P	N	R	O	U	C	A	N	O	Q
E	E	H	E	E	R	E	T	O	C	E	O	T	D
F	L	S	V	R	O	C	S	D	O	R	M	D	O
F	I	N	E	S	C	O	U	E	X	B	P	O	O
O	O	W	B	C	I	R	C	L	E	K	I	G	F
C	T	A	T	M	A	G	A	Z	I	N	E	S	R

Solution on Page 338

AMSTERDAM
AQUEDUCTS
BANK
BARGES
BASIN
BOATS
BRIDGES
CARGO
CHANNELS
COMMERCE
DEEP
DITCH
ERIE CANAL
FLOW
GATES
GOODS
IRRIGATION
LAKES
LAND
LEVEL
LOCKS
MANMADE
OCEANS
PANAMA
POUND LOCK
RIVERS
ROUTE
SEA
SHIPPING
SUEZ CANAL
SUPPLY
TRANSPORT
TRAVEL
TRENCH
TUNNEL
VENICE
WATERWAYS

Down a Canal

W	L	E	N	N	U	T	B	H	C	T	I	D	L
M	P	A	S	L	A	N	A	C	E	I	R	E	A
B	E	A	S	T	R	A	N	S	P	O	R	T	K
S	E	Q	M	U	A	B	K	V	E	N	I	C	E
F	D	U	P	S	E	O	B	R	I	D	G	E	S
L	A	E	G	D	T	Z	B	D	A	N	A	A	C
O	M	D	C	Q	S	E	C	R	M	A	T	B	A
W	N	U	O	V	K	H	R	A	A	L	I	Y	R
C	A	C	M	K	C	O	L	D	N	U	O	P	G
B	M	T	M	N	O	S	T	H	A	A	N	H	O
G	J	S	E	B	L	E	N	R	P	M	L	L	R
O	A	R	R	R	K	G	K	A	A	E	E	W	O
O	T	T	C	O	W	R	S	R	E	V	I	R	U
D	S	L	E	N	N	A	H	C	E	C	E	J	T
S	B	N	I	S	A	B	Y	L	N	H	O	L	E
V	G	N	I	P	P	I	H	S	U	P	P	L	Y

Solution on Page 339

ANDROMEDA
ASTEROIDS
BIG BANG
CELESTIAL
COMETS
COSMOS
EARTH
ECLIPSE
GALAXIES
GALILEO
GASES
GRAVITY
HEAVENS
HUBBLE
JUPITER
LENS
LIGHT
MARS
MERCURY
METEORS
MILKY WAY
MOONS
NASA
NEBULAE
NEPTUNE
NIGHT
ORBITS
PHYSICS
PLANETS
RESEARCH
SATURN
SCIENCE
SKY
SPACE
STARS
STUDY
SUPERNOVA
UNIVERSE
URANUS
VENUS

Space Journey

S	T	A	R	S	C	W	E	C	N	E	I	C	S
T	H	D	J	S	N	O	O	M	A	R	S	C	T
U	G	C	P	U	Y	A	W	Y	K	L	I	M	E
D	I	C	R	N	P	R	B	N	A	S	A	S	N
Y	N	O	K	A	E	I	M	I	Y	T	G	A	A
S	E	S	G	R	E	S	T	H	G	I	A	T	L
U	B	M	D	U	A	S	P	E	Q	B	L	U	P
N	U	O	U	I	E	V	E	I	R	R	A	R	T
E	L	S	M	L	O	N	O	R	L	O	X	N	H
V	A	D	E	M	O	R	D	N	A	C	I	N	G
L	E	C	R	M	E	T	E	O	R	S	E	E	I
E	A	O	C	S	L	D	P	T	A	E	S	P	L
C	R	M	U	N	I	V	E	R	S	E	P	T	Y
A	T	E	R	E	L	B	B	U	H	A	C	U	K
P	H	T	Y	L	A	N	H	E	A	V	E	N	S
S	E	S	A	G	G	R	A	V	I	T	Y	E	X

Solution on Page 339

ACCIDENTS
ATV
BOGGING
DANGEROUS
DIRT BIKE
DRIVING
DUNE BUGGY
ENGINE
FAST
FOREST
HANDLEBARS
HELMETS
HILLS
HONDA
KAWASAKI
MOTOCROSS
MOTORCYCLE
MUDDY
POLARIS
QUAD BIKE
RACING
RECREATION
ROUGH
SAFETY
SAND
SEAT
SPEED
SPORT
STEERING
SUSPENSION
SUZUKI
TRAILS
VEHICLE
WHEELS
WILDERNESS
WOODS
YAMAHA

All-Terrain Vehicles

S	D	R	I	V	I	N	G	T	S	E	R	O	F
T	D	A	E	L	C	Y	C	R	O	T	O	M	S
Y	R	O	N	O	I	T	A	E	R	C	E	R	P
S	A	A	O	G	E	B	O	G	G	I	N	G	O
P	Y	M	I	W	E	K	I	B	T	R	I	D	R
E	T	D	A	L	I	R	I	V	T	A	G	O	T
E	E	U	D	H	S	L	O	B	H	A	N	F	M
D	F	N	I	U	A	V	D	U	D	O	E	H	O
J	A	E	K	T	M	C	A	E	S	A	G	S	T
H	S	B	A	G	N	I	C	A	R	U	U	S	O
E	S	U	S	P	E	N	S	I	O	N	A	Q	C
L	L	G	A	D	N	O	H	R	D	F	E	W	R
M	L	G	W	N	E	L	C	I	H	E	V	S	O
E	I	Y	A	A	S	T	E	E	R	I	N	G	S
T	H	Z	K	S	S	W	H	E	E	L	S	T	S
S	U	Z	U	K	I	N	P	O	L	A	R	I	S

Solution on Page 339

ANTENNA
BATTERY
BILL
CALLING
CAMERA
CHARGERS
CONNECT
COVERAGE
DATA
E-MAIL
FAMILY
FLIP
GAMES
GPS
INTERNET
IPHONE
KEYBOARD
KEYPAD
MESSAGES
MODERN
MOTOROLA
NOKIA
NUMBERS
PICTURES
PLAN
PORTABLE
RECHARGE
ROAMING
SAMSUNG
SATELLITE
SERVICE
SIGNAL
SIM CARD
SPRINT
T-MOBILE
TALK
TEXTING
TRAVEL
WIRELESS

Mobile Phone

E	C	I	V	R	E	S	R	E	G	R	A	H	C
S	M	L	S	S	K	L	A	T	A	D	L	R	O
E	P	E	I	P	S	G	N	I	M	A	O	R	N
M	L	Y	S	A	R	E	E	L	O	T	R	P	N
A	A	R	E	S	M	I	L	L	D	M	O	F	E
G	N	E	I	L	A	E	N	E	E	O	T	A	C
G	I	T	P	Q	B	G	G	T	R	B	O	M	T
N	C	T	E	I	I	A	E	A	N	I	M	I	A
U	Q	A	S	N	C	K	T	S	R	L	W	L	R
S	K	B	L	I	N	T	E	R	N	E	T	Y	E
M	B	I	L	L	G	A	U	Y	O	O	V	P	M
A	T	E	X	T	I	N	G	R	B	P	K	O	A
S	R	E	B	M	U	N	A	P	E	O	I	I	C
K	E	Y	P	A	D	F	G	L	S	S	A	L	A
I	P	H	O	N	E	G	R	A	H	C	E	R	F
L	E	V	A	R	T	D	S	I	M	C	A	R	D

Solution on Page 339

ANCIENT
ARCHES
BIG
CENOTAPH
CITIES
EVENTS
GRAVE
HISTORICAL
HONOR
ICON
IMPORTANT
LANDMARKS
LARGE
LIBERTY
LOCATION
MAUSOLEUM
MEANING
MEMORIALS
MONOLITHS
MOUNDS
NATIONAL
OBELISKS
OLD
PARTHENON
PLACE
POLITICAL
PYRAMIDS
SCULPTURE
STONEHENGE
STRUCTURE
TAJ MAHAL
TOMBS
TOWER
WASHINGTON

Monuments

R	S	P	O	L	I	T	I	C	A	L	T	G	F
E	T	T	A	J	M	A	H	A	L	N	N	S	E
W	N	Y	T	R	E	B	I	L	A	I	L	C	U
O	E	N	N	M	T	C	Y	T	N	A	A	U	P
T	V	R	O	N	O	H	R	A	N	L	N	L	Y
N	E	E	T	N	L	O	E	D	P	O	C	P	R
O	R	G	G	Z	P	M	M	N	Y	I	I	T	A
I	U	R	N	M	M	A	U	S	O	L	E	U	M
T	T	A	I	E	R	O	Y	S	E	N	N	R	I
A	C	L	H	K	H	E	N	A	E	V	T	E	D
C	U	C	S	F	M	E	M	O	R	I	A	L	S
O	R	N	A	T	I	O	N	A	L	C	T	R	V
L	T	M	W	S	D	N	U	O	M	I	H	I	G
D	S	K	S	I	L	E	B	O	T	G	T	E	C
J	X	P	L	A	C	I	R	O	T	S	I	H	S
S	C	E	N	O	T	A	P	H	T	O	M	B	S

Solution on Page 340

ADVENTURE
AMERICAN
BUFFALO
CAMPING
CHILDREN
CHOLERA
DISEASE
EXPANSION
EXPEDITION
FAMILY
GOLD RUSH
HISTORY
HORSES
HUNTING
IDAHO
INDIANS
JOURNEY
MAP
MINERS
NEBRASKA
OREGON
OVERLAND
OXEN
PIONEERS
RAILROAD
RANCHERS
SETTLERS
SUPPLIES
TERRITORY
TRAPPERS
TRAVELERS
WESTWARD
WYOMING

On the Oregon Trail

H	H	H	I	S	T	O	R	Y	L	I	M	A	F
U	B	O	S	R	E	L	T	T	E	S	A	N	B
N	U	E	R	U	T	N	E	V	D	A	P	O	N
T	F	X	E	S	R	E	E	N	O	I	P	G	N
I	F	P	N	U	E	D	R	A	W	T	S	E	W
N	A	E	I	R	U	S	L	R	J	I	X	R	G
G	L	D	M	I	D	A	H	O	I	O	D	O	N
N	O	I	S	N	A	P	X	E	G	T	A	V	I
I	S	T	R	A	N	C	H	E	R	S	O	E	M
P	U	I	E	S	A	E	S	I	D	M	R	R	O
M	P	O	L	J	O	U	R	N	E	Y	L	L	Y
A	P	N	E	R	D	L	I	H	C	Q	I	A	W
C	L	Y	V	Q	B	X	I	N	D	I	A	N	S
A	I	M	A	M	E	R	I	C	A	N	R	D	O
N	E	B	R	A	S	K	A	R	E	L	O	H	C
A	S	D	T	R	A	P	P	E	R	S	U	N	M

Solution on Page 340

ARRIVAL
BAGGAGE
BOARDING
BUILDING
CARS
CITY
COMMUTER
DEPARTURE
ENGINEER
FOOD
FREIGHT
LATE
LINES
LOCOMOTIVE
LUGGAGE
METRO
PASSENGERS
PEOPLE
PLATFORMS
RAILROAD
RAILWAYS
ROUTE
SIGNS
STATION
STOPS
TERMINUS
TICKETS
TIMETABLE
TRACKS
TRAINS
TRANSPORT
TRAVEL
WAITING

Train Stations

E	J	P	L	A	T	F	O	R	M	S	R	A	C
M	N	L	T	R	O	P	S	N	A	R	T	U	A
E	E	G	A	G	G	U	L	B	A	E	H	X	L
T	R	A	I	N	S	G	D	O	R	G	G	R	U
R	U	L	I	N	E	S	E	A	R	N	I	O	K
O	S	W	P	H	E	J	P	R	I	E	E	U	A
K	Y	N	T	U	N	E	A	D	V	S	R	T	P
D	A	O	R	L	I	A	R	I	A	S	F	E	S
B	W	I	A	L	C	B	T	N	L	A	O	S	N
A	L	T	V	S	O	O	U	G	C	P	W	K	G
G	I	A	E	P	M	C	R	I	L	I	A	C	I
G	A	T	L	O	M	K	E	E	L	N	I	A	S
A	R	S	C	T	U	U	F	O	O	D	T	R	C
G	D	O	J	S	T	S	T	E	K	C	I	T	Y
E	L	B	A	T	E	M	I	T	Y	U	N	N	K
S	U	N	I	M	R	E	T	A	L	T	G	M	G

Solution on Page 340

ACCESS
ACCIDENT
ASPHALT
AUTOBAHN
BARRIER
BRIDGES
CARS
CITY
COMMUTE
CONCRETE
CROWDED
DIVIDED
DRIVERS
DRIVING
EXIT
FAST
GAS
HIGHWAY
LANES
MEDIAN
MERGE
NUMBERS
OVERPASS
PARKWAY
POLICE
RACE
RAMPS
ROADS
ROUTE
SAFER
SIGNS
SLOW LANE
TAR
TOLLS
TRAFFIC
TRAVEL
TRUCKS
TURNPIKE
UNDERPASS
VEHICLES

Highways

P	A	R	E	F	A	S	D	D	L	T	S	A	F
H	T	O	L	L	S	R	E	E	U	Y	I	E	A
V	L	A	C	C	I	D	E	N	T	A	G	A	S
T	M	D	R	V	W	T	D	A	I	W	N	T	K
R	E	S	I	O	E	E	X	L	X	K	S	U	C
A	R	N	R	R	R	W	Q	W	E	R	C	R	U
F	G	C	C	P	A	U	T	O	B	A	H	N	R
F	E	N	A	I	D	E	M	L	R	P	Y	P	T
I	O	S	T	L	A	H	P	S	A	B	A	I	R
C	S	S	R	E	B	M	U	N	F	R	W	K	A
O	R	A	M	P	S	S	E	L	C	I	H	E	V
M	E	P	S	D	E	D	I	V	I	D	G	T	E
M	V	R	E	I	R	R	A	B	N	G	I	U	L
U	I	E	N	U	P	O	L	I	C	E	H	O	S
T	R	V	A	W	A	C	C	E	S	S	E	R	N
E	D	O	L	Y	T	I	C	R	A	C	E	H	M

Solution on Page 340

ASTRONOMY
ATMOSPHERE
AXIAL TILT
CALORIS BASIN
CRATERS
DENSE
ECCENTRICITY
GAS
HEAT
HOTTEST
INNERMOST
MAGNETIC FIELD
MANTLE
MESSENGER
MOLTEN CORE
MOON
NASA
ORBITING
RED
ROCK
ROMAN GOD
ROTATION
RUPES
SATELLITE
SMALLEST PLANET
SOLAR NEBULA
SOLAR SYSTEM
SURFACE
TEMPERATURE
TERRESTRIAL
WEIRD TERRAIN

Trip to Mercury

T	S	O	L	A	R	S	Y	S	T	E	M	A	E
T	Y	T	I	C	I	R	T	N	E	C	C	E	L
E	D	O	G	N	A	M	O	R	N	H	E	A	T
R	E	D	N	I	N	O	I	T	A	T	O	R	N
R	N	E	I	S	T	L	I	T	L	A	I	X	A
E	S	T	A	A	E	T	S	E	P	U	R	S	M
S	E	I	R	B	C	E	G	R	T	I	R	O	A
T	L	L	R	S	A	N	N	U	S	N	E	L	T
R	D	L	E	I	F	C	I	T	E	N	G	A	M
I	C	E	T	R	R	O	T	A	L	E	N	R	O
A	R	T	D	O	U	R	I	R	L	R	E	N	S
L	A	A	R	L	S	E	B	E	A	M	S	E	P
R	T	S	I	A	M	S	R	P	M	O	S	B	H
O	E	A	E	C	O	L	O	M	S	S	E	U	E
C	R	N	W	H	O	T	T	E	S	T	M	L	R
K	S	Y	M	O	N	O	R	T	S	A	G	A	E

Solution on Page 341

BASEBALL
BEACHES
BIKING
BOATING
CAMPING
EVENTS
EXERCISE
FISHING
FOOTBALL
FUN
GAMBLING
GOLF
HIKING
HOBBIES
HUNTING
KNITTING
LEISURE
MOVIES
MUSIC
OUTDOORS
PARKS
PHYSICAL
PLAYING
PLEASURE
READING
RELAXING
REST
RUNNING
SAILING
SKIING
SLEEP
SOCCER
SPORTS
SURFING
SWIMMING
VACATION

Recreational Travel

V	S	K	I	I	N	G	N	I	F	R	U	S	S
W	A	Q	D	F	M	O	V	I	E	S	I	C	L
R	G	C	G	O	P	E	S	K	R	A	P	A	E
E	N	A	A	O	T	F	U	N	U	J	B	M	E
A	I	K	M	T	L	A	C	I	S	Y	H	P	P
D	K	G	B	B	I	F	Y	T	A	G	B	I	G
I	I	N	E	A	L	O	W	T	E	N	O	N	N
N	H	I	A	L	S	I	N	I	L	I	A	G	I
G	O	N	C	L	T	E	N	N	P	H	T	T	T
N	B	N	H	S	K	X	B	G	T	S	I	J	N
I	B	U	E	Q	R	E	L	A	X	I	N	G	U
Y	I	R	S	P	O	R	T	S	L	F	G	O	H
A	E	M	U	S	I	C	S	A	I	L	I	N	G
L	S	W	I	M	M	I	N	G	N	I	K	I	B
P	E	V	E	N	T	S	R	O	O	D	T	U	O
Y	B	S	O	C	C	E	R	U	S	I	E	L	J

Solution on Page 341

Answers

```
T I C E N J V T C L O W L I
R E T N I W H S R E I K S C
A E R A I K S K I L I F T S
V V A C A T I O N U R R S L
E C G T N E M P I U Q E E O
L G N I D R A O B J M S U P
P N I V I L L A G E O T G E
A I G I R E S O R T U A R S
S D D T A H T S F S N U G N
S D O Y I S K I P A T R O L
L E L L I I L O X N A A N I
I L L R I R R S E B I N D F
A S U N I T N V S S N T O T
R O G A M U D V H O T E L S
T C H D R A O B W O N S A F
S C O U N T R Y L I A V L B
```

Ski Resort

```
D A Z I M X T T I B E R E K
O T T A W A S D I P A R B F
H T U O M W E H E G U L L Y
P S A N D B A R A E R Z E P
R O T H S Y E T T L P I Z C
N N T H G F A Z E S L R S H
H A O O A H L N I R E O J D
P R H E M M N O G J W I W V
E I U V J A E I W T B A N K
L H D D H M C S L I Z V Y E
I V S C A J U O E P N E S R
N O O C O N I R O G O G H A
Y L N R I R U E R G N I M F
O G D G E C D B X A N A H T
R A E S O U R C E E Y O G O
N R Q C E E V E L A R U C N
```

River Trip

```
L Q T L L Q A A Y M Y P X S
S T E E R I N G H T G T V P
D E L L E B F I T N E S S E
P E C W C C U R I E S F B E
E R Y W H Y H L A E K A A D
D T C A L E C T R M L S L S
A S I V O Y E I L A E T A Q
L N R E C X T L N A N S R B
S P T H K M P C S U E E O F
T G N I R A E G F K S H R P
R N E C S E A T A I P S R A
O I O L G N I R U O T R I T
P C D E D X B R P M U P M C
S A A I M D C S T E M L E H
P R O B N T A N D E M O I N
L Y R D M G T S E L X A C O
```

Bikes

```
W C I T Y A B I L A S C G L
A N W Y R S D N A L S I J G
T N A T O H A F C O E A S L
E R I I T O E T I H N O T P
R E K S S T R I P A I C A A
L K I R I E A M O Y S E T C
M R K E H L N M R T U A E I
I O I V M S A Y T N B N N F
T T U I E L B H L U Y A I I
R R O N A N R C E O U I H C
A O O U T U U A L C P I S U
V P A S R A M E R I C A N L
E R K H E I I B S Z M W U T
L I W N U R S N B D N A S U
L A T I P A C T S L B H T R
T U N O C O C T S L A R G E
```

Honolulu

A	N	I	B	A	C	W	W	G	W	I	T	T	F
H	T	D	S	B	K	T	H	A	S	A	Q	O	R
W	T	F	L	O	C	N	S	E	Y	N	R	D	R
D	Y	H	I	A	O	F	O	A	E	E	U	K	Q
C	B	P	A	R	D	D	W	T	M	L	D	H	J
X	U	S	S	D	D	G	T	W	S	E	D	H	W
D	O	P	S	R	N	A	O	E	H	N	E	P	S
B	Y	O	H	A	B	J	A	R	O	B	R	A	H
B	A	R	G	W	P	G	T	C	T	F	A	B	A
O	I	T	N	E	Z	M	A	N	C	H	O	R	N
A	R	L	I	E	V	E	O	L	H	G	E	I	G
T	Q	K	G	L	B	O	L	C	L	T	H	D	L
U	R	E	G	E	E	C	F	L	A	E	R	G	J
K	I	V	I	A	B	E	A	M	L	Y	Y	E	I
S	T	E	R	N	A	A	K	M	G	U	A	A	B
V	K	V	D	H	L	N	P	K	G	S	H	I	P

Nautically Speaking

E	S	C	I	P	O	R	T	H	D	B	Y	K	S
E	U	M	R	A	I	N	F	A	L	L	T	N	N
E	N	W	R	C	O	N	D	I	T	I	O	N	S
R	S	O	E	O	A	N	Z	L	S	W	H	C	N
U	H	F	Z	T	T	Z	T	T	E	U	E	X	O
S	I	O	U	X	A	S	A	T	R	R	J	J	I
S	N	R	E	R	U	T	A	R	E	P	M	E	T
E	E	E	D	D	I	M	I	H	E	D	C	T	C
R	H	C	G	O	I	C	P	V	R	Y	L	S	I
P	U	A	N	L	A	S	A	O	C	O	O	T	D
R	M	S	C	N	O	W	U	L	O	W	U	R	E
E	I	T	E	P	T	G	O	C	D	T	D	E	R
T	D	S	O	A	H	N	E	W	S	O	Y	A	P
N	I	R	E	T	E	M	O	R	A	B	O	M	I
I	T	H	L	I	G	H	T	N	I	N	G	L	S
W	Y	W	A	R	M	T	O	R	N	A	D	O	F

Travel Forecast

Y	T	F	D	R	O	O	M	S	L	E	E	P	Q
U	R	M	K	B	R	E	A	K	F	A	S	T	Y
I	O	A	D	I	S	I	N	N	T	L	R	P	U
R	S	B	R	E	N	I	A	L	N	D	O	G	A
A	E	U	T	O	A	G	G	E	O	Z	L	O	E
T	R	I	T	H	P	V	E	V	I	L	E	N	R
E	U	L	C	L	I	M	M	A	S	U	T	V	B
S	I	D	V	E	L	H	E	R	I	X	O	A	E
H	T	I	W	G	T	A	N	T	V	U	M	C	L
Q	T	N	A	R	U	A	T	S	E	R	O	A	L
Y	O	G	U	E	S	T	S	U	L	Y	O	T	H
E	I	E	C	I	V	R	E	S	E	Q	R	I	O
K	R	E	L	C	L	G	I	F	T	S	H	O	P
T	R	I	P	N	T	S	I	R	U	O	T	N	I
H	A	K	L	O	D	G	I	N	G	N	A	A	T
V	M	E	X	C	L	U	S	I	V	E	B	S	Y

Staying at a Hotel

B	S	P	A	C	E	F	D	N	A	L	O	A	D
G	G	Y	U	N	S	R	T	R	A	V	E	L	F
N	A	V	S	J	M	A	M	N	O	B	L	W	E
A	S	A	G	T	O	Y	A	Y	P	U	G	A	R
S	G	N	B	G	E	C	T	R	A	C	T	O	R
T	R	N	R	N	G	M	I	N	S	W	C	E	Y
E	J	A	I	S	L	V	X	H	A	P	B	Q	S
J	C	G	D	V	A	X	U	D	U	M	P	U	V
M	N	O	G	T	I	T	I	B	P	I	U	Q	S
E	O	K	E	E	T	R	L	G	L	L	L	H	C
G	I	D	S	L	B	I	D	L	A	B	D	R	A
E	B	R	E	Y	C	T	Q	G	N	I	V	O	M
Z	O	S	H	S	R	Y	O	A	E	A	T	C	E
H	A	M	E	U	R	A	C	S	U	B	S	K	L
F	T	V	C	A	B	L	E	I	V	F	U	E	L
N	J	K	N	O	O	L	L	A	B	P	E	T	K

Transport

A	M	A	D	N	A	W	S	A	Y	I	H	S	P
N	U	L	E	V	A	R	T	A	F	R	I	C	A
T	O	E	W	A	N	A	D	U	S	Y	S	R	D
R	T	X	S	H	O	M	V	R	H	B	T	U	N
E	R	A	T	O	I	Z	E	P	S	L	O	I	A
S	A	N	A	N	T	T	A	R	L	U	R	S	W
E	H	D	O	Y	A	R	E	U	S	E	Y	E	R
D	K	R	B	W	G	V	X	N	D	N	H	M	W
K	R	I	D	O	I	O	I	A	I	I	U	P	C
S	D	A	E	R	R	F	L	G	M	L	G	H	R
A	E	G	I	X	R	U	R	O	A	E	E	A	O
H	L	X	G	N	I	S	A	B	R	T	G	R	S
A	T	A	N	Z	A	N	I	A	Y	D	I	A	S
R	A	A	D	N	A	G	U	E	P	A	Y	O	I
A	I	P	O	I	H	T	E	X	C	D	M	H	N
Z	N	O	R	T	H	F	L	O	O	D	I	N	G

Down the Nile

P	I	K	E	S	P	E	A	K	N	E	P	S	A
U	H	E	Z	C	S	N	I	A	T	N	U	O	M
E	N	V	L	B	R	E	D	L	U	O	B	H	T
B	R	F	S	T	E	O	N	L	J	Y	S	G	S
L	E	S	V	E	T	E	F	R	O	K	N	I	I
O	T	P	O	A	T	A	R	R	E	C	I	H	R
F	S	H	A	C	C	T	C	E	I	D	A	E	U
M	E	E	H	C	N	A	L	A	V	A	L	L	O
I	W	U	P	E	S	O	T	E	N	N	P	I	T
N	S	R	O	O	C	D	R	I	R	Y	E	M	W
I	S	T	E	G	G	U	N	B	O	S	O	D	S
N	H	I	S	T	O	R	Y	A	L	N	K	N	A
G	O	L	D	E	F	I	L	D	L	I	W	I	S
W	O	N	S	T	R	O	S	E	R	H	A	H	E
S	R	E	V	I	R	O	C	K	I	E	S	V	M
R	E	H	T	A	E	W	F	C	I	N	E	C	S

Come to Colorado

C	H	U	R	C	H	E	S	C	U	R	V	Y	T
A	H	I	S	T	O	R	Y	Z	A	T	T	T	K
P	E	R	E	L	I	G	I	O	U	S	N	S	S
E	N	G	L	A	N	D	E	Z	I	A	M	I	I
C	G	T	N	E	M	E	L	T	T	E	S	N	C
O	L	O	C	E	A	N	A	S	C	F	T	O	K
D	I	N	A	C	I	R	E	M	A	N	A	L	N
S	S	U	O	N	A	T	I	V	E	W	H	O	E
A	H	A	I	P	O	C	U	N	R	O	C	C	S
B	F	I	E	R	I	P	U	R	I	T	A	N	S
V	R	S	P	I	L	G	R	I	M	S	T	A	T
O	E	I	M	A	Y	F	L	O	W	E	R	I	U
Y	E	O	T	N	A	U	Q	S	D	M	A	D	R
A	D	L	C	I	T	N	A	L	T	A	V	N	K
G	O	D	D	I	S	E	A	S	E	J	E	I	E
E	M	P	F	I	S	H	I	N	G	J	L	X	Y

Pilgrim's Journey

T	U	G	B	O	A	T	R	O	W	B	O	A	T
E	R	O	R	T	T	A	O	B	E	F	I	L	R
L	E	N	I	R	A	M	B	U	S	R	C	Z	A
D	N	D	V	A	O	O	I	U	B	O	A	T	W
D	O	O	E	F	B	N	B	O	P	U	N	T	L
A	O	L	R	T	S	Y	A	R	G	J	O	R	E
P	H	A	B	T	S	T	T	R	O	T	E	T	R
O	C	T	O	N	A	R	A	M	A	T	A	C	E
N	S	D	A	E	B	O	O	O	H	M	O	H	W
T	L	C	T	O	E	D	B	G	B	C	I	M	O
O	O	A	D	G	B	L	I	M	Y	D	T	R	P
O	O	R	R	O	I	E	K	K	A	R	E	E	T
N	P	A	X	A	R	G	S	N	A	E	R	E	K
X	B	V	S	F	S	Y	B	U	U	Y	T	E	R
P	R	E	G	G	I	R	T	U	O	J	A	S	F
Z	I	L	W	O	H	D	I	N	G	H	Y	K	Q

All Kinds of Boats

F	N	S	B	L	P	R	N	E	A	Q	N	X	O
H	I	M	A	L	A	Y	A	S	L	I	O	K	T
J	Y	C	S	A	U	W	T	D	T	H	I	G	H
C	S	I	T	F	S	E	U	G	I	I	T	N	D
E	U	S	E	R	Q	A	R	N	T	K	A	I	W
G	M	D	E	E	A	T	E	I	U	I	V	I	E
N	M	V	P	T	N	H	H	B	D	N	E	K	I
A	I	N	M	A	I	E	G	M	E	G	L	S	V
R	T	W	R	W	M	R	U	I	C	E	E	E	O
F	P	Z	O	D	A	R	O	L	O	C	T	I	L
I	E	E	F	N	L	O	R	C	S	S	A	K	C
G	A	S	D	D	S	P	K	E	E	M	M	C	A
A	K	E	N	W	W	E	E	R	O	S	I	O	N
Y	S	K	A	F	O	R	E	S	T	Y	L	R	O
M	T	A	L	L	T	V	O	P	C	E	C	A	F
H	I	L	L	H	E	I	G	H	T	S	P	L	A

On a Mountain

N	R	M	V	T	B	U	D	A	P	E	S	T	A
L	E	V	A	R	T	G	N	I	J	I	E	B	N
S	E	O	U	L	A	E	R	T	N	O	M	I	N
K	D	U	B	L	I	N	X	G	C	Y	U	M	E
T	I	E	R	O	M	E	A	B	H	K	R	A	I
R	R	T	U	S	L	P	A	O	I	O	B	I	V
A	D	O	S	T	O	A	B	S	C	T	A	M	E
F	A	R	S	R	H	R	I	T	A	H	N	S	N
F	M	O	E	O	K	I	D	O	G	G	N	N	I
I	A	N	L	P	C	S	J	N	O	E	M	O	C
C	B	T	S	R	O	B	A	G	H	D	A	D	E
A	H	O	N	I	T	H	N	T	S	S	P	N	M
I	O	I	R	A	S	E	A	T	T	L	E	O	I
R	N	A	M	I	L	M	O	S	C	O	W	L	L
O	T	T	A	W	A	T	S	Y	D	N	E	Y	A
S	J	K	O	K	G	N	A	B	E	R	L	I	N

Major Cities

T	A	F	O	R	E	S	T	S	H	U	M	I	D
I	N	T	D	J	N	A	T	U	R	A	L	R	I
N	A	E	L	S	O	U	T	H	E	R	N	U	A
D	M	R	D	E	S	N	I	A	T	N	U	O	M
I	O	Y	I	I	D	I	E	E	T	A	T	S	O
A	H	R	W	V	S	V	T	S	T	S	E	S	N
N	A	T	M	P	E	E	U	Y	B	U	X	I	D
S	L	N	I	A	E	R	R	H	G	O	A	M	S
O	K	U	K	M	S	S	M	P	N	I	R	N	G
G	O	O	E	E	S	I	S	A	I	G	K	O	N
N	Z	C	B	R	E	T	I	R	M	I	A	T	I
I	A	X	E	I	N	Y	R	G	R	L	N	N	H
T	R	U	E	C	N	N	U	O	A	E	A	I	S
N	K	O	B	A	E	N	O	E	F	R	D	L	I
U	S	I	E	N	T	P	T	G	T	O	H	C	F
H	I	S	T	O	R	Y	M	O	N	O	C	E	X

Visit Arkansas

T	T	H	C	N	U	A	L	A	N	D	I	N	G
Y	C	L	F	F	O	E	K	A	T	B	G	L	U
S	T	E	K	C	O	R	V	T	R	A	V	E	L
H	A	I	R	G	L	I	D	E	R	S	N	U	L
G	I	S	V	I	G	S	E	D	H	G	B	F	V
L	L	S	C	A	D	C	G	N	I	R	A	O	S
I	N	C	T	I	R	E	G	N	I	Y	L	F	W
D	O	I	I	O	N	G	E	L	I	A	L	Q	R
I	O	N	F	N	R	O	O	P	I	W	I	P	I
N	L	O	Y	K	S	Y	S	R	S	F	S	H	G
G	L	S	P	A	C	E	C	R	A	F	T	Y	H
P	A	R	I	W	W	R	C	I	E	G	I	S	T
M	B	E	L	S	A	F	E	T	Y	P	C	I	S
I	O	P	O	F	B	I	R	D	S	A	U	C	T
L	Q	Y	T	A	I	R	P	L	A	N	E	S	E
B	P	H	E	L	I	C	O	P	T	E	R	U	J

Flight

L	H	T	R	A	E	C	N	E	D	I	V	E	X
O	A	S	M	Y	G	O	L	O	I	B	O	X	E
U	Y	C	A	R	I	P	S	N	O	C	P	P	N
T	C	A	I	R	E	T	C	A	B	M	L	W	O
E	N	L	Q	M	S	N	A	I	T	R	A	M	B
R	A	E	I	C	O	N	T	A	C	T	N	E	I
S	G	V	G	F	D	N	O	Y	E	B	E	T	O
P	A	A	S	I	E	B	O	R	P	T	T	S	L
A	S	R	E	I	L	O	R	R	E	N	S	Y	O
C	L	T	T	W	G	L	N	L	T	A	S	S	G
E	R	B	I	O	C	H	E	M	I	S	T	R	Y
S	A	T	U	R	N	S	T	T	A	A	A	A	X
U	C	B	P	F	C	A	U	I	N	R	R	L	A
S	E	I	R	O	E	H	T	N	N	I	S	O	L
W	J	U	P	I	T	E	R	I	E	G	S	S	A
T	D	E	C	N	A	V	D	A	T	V	S	I	G

Alien Travelers

Y	A	W	H	G	I	H	K	C	U	R	T	J	Q
N	O	I	T	A	T	S	S	R	I	A	P	E	R
L	E	V	A	R	T	R	G	A	L	L	O	N	S
U	C	A	P	A	Y	T	A	N	W	A	T	E	R
S	L	F	R	G	M	U	E	L	O	R	T	E	P
D	E	D	A	E	L	N	U	N	U	Z	A	S	K
I	R	R	S	L	S	A	P	H	D	G	Z	C	O
U	K	E	I	E	S	T	V	M	O	A	E	L	N
L	S	U	I	T	R	E	R	C	U	S	N	R	E
F	M	F	S	H	H	V	T	O	F	P	E	T	E
T	U	I	E	I	S	A	I	V	O	U	R	O	T
A	I	L	C	I	N	A	H	C	E	M	E	I	H
N	M	L	I	E	M	M	C	J	E	P	S	L	A
K	E	U	R	A	E	N	I	L	O	S	A	G	N
S	R	P	P	Y	E	N	O	M	F	O	O	D	O
N	P	S	E	R	O	T	S	D	I	E	S	E	L

Filling Stations

M	A	Z	T	E	C	S	N	A	E	B	A	J	A
S	E	L	A	M	A	T	I	J	U	A	N	A	F
I	T	Y	I	X	E	N	I	S	I	U	C	Z	I
R	A	R	E	U	C	S	O	A	X	A	C	A	E
U	C	T	O	F	Q	G	N	I	P	P	O	H	S
O	O	N	E	S	E	E	Z	A	T	F	L	F	T
T	S	U	Z	H	E	S	T	V	C	A	O	G	A
S	S	O	C	C	E	R	T	O	C	I	C	O	N
K	D	C	I	N	A	P	S	I	H	T	X	A	D
H	S	I	N	A	P	S	P	C	V	R	T	E	V
X	C	E	M	L	O	O	A	O	E	A	F	S	M
W	S	X	L	A	R	I	W	Z	C	V	L	O	A
A	L	L	I	T	R	O	T	U	I	E	U	U	Y
N	U	C	N	A	C	Y	Y	M	R	L	G	T	A
Q	I	Z	M	O	L	E	P	E	S	O	S	H	N
B	O	R	D	E	R	U	T	L	U	C	W	S	S

Tour of Mexico

S	A	N	T	A	R	C	T	I	C	O	L	D	E
A	O	D	P	Z	U	D	W	R	V	N	I	G	D
Y	R	E	V	O	C	S	I	D	Q	F	I	A	Y
A	O	X	U	E	L	O	P	H	T	U	O	S	D
L	T	P	Y	S	N	I	A	T	N	U	O	M	C
A	A	L	C	K	T	T	C	P	B	D	R	E	L
M	G	O	E	N	S	D	U	E	A	I	X	S	I
I	I	R	L	I	E	H	S	R	S	P	L	H	M
H	V	I	O	G	R	E	P	E	E	K	E	E	B
S	A	N	P	H	E	R	H	D	C	R	V	R	I
I	N	G	H	T	V	O	I	B	A	O	A	P	N
T	E	S	T	H	E	T	S	O	M	P	R	A	G
I	P	N	R	O	I	H	T	O	P	E	T	B	F
R	A	O	O	O	P	G	O	T	I	M	M	U	S
B	L	W	N	D	F	I	R	S	T	I	B	E	T
F	R	M	S	J	Z	H	Y	K	A	E	P	Q	P

Sir Edmund Hillary

Postcards

B	Y	P	P	I	C	T	U	R	E	S	S	Y	P
E	V	U	H	O	T	O	U	R	I	S	T	R	A
Y	G	O	L	O	I	T	L	E	D	S	E	I	P
L	E	V	A	R	T	Y	T	L	E	V	O	N	E
K	R	A	M	T	S	O	P	L	E	T	T	E	R
M	G	U	Q	L	W	D	G	D	P	C	U	V	L
E	N	V	E	L	O	P	E	R	L	G	T	U	D
S	I	N	O	T	E	S	I	A	A	V	S	O	G
S	T	R	A	L	S	B	N	O	C	P	L	S	R
A	I	Y	T	O	L	O	Y	B	E	D	H	P	E
G	R	S	B	S	S	E	R	D	D	A	L	A	E
E	W	M	P	R	G	P	O	R	T	P	F	E	T
S	E	A	E	A	M	S	T	A	M	P	S	H	I
E	I	P	M	D	D	K	S	C	E	N	I	C	N
N	V	I	M	A	I	L	I	N	G	I	Y	M	G
T	O	U	P	T	Q	Q	H	Q	U	I	C	K	S

Tour de France

J	N	A	N	N	U	A	L	G	N	I	C	A	R
S	E	G	A	T	S	E	K	I	B	Z	R	V	O
W	Y	R	O	U	T	E	A	M	S	U	I	I	A
S	R	E	T	E	M	O	L	I	K	C	D	C	D
U	K	V	S	S	J	S	D	I	O	R	E	T	S
M	G	E	V	R	N	E	T	S	M	D	R	O	D
M	S	N	E	N	E	I	P	I	N	P	S	R	I
E	G	T	I	W	O	J	A	O	U	A	E	Y	S
R	N	Y	S	N	E	H	M	T	R	C	F	G	T
W	I	U	L	I	I	E	T	W	N	U	R	N	A
I	P	O	P	U	L	A	R	A	S	U	E	I	N
N	O	P	J	G	J	C	R	H	R	L	O	B	C
N	D	E	E	P	S	U	Y	T	T	A	L	M	E
E	P	R	P	E	D	A	L	C	T	U	M	I	G
R	G	R	A	N	D	T	O	U	R	S	L	L	H
S	T	R	E	N	G	T	H	F	R	A	N	C	E

World's Fair

O	E	X	H	I	B	I	T	I	O	N	S	H	K
S	K	N	I	N	V	E	N	T	I	O	N	S	R
P	U	R	E	X	P	O	S	I	T	I	O	N	O
E	L	D	E	E	N	E	C	A	P	S	I	K	Y
C	I	B	A	O	G	A	C	I	H	C	T	R	W
I	N	F	U	N	E	R	U	T	L	U	C	A	E
A	N	N	F	P	I	C	B	S	I	R	A	P	N
L	O	E	L	E	E	H	W	S	I	R	R	E	F
I	V	C	A	O	L	I	C	I	Z	G	T	D	H
Z	A	N	R	P	S	T	N	E	V	E	T	Y	O
E	T	E	G	L	T	E	O	D	D	Q	A	H	S
D	I	I	E	E	I	C	D	W	U	O	S	H	T
L	O	C	O	U	N	T	R	I	E	S	A	L	C
R	N	S	T	L	O	U	I	S	R	R	T	N	I
O	A	K	L	A	S	R	E	V	I	N	U	R	T
W	P	R	I	N	C	E	A	L	B	E	R	T	Y

Climb a Mountain

Y	T	E	F	A	S	T	H	G	I	E	H	Y	Y
S	R	O	C	K	Y	X	S	O	D	F	E	B	V
K	A	W	H	I	T	E	O	U	T	S	N	B	M
I	V	E	I	I	V	I	T	S	I	E	U	O	S
I	E	A	X	A	M	I	K	C	P	E	U	H	E
N	L	T	C	A	T	A	R	A	T	N	B	W	P
G	S	H	R	L	E	E	L	R	T	I	E	O	O
U	T	E	A	P	X	C	A	A	O	P	L	N	R
I	E	R	M	E	S	I	I	T	Y	L	A	S	N
D	N	E	P	T	N	N	S	T	G	A	Y	U	E
E	T	Q	O	I	S	E	N	N	E	R	S	M	G
S	E	O	N	S	R	E	I	C	A	L	G	M	Y
T	B	G	S	E	C	P	O	L	R	G	H	I	X
E	I	M	V	S	M	L	L	S	P	O	R	T	O
E	T	E	E	A	D	I	Z	T	N	E	C	S	A
P	E	D	C	T	H	I	K	I	N	G	Y	Q	E

Scenic National Parks

C	C	M	O	U	N	T	A	I	N	S	N	I	Y
I	A	I	D	A	C	A	R	L	S	B	A	D	E
R	P	R	O	T	E	C	T	E	D	R	A	S	C
O	A	R	C	H	E	S	N	R	L	L	A	H	Y
T	D	K	S	F	V	R	G	L	A	C	I	E	R
S	V	A	L	L	E	Y	S	K	S	I	D	N	B
I	R	N	R	D	R	A	A	D	S	R	L	A	S
H	E	O	L	O	G	E	E	M	E	O	D	N	Y
S	D	I	I	U	L	N	V	V	N	L	N	D	O
T	W	Z	A	A	A	O	A	F	A	Y	E	O	S
S	O	R	H	L	D	S	C	N	T	M	B	A	E
E	O	R	I	V	E	R	D	I	I	P	G	H	M
R	D	W	F	M	S	S	N	R	O	I	I	Q	I
O	E	N	Y	A	C	S	I	B	N	C	B	Y	T
F	G	N	I	K	I	H	W	P	A	R	K	S	E
Q	E	Y	Q	E	F	I	L	D	L	I	W	Q	B

Haiti

S	D	N	A	L	S	I	C	S	D	H	E	L	P
C	S	A	Y	A	R	E	L	O	H	C	N	H	O
I	S	E	O	G	N	A	M	C	U	W	A	C	V
T	O	B	L	E	B	I	H	C	Q	N	I	N	E
I	C	B	S	E	N	A	H	E	W	A	T	E	R
L	E	I	F	I	M	A	B	R	B	C	I	R	T
O	A	R	C	L	R	O	C	Y	D	S	A	F	Y
P	N	A	T	I	O	N	H	I	D	S	H	C	M
T	N	C	T	G	X	O	S	T	R	O	P	I	A
R	C	Y	P	A	P	A	D	O	C	R	C	L	L
O	U	V	D	I	S	E	A	S	E	C	U	O	A
P	L	A	N	T	A	I	N	A	I	D	S	H	R
I	T	W	E	C	H	I	L	D	R	E	N	T	I
C	U	R	C	I	L	B	U	P	E	R	A	A	A
A	R	A	G	U	S	U	B	M	U	L	O	C	S
L	E	E	F	F	O	C	R	E	O	L	E	Q	L

Let's Go to Disneyland

S	U	S	T	E	K	C	I	T	M	U	S	I	C
T	H	O	T	E	L	S	Z	Y	L	I	M	A	F
S	C	U	O	B	M	U	D	E	A	R	S	C	V
E	R	V	N	R	O	H	R	E	T	T	A	M	X
U	M	E	M	O	R	I	E	S	L	L	R	Y	L
G	O	N	T	T	S	B	A	E	I	E	K	A	X
R	N	I	P	C	R	N	M	F	S	J	N	E	P
I	O	R	X	T	A	D	O	O	F	I	O	F	C
D	R	S	V	P	L	R	R	W	G	B	I	Z	H
E	A	D	A	R	N	T	A	I	W	R	S	J	I
S	I	W	C	I	Y	X	R	H	E	H	S	E	L
H	L	O	A	N	P	O	Q	W	C	F	I	N	D
O	I	R	T	C	G	O	O	F	Y	X	M	T	R
W	N	C	I	E	L	R	T	O	U	E	D	Y	E
S	E	Y	O	S	K	M	U	U	E	N	A	K	N
W	S	H	N	S	Z	P	A	R	A	D	E	S	L

Autos

T	Z	D	I	E	S	E	L	C	I	H	E	V	T
C	L	O	I	L	I	C	E	N	S	E	W	Y	I
W	I	E	C	H	R	Y	S	L	E	R	H	R	R
B	I	F	B	T	S	U	A	H	X	E	E	E	E
R	W	N	F	T	R	D	E	E	P	S	E	T	S
A	E	B	D	A	A	N	S	U	V	L	L	T	N
K	C	P	N	S	R	E	G	N	E	S	S	A	P
E	H	C	M	Y	H	T	S	C	A	P	V	B	C
S	E	H	F	U	C	I	T	A	M	O	T	U	A
W	V	O	I	X	B	R	E	O	S	L	E	A	L
O	R	T	R	G	I	M	T	L	E	L	N	T	L
D	O	R	E	C	H	O	W	U	D	U	I	O	I
N	L	U	V	V	R	W	F	F	A	T	G	Y	D
I	E	N	I	L	O	S	A	G	N	I	N	O	A
W	T	K	R	D	I	R	B	Y	H	O	E	T	C
R	O	A	D	S	M	E	C	H	A	N	I	C	I

M	A	G	L	E	V	G	C	O	N	N	E	C	T
B	G	O	E	C	O	N	D	U	C	T	O	R	K
O	N	D	V	L	E	S	E	I	D	A	L	O	A
G	J	P	I	L	F	R	E	D	L	K	F	S	R
I	E	U	T	N	I	E	P	E	M	R	E	S	T
E	L	L	O	B	I	G	S	P	O	A	C	I	M
S	U	L	M	O	M	N	H	O	N	I	N	N	A
E	D	M	O	X	A	E	G	T	O	L	A	G	C
L	E	A	C	C	E	S	I	C	R	C	T	E	F
C	H	N	O	A	T	S	H	Z	A	A	S	N	N
I	C	H	L	R	S	A	P	R	I	R	I	I	O
H	S	O	A	E	L	P	S	A	L	F	D	L	I
E	V	V	R	J	C	I	R	T	C	E	L	E	T
V	E	P	C	T	S	Y	A	W	L	I	A	R	A
L	X	S	T	A	E	S	F	R	E	I	G	H	T
E	N	I	G	N	E	M	T	U	N	N	E	L	S

Train Travel

L	O	R	R	Y	S	E	M	I	V	T	R	S	T
S	C	W	W	E	I	G	H	E	A	V	Y	R	I
P	A	D	C	T	L	A	R	G	E	A	U	R	R
E	R	R	W	H	E	E	L	S	W	C	E	E	E
E	G	I	R	G	I	B	S	H	K	P	U	L	S
D	O	V	E	I	N	C	G	E	E	K	E	I	P
R	T	E	C	E	B	I	R	E	I	U	F	A	E
C	O	R	N	R	H	G	L	O	F	D	I	R	T
O	G	U	A	F	S	S	N	P	A	H	N	T	E
N	N	D	T	N	E	E	G	I	U	D	K	F	R
V	I	A	S	E	S	T	N	I	L	O	K	S	B
O	K	O	I	L	N	P	A	I	R	U	C	M	I
Y	A	L	D	X	E	L	O	N	G	H	A	U	L
F	R	T	R	A	C	T	O	R	K	N	J	H	T
K	B	V	E	H	I	C	L	E	T	E	E	Z	E
S	T	H	G	I	L	I	L	E	V	A	R	T	C

Semi Trucks

T	S	E	I	K	O	O	C	V	J	E	R	K	Y
C	T	E	G	A	B	M	A	E	R	C	E	C	I
R	O	S	L	Q	D	O	U	G	H	N	U	T	S
A	R	R	W	P	R	O	C	E	S	S	E	D	A
C	R	U	N	E	P	S	N	T	E	N	Y	E	N
K	A	P	E	C	E	A	R	A	R	I	H	G	D
E	C	C	T	E	H	T	O	B	F	C	T	A	W
R	D	P	A	C	H	I	C	L	X	K	L	K	I
S	P	O	L	N	D	S	P	E	I	E	A	C	C
Q	S	R	O	K	D	F	O	S	M	R	E	A	H
U	D	T	C	F	N	Y	P	J	L	S	H	P	E
I	N	A	O	R	K	I	B	Z	I	D	B	L	E
C	O	B	H	U	M	N	R	A	A	E	C	L	T
K	M	L	C	I	F	G	U	D	R	E	A	A	O
S	L	E	Z	T	E	R	P	J	T	S	K	M	S
K	A	E	R	B	N	N	O	O	D	L	E	S	G

Travel Snack

R	S	W	S	U	N	T	A	N	S	K	C	O	D
E	T	E	H	N	D	A	N	C	I	N	G	W	I
A	S	R	O	R	E	L	A	X	A	T	I	O	N
D	I	C	P	E	X	K	C	I	S	A	E	S	I
I	R	L	P	T	C	A	P	T	A	I	N	R	N
N	U	I	I	S	U	N	B	A	T	H	I	N	G
G	O	F	N	C	R	C	A	B	I	N	S	W	X
J	T	E	G	K	S	E	A	B	R	E	E	Z	E
B	P	B	G	N	I	L	B	M	A	G	R	B	N
E	S	O	E	O	O	N	I	S	A	C	B	A	I
A	T	A	R	D	N	E	G	A	G	G	U	L	H
C	E	T	L	T	S	E	V	E	F	I	L	C	S
H	F	C	A	T	H	V	A	C	A	T	I	O	N
E	F	Y	E	T	A	O	B	G	U	T	G	N	U
S	U	U	M	S	A	I	L	I	N	G	F	Y	S
I	B	A	N	C	H	O	R	E	T	A	W	A	H

Pleasure Cruise

T	N	E	V	A	D	A	S	E	K	A	N	S	Y
S	A	A	R	I	Z	O	N	A	R	O	N	O	S
S	A	E	I	R	L	A	N	D	S	C	A	P	E
K	E	H	H	B	K	I	Z	H	U	M	I	D	N
T	M	N	A	S	A	N	D	S	T	O	R	M	S
H	E	A	U	R	L	R	W	L	C	R	M	N	D
G	R	M	F	D	A	O	A	I	A	A	O	E	I
U	T	A	P	X	H	F	T	Z	C	I	U	R	U
O	X	C	F	E	A	I	E	A	P	N	N	R	R
R	E	A	C	R	R	L	R	R	K	F	T	A	N
D	E	T	N	O	I	A	O	D	K	A	A	B	A
E	T	A	M	I	L	C	T	S	N	L	I	W	L
G	O	B	I	X	S	D	A	U	Y	L	N	I	I
Y	Y	H	O	T	D	E	S	E	R	T	S	N	F
P	O	X	P	B	N	I	U	O	D	E	B	D	E
T	C	M	O	J	A	V	E	R	E	G	I	O	N

Desert Journey

D	K	R	O	A	D	W	A	Y	E	T	A	L	M
R	E	G	N	A	C	C	I	D	E	N	T	S	O
U	L	E	C	O	N	G	E	S	T	I	O	N	V
L	T	A	P	H	I	G	H	W	A	Y	S	T	I
E	E	S	N	S	T	E	E	R	T	S	T	D	N
S	K	V	R	E	J	H	P	A	S	S	I	N	G
G	C	C	A	A	S	H	O	H	R	R	S	S	I
N	I	S	O	R	C	T	I	X	E	T	R	V	R
I	T	N	M	L	T	I	H	C	T	A	E	V	E
V	T	G	S	A	D	F	T	G	N	H	V	C	N
I	R	I	Y	L	J	I	B	I	I	Y	I	Y	E
R	U	S	H	H	O	U	R	C	E	L	R	D	W
D	C	P	E	N	S	W	L	G	O	S	D	Q	Y
K	K	O	X	E	P	E	O	P	L	E	P	E	O
W	S	T	S	H	S	E	G	A	R	D	A	O	R
H	Z	S	Y	A	W	E	E	R	F	A	S	T	K

Driving

S	R	K	L	C	T	S	A	O	C	R	W	B	P
K	R	V	F	A	N	C	H	O	R	B	N	I	F
C	B	S	N	R	R	Y	D	E	O	A	E	V	F
K	T	A	T	G	A	U	W	A	L	R	N	Q	S
E	I	S	R	O	S	H	T	M	S	T	R	O	P
U	N	P	E	G	R	S	W	A	G	I	E	G	I
W	L	R	H	D	E	M	E	R	N	F	L	R	H
H	A	O	T	L	A	S	D	I	I	I	H	C	S
M	N	T	A	F	G	R	I	N	D	C	H	I	E
N	D	E	E	Y	W	N	T	A	A	I	S	T	A
F	O	C	W	R	T	O	I	E	O	A	E	I	N
A	T	T	D	Y	Z	T	B	G	L	L	V	E	E
L	T	K	S	D	O	G	E	I	D	N	A	S	V
W	A	U	C	O	N	R	V	J	Z	E	W	U	A
C	B	F	I	O	B	W	K	R	O	B	R	A	H
Y	M	L	L	M	D	U	O	S	Z	K	W	D	B

Harbor

G	L	Q	S	W	O	S	J	L	O	O	W	S	P
S	W	U	T	O	W	A	R	M	T	H	I	A	L
N	A	L	Y	N	C	A	S	U	A	L	N	U	S
N	H	B	L	K	C	K	P	C	K	T	S	T	N
R	S	G	E	E	O	T	S	P	S	R	E	N	O
E	T	T	B	L	T	J	G	Z	A	N	S	P	T
P	R	I	R	L	T	L	X	X	M	R	S	R	T
P	O	N	C	H	O	S	S	R	A	R	E	A	U
I	H	M	R	V	N	U	O	C	J	T	R	L	B
Z	S	S	E	T	I	F	S	C	A	G	D	F	Z
F	L	S	P	H	I	N	O	E	P	R	A	S	M
D	E	E	M	N	A	A	W	J	U	B	V	L	N
Q	E	W	U	E	T	S	H	I	R	T	S	E	H
E	V	I	J	S	I	Z	E	I	S	I	T	D	S
M	E	N	K	A	O	L	C	W	E	E	A	O	W
S	H	G	L	S	T	R	I	K	S	F	H	M	D

Clothes to Pack

T	D	H	S	S	F	L	O	R	I	D	A	S	R
S	G	I	N	L	N	E	W	Y	O	R	K	M	H
I	P	K	I	A	H	V	R	E	T	A	W	U	I
R	T	I	A	V	V	A	B	E	A	C	H	E	S
U	S	N	R	I	I	R	W	I	F	N	N	S	T
O	N	G	T	T	V	T	N	A	O	S	G	U	O
T	O	H	V	S	K	R	M	I	I	N	I	M	R
L	I	O	W	E	O	I	T	G	A	I	E	R	Y
J	T	T	H	F	L	A	N	D	M	A	R	K	S
C	A	E	I	I	E	I	S	L	E	T	O	M	A
H	C	L	E	R	L	T	J	O	F	N	F	K	V
I	A	S	C	B	A	Y	R	T	S	U	D	N	I
C	V	E	M	T	N	E	M	U	N	O	M	G	N
A	R	A	E	K	C	Y	O	S	E	M	I	T	E
G	G	S	T	R	O	S	E	R	E	M	M	U	S
O	R	L	A	N	D	O	S	E	I	T	I	C	W

Touristy

D	E	E	P	S	G	A	H	A	M	A	Y	G	L
A	L	B	S	T	R	A	P	J	A	C	K	E	T
O	C	X	S	E	I	L	E	E	H	W	V	N	I
R	Y	C	S	S	K	A	W	A	S	A	K	I	K
V	C	R	U	I	S	I	N	G	R	S	F	G	U
P	V	S	E	K	A	R	B	T	U	E	R	N	Z
P	A	S	S	E	N	G	E	R	R	A	E	E	U
S	G	N	A	G	R	S	C	O	O	T	E	R	S
U	W	I	N	D	I	A	N	H	H	T	D	T	I
O	U	I	H	I	G	H	W	A	Y	R	O	E	D
C	H	O	P	P	E	R	S	R	B	A	M	M	E
L	E	A	T	H	E	R	A	L	Y	F	O	L	C
R	E	W	O	P	E	C	S	E	E	F	P	E	A
D	G	N	I	D	I	R	R	Y	S	I	E	H	R
Q	D	R	I	N	E	M	O	R	H	C	D	Y	T
A	G	R	G	F	R	Y	T	E	F	A	S	T	S

Motorcycle Touring

L	P	R	K	S	P	E	E	D	D	T	L	D	O
G	O	R	F	Q	L	B	F	C	H	W	E	C	X
O	I	K	E	C	A	O	L	S	L	M	E	L	C
N	R	R	E	A	K	A	O	I	H	A	K	R	U
U	O	E	H	T	E	T	A	P	N	I	X	G	C
F	Y	I	P	B	C	S	T	E	N	N	P	N	G
P	O	R	T	O	D	H	R	A	O	S	V	I	A
E	R	T	F	A	R	C	R	E	T	A	W	C	L
P	G	E	E	T	E	A	W	D	E	I	D	A	L
W	N	H	K	R	M	R	G	S	X	L	I	R	E
J	I	B	U	A	E	S	C	H	O	O	N	E	R
N	T	N	T	L	N	D	T	E	B	Y	G	T	Y
K	H	A	D	G	L	N	D	E	R	E	H	T	A
Q	C	L	G	N	I	S	I	U	R	C	Y	U	W
Q	A	L	E	S	S	E	V	P	R	N	L	C	L
T	Y	T	G	N	I	L	I	A	S	T	S	A	M

Sails Up

F	O	O	T	B	A	L	L	S	E	N	E	C	A
T	Z	H	L	E	G	D	I	R	B	M	A	C	V
O	B	E	L	L	W	E	T	H	E	R	B	W	I
L	N	T	A	A	P	N	A	C	I	R	E	M	A
E	O	A	B	N	O	U	N	Y	E	P	N	D	T
D	T	T	E	I	P	L	N	P	I	O	G	X	I
O	Y	S	S	D	U	Y	I	G	R	R	A	E	O
H	A	O	A	R	L	T	C	O	E	T	L	M	N
I	D	I	B	A	A	I	N	V	E	S	S	F	L
O	C	H	L	C	T	S	I	E	K	M	N	I	O
A	A	O	H	N	I	R	C	R	A	O	I	N	T
N	N	A	E	N	O	E	O	N	L	U	A	D	T
S	T	K	S	I	N	V	R	O	N	T	L	I	E
Z	O	R	H	U	C	I	N	R	T	H	P	A	R
G	N	O	Y	O	U	N	G	S	T	O	W	N	Y
H	Q	N	C	O	L	U	M	B	U	S	X	S	T

The Buckeye State

Railroad History

Y	N	O	I	T	U	L	O	V	E	R	E	A	Q
Z	Y	K	H	Q	E	O	D	K	M	K	X	M	L
L	E	S	E	I	D	C	S	E	Z	J	P	T	E
T	R	A	C	K	S	O	H	E	E	R	A	R	E
T	R	A	I	N	S	M	B	N	A	P	N	A	T
Q	G	W	F	L	A	O	C	W	O	P	S	K	S
F	R	E	I	G	H	T	L	L	A	L	I	R	J
P	A	N	C	C	T	I	E	S	B	D	O	E	J
U	I	G	A	R	V	V	S	U	S	T	N	G	A
L	L	I	P	I	A	E	S	T	C	W	L	U	Y
L	R	N	C	R	N	I	A	U	A	E	I	A	G
M	O	E	T	G	N	T	D	T	R	S	A	G	O
A	A	E	E	E	I	N	D	U	S	T	R	Y	U
N	D	R	S	O	O	N	O	R	I	E	N	S	L
E	S	S	N	C	D	L	I	U	B	R	O	D	D
Y	P	V	S	T	R	I	K	E	S	N	C	H	L

Capitals Around the World

G	M	A	D	R	I	D	B	S	A	M	M	A	N
Z	R	N	U	U	V	V	I	E	N	N	A	A	H
R	O	O	B	S	I	R	A	P	I	E	R	R	E
A	M	D	L	Q	U	I	T	O	T	R	H	Z	C
B	E	N	I	L	R	E	B	H	S	A	U	T	N
A	M	O	N	A	C	O	J	A	K	A	R	T	A
T	O	L	I	I	P	B	A	N	G	K	O	K	S
O	S	U	S	L	R	B	S	O	J	H	K	T	S
K	C	O	N	O	A	E	K	I	E	V	D	S	A
Y	O	E	O	P	G	I	V	L	A	H	A	A	U
O	W	S	B	I	U	J	S	H	R	C	L	F	D
L	A	P	S	R	E	I	G	L	A	L	I	L	A
S	S	T	I	T	N	N	A	R	K	V	N	E	R
O	R	O	L	K	A	G	A	D	N	J	A	B	C
I	A	L	I	M	A	C	R	H	A	V	M	N	C
U	W	Q	C	C	A	I	R	O	T	T	A	W	A

On the Street

Y	C	U	R	B	S	O	N	E	W	A	Y	X	P
E	T	C	N	W	O	T	U	H	S	S	A	P	A
C	B	I	H	Q	P	N	H	K	H	P	L	S	V
A	C	R	C	I	E	S	L	G	A	H	Y	E	E
L	L	C	I	V	L	A	R	G	I	A	B	N	M
P	R	L	A	C	W	D	R	A	W	L	U	A	E
U	O	E	E	E	K	A	R	R	C	T	S	L	N
T	A	H	D	Y	V	R	O	E	O	G	Y	G	T
S	D	I	R	E	C	T	I	O	N	N	S	N	R
N	S	G	L	A	O	I	R	I	C	A	E	I	A
G	E	H	M	M	T	D	D	E	R	M	L	K	F
I	N	W	P	U	B	L	I	C	E	E	C	R	F
S	I	A	D	R	I	V	E	S	T	S	I	A	I
D	L	Y	F	U	T	R	A	V	E	L	H	P	C
X	Y	S	B	S	S	E	R	D	D	A	E	A	S
N	A	B	R	U	H	R	O	D	N	E	V	I	J

Stop at McDonald's

M	C	R	I	B	F	A	S	T	F	O	O	D	S
R	H	M	C	G	R	I	D	D	L	E	O	G	P
S	E	K	A	H	S	K	L	I	M	L	O	U	A
E	E	L	B	U	O	D	C	M	L	L	H	T	R
I	S	E	A	D	N	U	S	A	D	C	U	J	W
R	E	D	N	U	O	P	R	E	T	R	A	U	Q
F	B	C	O	K	E	M	N	E	Y	T	S	A	T
H	U	O	B	R	E	A	K	F	A	S	T	W	E
C	R	F	K	N	R	B	I	G	M	A	C	T	L
N	G	F	U	C	H	M	A	E	R	C	E	C	I
E	E	E	H	A	P	P	Y	M	E	A	L	S	F
R	R	E	G	G	M	C	M	U	F	F	I	N	H
F	S	R	E	G	R	U	B	M	A	H	T	J	S
A	D	O	S	E	H	C	I	W	D	N	A	S	I
Y	S	N	A	C	K	W	R	A	P	I	E	S	F
N	E	K	C	I	H	C	C	M	C	C	A	F	E

T	S	S	X	Z	T	C	A	T	N	O	C	O	P
A	E	T	D	R	C	A	F	P	I	L	O	T	S
K	N	R	H	I	F	A	S	R	E	W	O	T	L
E	I	O	S	D	R	E	C	A	P	S	R	I	A
O	L	P	A	C	T	E	R	M	I	N	A	L	N
F	R	R	R	T	S	A	C	D	A	O	R	B	G
F	I	I	C	E	N	O	I	T	A	I	V	A	U
D	A	A	D	C	A	L	L	S	I	G	N	L	A
E	P	S	E	H	R	Y	D	R	Y	O	D	A	G
F	P	Y	P	N	R	R	E	E	T	S	N	N	E
E	R	A	A	O	I	A	L	T	I	T	U	D	E
N	O	W	R	L	V	T	A	U	R	H	O	I	I
S	A	N	T	O	A	I	Y	P	U	G	R	N	X
E	C	U	U	G	L	L	S	M	C	I	G	G	A
F	H	R	R	Y	P	I	B	O	E	L	W	Z	T
S	A	F	E	T	Y	M	N	C	S	F	L	O	W

Air Traffic Control

E	L	A	T	I	N	O	T	R	A	V	E	L	I
R	O	D	A	U	C	E	L	I	H	C	I	L	D
U	C	L	B	R	A	Z	I	L	V	M	C	A	A
T	B	O	L	I	V	I	A	A	A	I	G	M	D
L	T	G	C	S	S	N	N	R	L	N	S	A	I
U	O	C	Y	A	D	A	A	G	D	D	V	S	N
C	U	U	Y	M	M	L	C	E	I	I	E	P	I
O	R	I	A	B	U	A	O	N	V	A	N	A	R
U	I	S	U	A	C	O	N	T	I	N	E	N	T
N	S	I	G	H	R	Y	D	I	A	S	Z	I	A
T	M	N	A	I	E	M	A	N	I	R	U	S	U
R	H	E	R	S	E	H	C	A	E	B	E	H	H
Y	K	V	A	T	B	A	I	B	M	O	L	O	C
U	R	E	P	O	S	L	A	M	I	N	A	I	E
A	H	N	A	R	I	P	Y	A	U	G	U	R	U
O	A	N	A	Y	U	G	R	A	U	G	A	J	Q

Explore South America

T	A	E	H	R	T	H	G	I	E	R	F	D	R
T	T	X	O	B	E	R	I	F	U	E	L	E	A
L	R	S	S	U	C	E	B	E	L	L	V	E	S
O	A	A	A	F	H	I	N	F	C	I	T	P	L
C	C	C	V	F	N	N	E	I	R	O	E	S	E
O	K	A	I	E	O	V	X	D	G	B	N	L	E
M	P	V	R	R	L	E	H	A	O	N	D	Q	H
O	O	A	Q	S	O	N	A	O	C	S	E	B	W
T	L	L	S	V	G	T	U	R	O	R	R	L	L
I	L	V	C	S	Y	I	S	L	A	E	U	A	U
V	U	E	H	R	E	O	T	I	L	K	S	C	P
E	T	S	A	A	E	N	L	A	H	O	S	K	I
D	I	E	S	E	L	W	G	R	N	T	E	D	S
O	O	W	S	G	A	K	O	E	I	S	R	Y	T
O	N	I	I	Y	Q	T	W	P	R	I	P	E	O
W	H	I	S	T	L	E	S	T	A	T	I	O	N

Steam Train

K	D	N	A	L	N	I	J	D	Q	B	D	Q	F
K	S	A	M	O	U	N	T	A	I	N	A	U	E
P	U	T	E	A	G	L	A	M	B	M	R	S	A
O	M	U	S	A	N	D	N	G	A	K	G	S	S
N	M	R	E	S	E	R	V	O	I	R	L	K	T
D	E	A	E	E	Z	G	T	R	K	H	A	I	R
S	R	L	P	C	N	U	E	E	A	M	C	O	E
S	H	O	R	E	R	T	G	T	L	E	I	I	A
Z	M	U	I	T	A	E	R	A	E	T	A	R	M
F	G	D	L	R	G	I	A	W	D	S	L	A	S
S	K	E	C	I	E	R	L	T	C	Y	T	T	T
O	B	P	O	V	A	P	E	L	I	S	F	N	N
G	F	T	O	E	E	W	U	A	Y	O	U	O	A
U	A	H	L	R	M	O	S	S	T	C	N	R	L
L	F	C	I	S	A	V	A	L	L	E	Y	U	P
R	Z	E	E	C	H	W	O	L	F	I	S	H	K

At the Lake

E	U	L	B	T	E	J	Y	T	E	F	A	S	F
C	N	A	G	E	N	T	H	G	I	E	R	F	U
R	O	V	V	N	R	G	S	E	C	I	R	P	E
E	I	I	Q	O	I	F	E	G	A	G	G	U	L
W	T	R	P	L	R	U	N	W	A	Y	K	S	A
N	A	R	F	A	T	T	E	N	D	A	N	T	N
I	I	A	Y	U	S	A	I	R	W	A	Y	S	I
A	V	Y	T	W	E	S	D	X	B	E	S	E	M
T	A	M	I	A	N	T	E	G	A	L	E	W	R
P	M	O	R	I	A	E	P	N	G	U	C	H	E
A	E	N	U	R	L	K	A	I	G	D	I	T	T
C	R	O	C	C	P	C	R	E	A	E	V	U	A
A	I	C	E	R	R	I	T	O	G	H	R	O	G
B	C	E	S	A	I	T	U	B	E	C	E	S	Y
I	A	I	K	F	A	T	R	O	P	S	S	A	P
N	N	O	R	T	H	W	E	S	T	O	L	I	P

Airlines

S	K	I	I	N	G	A	T	S	P	E	E	D	C
W	I	T	T	R	A	C	K	G	P	H	V	B	J
I	E	X	X	E	Y	G	Y	H	O	R	S	E	J
M	D	G	H	C	L	L	N	L	K	A	I	P	M
M	F	N	L	N	L	I	Y	I	M	U	Q	N	O
I	O	I	U	A	Q	M	B	A	W	T	C	D	T
N	N	T	R	O	P	S	R	O	T	O	M	Y	O
G	F	A	O	I	H	A	L	Y	M	Y	R	V	C
N	O	K	C	R	T	Y	D	E	A	W	N	L	R
I	O	S	Z	H	C	Y	E	L	D	U	O	A	O
N	T	A	O	B	B	Y	E	R	Q	D	C	N	S
N	R	N	M	R	D	R	C	B	G	K	O	M	S
U	A	X	E	C	A	M	E	L	C	A	E	G	A
R	K	D	A	O	R	F	F	O	E	V	R	S	P
C	K	V	B	R	U	O	T	B	I	R	X	D	V
G	N	I	L	I	A	S	B	I	C	Y	C	L	E

At the Races

E	B	C	I	F	I	T	N	E	I	C	S	O	X
R	E	U	C	A	N	T	I	Q	U	E	R	A	R
U	N	T	A	P	A	I	N	T	I	N	G	S	J
T	A	B	S	C	U	L	P	T	U	R	E	S	G
L	T	A	E	E	X	H	I	B	I	T	S	U	A
U	U	R	S	S	H	V	C	U	R	A	T	O	R
C	R	T	N	O	I	T	C	E	L	L	O	C	T
D	A	I	D	T	S	R	O	T	I	S	I	V	I
V	L	F	C	L	T	R	E	A	S	U	R	E	S
N	E	A	D	N	O	I	S	S	I	M	D	A	T
N	A	C	E	S	R	U	A	S	O	N	I	D	I
R	R	T	N	O	I	T	A	C	U	D	E	A	C
E	N	S	A	N	C	I	E	N	T	O	U	R	S
D	I	S	P	L	A	Y	S	T	C	E	J	B	O
O	N	E	R	D	L	I	H	C	I	L	B	U	P
M	G	A	L	L	E	R	Y	F	A	M	O	U	S

Going to Museums

G	F	L	J	G	N	I	T	A	O	L	F	L	E
N	G	A	K	N	R	C	S	R	E	D	D	A	L
I	N	P	M	I	E	H	K	O	X	L	E	N	I
D	I	S	D	N	M	E	S	L	E	I	P	E	T
A	X	S	E	A	M	M	W	O	R	E	T	S	R
W	A	B	T	E	U	I	I	P	C	N	H	E	Y
D	L	S	A	L	S	C	M	R	I	I	C	L	C
I	E	R	E	C	R	A	S	E	S	R	O	H	L
V	R	E	H	E	K	L	U	T	E	O	I	O	O
I	O	M	P	T	R	S	I	A	C	L	S	T	U
N	O	M	H	E	K	E	T	W	D	H	K	T	N
G	D	I	S	R	N	I	T	R	A	C	I	U	G
D	T	W	A	C	O	D	E	L	O	P	M	B	E
E	U	S	L	N	T	N	L	D	I	K	M	F	P
C	O	J	P	O	E	O	J	K	J	F	E	U	D
K	I	D	S	C	W	I	N	D	O	O	R	N	P

Motel Pool

Z	O	T	S	I	L	L	S	I	D	O	O	W	L
M	F	H	G	U	O	R	O	A	D	M	S	H	N
D	A	T	A	R	M	A	C	P	N	U	V	I	U
T	I	D	T	L	A	S	A	N	S	D	K	T	S
Z	N	Z	A	P	V	V	M	R	X	C	L	E	B
C	S	E	L	C	I	H	E	V	I	A	C	Y	G
R	T	L	M	N	A	D	V	L	H	C	O	A	O
A	R	O	G	E	N	M	S	P	C	D	N	W	M
C	E	H	B	I	V	U	S	B	A	R	C	H	S
K	E	T	C	W	R	A	L	U	N	A	R	G	K
S	T	O	C	F	Z	S	P	O	X	H	E	I	G
E	K	P	A	E	C	I	F	F	A	R	T	H	O
N	D	C	C	O	M	P	O	S	I	T	E	T	K
I	E	I	I	A	R	E	B	B	U	R	O	C	K
L	C	E	R	R	R	E	N	O	T	S	V	H	N
R	R	Y	B	W	B	S	H	T	O	O	M	S	Z

Road Surface

T	P	N	I	A	P	S	E	I	N	E	P	L	P
R	L	F	R	A	N	C	I	S	C	A	I	O	M
A	O	X	D	H	I	S	T	O	R	Y	N	U	U
V	I	R	G	N	A	P	O	L	E	O	N	V	E
E	R	A	O	R	X	M	I	U	I	J	W	R	S
L	E	R	V	A	U	A	A	T	T	E	I	E	U
Y	N	T	E	E	M	O	U	R	R	O	N	G	M
O	G	I	R	E	R	L	B	U	I	I	E	A	U
N	A	S	N	A	O	S	T	M	S	A	Y	U	I
G	P	T	M	V	P	A	A	I	E	R	N	G	G
E	M	S	E	X	R	A	U	I	T	X	Z	N	L
R	A	R	N	E	G	C	N	N	L	D	U	A	E
M	H	S	T	S	I	R	U	O	T	L	N	L	B
A	C	I	G	F	O	O	D	C	B	G	E	P	K
N	L	O	V	E	C	U	L	T	U	R	E	S	M
Y	M	O	N	O	C	E	T	A	N	E	S	L	T

French Vacation

Y	O	S	E	M	I	T	E	R	M	I	N	U	S
R	N	O	G	E	R	O	F	O	R	E	S	T	S
O	C	A	N	A	D	A	O	C	I	X	E	M	E
T	P	A	I	W	A	S	H	I	N	G	T	O	N
S	E	L	S	E	T	U	O	R	A	A	J	U	R
I	S	R	E	C	R	E	A	T	I	O	N	N	E
H	U	C	O	L	A	N	T	N	R	T	I	T	D
I	B	A	M	L	G	D	R	S	T	L	A	A	L
K	A	J	D	E	P	O	E	R	S	W	R	I	I
E	C	O	N	V	F	X	S	O	E	I	R	N	W
R	K	N	C	I	E	P	E	O	U	L	E	S	H
S	P	P	L	G	A	N	D	D	Q	D	T	C	I
B	A	A	A	R	P	C	T	T	E	L	S	E	K
Q	C	S	K	M	Z	A	O	U	K	I	E	N	I
Q	K	S	E	S	R	O	H	O	R	F	W	I	N
W	O	N	S	D	R	A	O	B	A	E	S	C	G

Pacific Crest Trail

P	G	Y	A	M	A	H	A	S	K	I	S	D	S
A	T	A	K	E	X	T	E	L	C	I	H	E	V
T	R	B	S	A	V	A	L	A	N	C	H	E	A
H	I	O	A	O	V	C	O	L	D	C	K	P	F
S	D	M	L	T	L	C	F	U	N	O	M	S	T
H	E	B	A	D	R	I	V	E	R	U	D	N	A
T	R	A	V	E	L	T	N	T	J	A	A	O	C
F	O	R	E	S	T	C	S	E	C	I	N	W	W
D	T	D	R	A	G	R	A	C	I	N	G	S	O
N	O	I	S	E	U	A	I	C	E	I	E	L	N
A	M	E	K	O	D	D	P	O	L	A	R	I	S
L	E	R	F	P	E	U	F	A	S	T	O	A	K
Y	T	R	A	N	S	P	O	R	T	N	U	R	C
W	I	N	T	E	R	D	E	L	S	U	S	T	A
P	A	S	S	E	N	G	E	R	A	O	M	Y	R
E	N	I	G	N	E	X	T	R	E	M	E	D	T

Snowmobile

K I N G D O M C U L T U R E
S Y R T N U O C U I A D L U
R D A N C E C H O I P R A Q
E A T L A N T I C C S X T S
R H W E J I S N L A N I I A
O N C L Q W E D P O P A N B
L F O L I L B E A C H Z R E
P O B I A V N M E M S T A F
X O L V T I I O L U E F A G
E T A E N I M C L S E L E C
C B G S L S D R A I N A P S
I A U U R O M A N C E M O I
R L T T S A O C R X R E R B
A L R W A R M Y L T Y N U I
Y R O T S I H U K C P C E Z
S A P A T Y H C R A N O M A

Going to Spain

R T F A R C R I A X A J Y J
B M I L I T A R Y Q Y F B S
S W B E T R G N I Y L F B H
Z T E V N O I T A I V A O Q
P X R I T A W A G G T L H E
L R G O G G L H G G H I A T
I P L N P H T P D N G A N U
M I A S I S T E L O I T G H
P S S R L D R T F I L S A C
V L S G A E I I H T A X I A
K O A S W G D L A A R S R R
L R A O S R L O G E T G P A
D T P A P E R I M R L N L P
G N I N I A R T D C U I A N
U O W F E N G I N E Q W N J
H C N U A L A N D R R V E T

Glider Aircraft

X H O L S C H O O L S P S K
B C U W F S D R A Y O A S G
P I T A A S R R A U I E P F
E R S R M A U W T B M O Q E
R F K P I R H S R O P U L N
F S I S L G I U H U I H E C
E T R W I D B O L E Y P O E
C E T H E U U A T T O M P S
T E S C S S T R I P M A L L
R R D C I I U N X U R A B W
A T B N O R U O T K W N O E
F S G N A M T I H N M W R L
F R W B M L N S S P A O O P
I A D O B G G N I Y L T U O
C C C I T I E S V D L C G E
Z O N I N G T R E E S I H P

Suburbs

C A S I N O I T A C A V I G
F L O G O A G N I I K S C U
G N I N I D M P O O L L A E
S C B T T H F E N A U C V S
Y O E R A E K U N B T I L T
A N A O X A S D M I S E N S
D C C S A L E E V U T O G E
I A H E L T D I L O I I I V
L R E R E H T C H T S S E I
O I S I R I N R A P G H R S
H B I K E I O E A Z F O O N
I B D S S E R V I C E P F E
S E A X S C F O O D T P P P
V A R R E M O U N T A I N X
T N A R U A T S E R L N O E
I B P N S W I M M I N G L N

Resort

R	A	I	N	R	O	F	I	L	A	C	N	H	A
S	M	U	E	S	U	M	Z	O	O	S	L	O	R
B	U	I	L	D	I	N	G	O	O	N	A	L	A
A	S	N	I	A	T	N	U	O	M	I	S	L	G
D	E	E	J	N	O	I	T	A	C	A	V	Y	A
I	M	W	C	A	S	I	N	O	S	L	E	W	I
R	E	Y	O	S	E	M	I	T	E	P	G	O	N
O	N	O	U	K	K	L	A	W	D	R	A	O	B
L	T	R	G	N	I	L	B	M	A	G	S	D	E
F	H	K	D	I	S	N	E	Y	L	A	N	D	A
C	I	S	A	C	H	I	C	A	G	O	C	D	C
A	S	K	L	A	N	D	M	A	R	K	S	D	H
N	T	R	A	M	O	N	U	M	E	N	T	S	E
Y	O	A	M	R	E	I	P	Y	V	A	N	K	S
O	R	P	O	T	H	C	A	P	E	C	O	D	Q
N	Y	O	R	L	A	N	D	O	D	D	Q	B	S

Tourist Attractions

P	V	A	C	A	T	I	O	N	K	S	T	C	P
A	E	U	R	O	P	E	R	C	N	R	W	A	I
C	I	T	M	A	P	S	O	O	O	A	S	E	R
K	H	O	T	E	L	M	I	P	L	S	R	S	T
I	P	M	A	C	M	T	S	K	P	U	H	A	D
N	C	O	J	U	A	N	I	O	T	I	S	I	N
G	O	B	T	C	A	N	R	N	P	N	S	R	U
E	U	I	O	R	G	T	E	S	I	C	E	P	O
O	N	L	T	H	T	V	C	A	O	L	S	L	R
G	T	E	O	C	D	N	R	V	A	G	G	A	Y
R	R	I	U	A	A	T	E	X	I	N	U	N	A
A	I	M	R	E	D	R	A	M	I	S	D	E	D
P	E	M	I	B	Y	T	T	K	E	M	I	S	I
H	S	T	S	A	I	J	I	T	E	V	M	T	L
Y	L	E	T	O	M	H	O	H	A	I	O	A	O
A	B	S	N	S	S	E	N	I	S	U	B	M	H

Let's Go!

N	W	Q	A	N	E	X	C	I	T	I	N	G	X
Y	K	S	I	R	W	Y	E	N	R	U	O	J	S
D	L	O	B	E	X	P	E	R	I	E	N	C	E
N	A	O	K	R	O	M	J	F	Q	W	G	X	G
A	L	R	V	U	E	O	D	A	N	G	E	R	N
L	S	E	I	T	I	V	I	T	C	A	N	N	I
I	I	B	I	N	O	I	T	A	E	R	C	E	R
F	R	C	E	E	G	O	L	G	P	A	O	X	O
E	X	W	A	V	L	E	D	C	F	C	U	O	L
E	N	U	A	D	V	E	L	E	N	I	N	T	P
M	Z	N	W	A	L	I	A	A	W	N	T	I	X
E	H	V	R	W	M	R	G	R	U	G	E	C	E
R	X	T	O	B	O	O	K	S	N	S	R	R	X
T	G	N	I	V	I	D	Y	K	S	I	U	G	L
X	K	N	P	H	Y	S	I	C	A	L	N	N	B
E	G	N	I	K	I	H	Q	Y	L	Q	R	G	U

Adventure Travel

S	E	L	C	S	U	M	K	E	N	E	R	G	Y
W	G	N	I	K	L	A	W	R	O	W	I	N	G
I	S	R	V	H	Y	A	L	O	D	N	O	G	Z
M	R	E	Y	A	H	A	N	D	C	A	R	C	F
M	U	S	K	S	B	I	C	Y	C	L	E	S	U
I	N	I	K	R	E	T	O	O	C	S	K	N	N
N	N	C	W	H	E	E	L	C	H	A	I	R	I
G	I	R	L	S	P	R	I	N	T	I	N	G	C
R	N	E	E	T	A	K	S	E	C	I	Z	N	Y
O	G	X	F	G	N	I	B	M	I	L	C	I	C
W	T	E	C	H	N	O	L	O	G	Y	W	L	L
B	I	K	E	C	A	N	O	E	I	N	G	W	E
O	D	P	T	R	O	P	S	N	A	R	T	A	T
A	L	A	D	E	P	K	L	E	I	S	U	R	E
T	R	I	C	Y	C	L	E	T	S	W	A	C	A
P	U	S	H	I	N	G	N	I	L	C	Y	C	D

Human Powered

T	H	P	A	R	K	R	A	M	D	N	A	L	P
G	E	O	R	G	E	C	N	E	D	I	S	E	R
H	D	I	S	T	I	L	L	E	R	Y	B	S	O
V	I	R	G	I	N	I	A	D	N	M	Q	U	P
A	Y	S	S	O	F	W	N	H	O	M	T	O	E
C	H	A	T	T	R	A	C	T	I	O	N	H	R
I	B	H	A	O	X	S	O	B	T	N	E	L	T
R	L	T	B	E	R	H	G	M	A	U	D	A	Y
E	A	R	L	O	F	I	A	M	T	M	I	N	F
M	I	A	E	A	F	N	C	R	N	E	S	O	A
A	N	M	M	T	S	G	E	A	A	N	E	I	I
J	O	I	S	I	E	T	L	F	L	T	R	T	R
V	L	H	O	M	A	O	I	W	P	W	P	A	F
Y	O	N	O	T	G	N	I	L	R	A	O	N	A
P	C	H	S	K	K	C	O	D	D	A	P	O	X
S	N	E	D	R	A	G	R	O	U	N	D	S	D

Mount Vernon

T	E	G	I	I	S	L	A	N	D	S	X	N	E
R	R	T	U	N	L	E	V	A	R	T	A	T	X
D	E	O	R	L	D	P	E	E	D	E	S	R	P
E	H	N	P	E	F	I	F	C	C	A	U	E	L
P	P	T	I	L	N	I	A	O	V	M	R	T	O
T	S	A	O	L	L	C	C	N	A	F	F	A	R
H	O	O	C	A	A	I	H	R	O	P	A	W	A
U	R	B	E	I	T	S	I	E	I	C	C	T	T
R	D	S	D	N	F	N	W	H	S	B	E	L	I
R	Y	X	A	Q	E	I	S	T	G	L	S	A	O
I	H	L	A	R	G	E	C	U	W	U	B	S	N
C	T	A	R	C	T	I	C	O	C	E	A	N	N
A	C	U	R	R	E	N	T	S	C	O	R	A	L
N	Y	H	P	A	R	G	O	N	A	E	C	O	F
E	R	O	H	S	L	N	O	T	K	N	A	L	P
W	H	A	L	E	S	D	O	L	P	H	I	N	S

Ocean Voyage

T	G	Z	S	S	E	N	R	E	D	L	I	W	M
R	R	C	H	L	G	L	A	K	E	S	O	O	M
A	E	A	W	U	N	N	Z	T	N	R	U	L	C
I	S	M	M	F	I	O	I	O	U	N	E	V	A
L	L	P	S	H	B	I	I	R	T	R	G	E	L
S	L	I	T	T	A	T	V	A	P	V	E	S	D
L	A	N	S	I	C	A	I	B	L	S	O	E	E
A	F	G	I	A	S	N	C	O	L	D	T	C	R
M	R	S	R	F	S	I	N	A	E	E	H	O	A
I	E	T	U	D	M	T	H	T	F	B	E	S	H
N	T	L	O	L	N	S	C	I	A	U	R	Y	I
A	A	Y	T	O	R	E	L	N	M	F	M	S	K
R	W	Q	S	E	T	D	L	G	O	F	A	T	I
O	U	I	V	O	L	M	M	K	U	A	L	E	N
L	B	I	R	I	D	A	H	O	S	L	E	M	G
F	R	P	W	R	V	I	S	I	T	O	R	S	B

Yellowstone National Park

P	C	P	B	C	D	E	T	D	I	N	N	E	R
I	S	U	A	G	S	R	E	V	O	T	F	E	L
C	Y	O	N	D	E	A	F	S	Y	H	Z	L	F
N	A	S	Q	O	M	P	F	I	U	I	J	B	W
I	D	F	U	O	O	E	U	D	T	P	F	A	K
C	I	K	E	F	H	R	B	E	N	D	P	T	N
K	L	I	T	T	B	P	P	D	A	X	H	E	I
C	O	T	N	S	E	P	E	I	R	D	C	G	R
A	H	C	U	A	A	R	N	S	U	E	N	E	D
N	P	H	T	F	X	I	I	H	A	S	U	V	X
S	D	E	R	A	H	S	W	A	T	S	L	G	H
J	G	N	I	K	O	O	C	D	S	E	L	D	F
M	E	A	T	S	A	F	K	A	E	R	B	R	U
K	E	N	I	S	I	U	C	L	R	T	U	W	L
K	T	C	O	U	R	S	E	A	T	I	N	G	L
J	H	C	N	U	R	B	Y	S	T	H	G	I	L

Stop for a Bite

S	G	E	L	T	I	M	E	D	X	Y	B	V	X
O	N	R	S	T	R	O	P	S	T	N	E	V	E
C	I	P	A	C	E	N	D	U	R	A	N	C	E
K	G	D	B	Q	E	E	H	V	O	O	N	E	S
S	G	F	R	U	S	U	R	L	I	A	N	A	I
W	O	I	U	A	R	N	Y	T	T	K	T	G	C
E	J	T	N	D	C	M	O	S	S	H	N	L	R
A	F	N	L	R	P	M	I	H	L	I	A	L	E
T	A	E	E	I	O	D	D	E	T	P	I	I	X
E	S	S	C	C	S	E	T	N	S	A	U	M	E
E	T	S	O	E	E	I	I	Y	E	Q	R	D	B
F	D	L	O	P	C	R	G	N	I	K	L	A	W
C	J	H	S	S	P	R	M	U	S	C	L	E	M
O	S	U	Q	S	E	G	N	I	N	I	A	R	T
R	A	C	I	N	G	S	S	H	E	A	L	T	H
M	I	L	E	D	I	R	T	S	F	O	O	T	I

Run Away

Q	V	E	K	G	G	T	O	H	C	O	I	R	Q
R	F	R	O	Z	E	N	C	H	O	I	C	E	S
R	F	I	S	H	U	N	I	E	X	N	J	P	J
X	O	B	H	E	U	C	G	R	I	Y	O	P	E
K	O	D	E	L	K	A	N	K	E	R	T	E	C
A	D	E	R	E	R	R	P	O	K	T	S	P	I
E	S	S	N	E	N	A	L	P	R	I	A	N	V
T	B	S	V	M	N	V	C	N	A	D	F	C	R
S	P	E	C	O	N	O	M	Y	N	L	K	A	E
A	B	R	E	R	F	A	T	A	I	I	A	R	S
L	M	T	E	F	I	I	L	G	T	K	E	T	N
T	E	T	E	T	L	B	H	C	N	W	R	R	A
O	A	E	W	A	Z	T	H	I	O	F	B	A	C
W	T	C	U	T	L	E	R	Y	B	H	R	V	K
K	F	Q	Q	J	N	D	L	L	O	R	O	E	W
L	L	A	M	S	P	L	A	S	T	I	C	L	E

Airline Meals

S	K	J	N	O	T	G	N	I	M	L	I	W	Q
E	I	O	E	F	R	S	O	U	T	H	E	R	N
N	T	T	U	E	Q	O	A	F	L	I	G	H	T
A	T	W	S	T	A	C	B	O	B	M	S	G	P
C	Y	G	T	A	E	P	I	S	C	B	D	I	E
I	H	G	E	R	F	R	A	R	N	T	N	E	L
R	A	A	H	E	H	S	B	N	O	E	S	L	B
R	W	R	P	D	E	E	E	A	T	T	E	A	H
U	K	B	C	E	F	R	U	H	N	H	S	R	E
H	D	T	A	F	L	J	U	C	C	K	E	I	G
C	O	R	R	N	O	H	C	T	E	A	S	R	H
O	O	O	D	O	G	K	I	T	I	B	E	J	S
T	W	F	I	C	Y	M	B	L	G	N	R	B	X
T	G	F	N	F	T	A	N	I	L	O	R	A	C
O	O	D	A	M	L	C	O	L	O	N	Y	U	B
N	D	E	L	L	I	V	E	H	S	A	N	D	F

North Carolina

D	I	E	S	E	L	A	N	G	I	S	E	I	T
A	A	B	T	O	K	E	N	K	V	C	F	F	M
O	P	O	O	L	R	A	C	X	O	B	I	T	J
R	E	O	D	R	E	F	F	U	B	R	R	S	W
L	G	S	S	S	E	R	P	X	E	A	E	E	H
I	U	T	S	A	L	L	A	B	I	I	M	K	E
A	A	E	N	A	E	L	O	N	T	L	A	I	E
R	G	R	O	R	E	X	S	C	Y	W	N	P	L
E	O	C	I	E	C	F	A	N	T	A	O	S	S
P	N	C	T	R	L	B	R	R	B	Y	T	T	B
E	D	S	A	A	O	A	A	E	O	G	S	E	G
E	O	E	T	O	C	C	I	T	I	B	I	K	L
L	L	C	S	D	K	A	L	N	L	G	P	C	I
S	A	E	N	S	T	R	C	A	E	B	H	I	N
R	Y	A	W	B	U	S	A	L	R	O	U	T	E
W	H	I	S	T	L	E	R	S	W	I	T	C	H

Railroad Words

K	T	Z	X	M	P	F	U	E	L	A	S	E	G
W	H	E	E	L	S	E	E	V	T	D	B	N	T
S	S	T	J	N	M	D	O	R	E	V	I	R	D
F	R	E	I	G	H	T	A	P	R	K	C	H	T
O	E	A	G	Q	W	C	O	O	L	Y	Y	U	E
G	R	R	C	D	K	T	S	A	R	E	C	S	K
T	T	B	A	S	I	Y	W	P	U	B	L	I	C
M	A	R	T	F	A	R	C	R	I	A	E	S	O
E	O	L	A	W	Q	L	B	T	N	I	S	H	R
S	B	V	H	I	B	I	R	I	S	R	E	I	E
R	L	G	E	U	L	A	M	L	A	P	L	P	T
O	I	N	S	M	F	R	B	E	G	L	C	S	A
H	A	E	Y	F	E	O	O	V	O	A	I	V	W
V	S	C	I	T	C	N	A	A	O	N	H	M	Q
S	K	C	U	R	T	O	T	R	D	E	E	P	S
L	Z	Q	J	R	Q	M	S	T	S	E	V	G	J

Getting Around

H	U	R	R	I	C	A	N	E	T	A	E	H	D
M	N	W	O	T	N	W	O	D	H	T	D	V	E
O	O	S	U	N	B	E	L	T	E	T	L	K	S
R	Y	D	B	E	A	C	H	S	M	R	R	N	T
L	E	C	G	M	F	U	N	L	E	A	O	A	I
A	N	T	D	N	M	B	M	E	P	C	W	T	N
N	S	R	S	I	I	C	L	T	A	T	Y	I	A
D	I	O	D	A	I	K	N	O	R	I	E	L	T
O	D	P	Q	T	O	E	C	H	K	O	N	O	I
M	T	R	Y	R	M	C	G	I	S	N	S	P	O
A	L	I	L	E	V	A	R	T	G	S	I	O	N
G	A	A	S	T	R	O	S	E	R	A	D	R	A
I	W	U	Q	N	F	A	M	I	L	Y	M	T	E
C	M	Q	S	E	N	T	I	N	E	L	Q	E	C
A	N	I	M	A	L	K	I	N	G	D	O	M	O
G	P	Y	T	N	U	O	C	E	G	N	A	R	O

Orlando

C	Y	D	E	X	P	E	D	I	T	I	O	N	T
E	F	I	N	I	A	P	S	H	D	T	R	A	F
Z	L	S	D	A	G	R	K	I	L	A	S	V	A
E	A	C	N	I	N	A	O	S	R	L	N	I	E
U	T	O	A	V	I	I	A	T	O	I	A	G	S
R	H	V	L	C	L	C	D	O	W	A	I	A	P
O	O	E	G	G	I	E	S	R	W	N	D	T	I
P	L	R	N	R	A	T	V	Y	E	A	N	O	H
E	I	Y	E	I	S	O	N	A	N	F	I	R	S
F	D	M	K	Z	S	P	N	A	R	C	A	E	E
N	A	E	C	O	I	A	I	E	L	T	T	R	G
J	Y	Q	U	E	E	N	B	C	G	T	P	O	A
T	R	E	B	O	T	C	O	E	E	X	A	L	Y
Y	P	O	R	T	U	G	A	L	L	S	C	P	O
D	U	H	I	S	P	A	N	I	O	L	A	X	V
L	K	T	R	A	D	I	N	G	C	C	A	E	Y

Christopher Columbus

R	E	S	I	H	P	M	E	M	E	D	K	L	V
M	A	M	O	T	O	W	N	F	C	N	C	B	G
H	G	U	T	F	H	R	U	O	N	A	O	Z	B
T	G	R	O	V	P	S	T	L	A	B	R	Z	E
Y	E	D	G	N	I	W	S	K	D	G	K	A	B
H	R	Y	N	O	H	P	M	Y	S	I	N	J	O
R	E	P	N	N	N	C	L	Q	C	B	U	N	P
A	C	M	B	A	A	A	E	S	L	E	P	A	A
T	O	W	I	R	N	S	I	T	A	I	O	I	T
I	R	H	P	T	O	N	H	T	S	D	I	I	R
U	D	R	O	S	G	A	N	V	S	N	D	A	I
G	O	S	P	E	L	A	D	J	I	I	A	W	O
E	J	S	R	H	C	B	R	W	C	L	R	A	T
N	N	S	K	C	O	R	D	R	A	H	L	H	I
R	A	L	G	R	U	N	G	E	L	Y	U	E	C
E	B	I	C	O	N	C	E	R	T	S	O	U	L

Car Radio Music

P	H	E	A	L	T	H	Y	U	M	E	F	P	Y
L	G	N	O	I	T	I	R	T	U	N	N	G	T
A	R	I	T	R	E	S	S	E	D	R	R	R	I
T	O	S	E	L	B	A	T	E	G	E	V	E	U
E	W	I	I	S	F	R	L	N	N	Z	L	G	R
U	T	U	D	K	E	D	I	E	D	I	N	N	F
Q	H	C	A	N	S	W	J	I	R	T	O	U	T
N	Z	E	N	M	O	E	N	B	I	E	I	H	A
A	R	I	R	L	G	I	R	N	N	P	T	C	Y
B	D	B	L	B	N	G	T	O	K	P	S	N	T
P	Q	A	E	G	I	A	N	S	V	A	E	U	I
A	W	L	S	W	K	V	V	I	E	I	G	L	S
S	W	A	E	E	C	O	O	K	W	G	N	Z	E
T	L	N	E	C	A	L	O	R	I	E	I	M	B
A	G	C	H	C	N	U	R	B	E	Y	H	D	O
U	F	E	C	F	S	B	U	F	F	E	T	C	Z

Eating on the Road

E	C	A	P	S	C	I	E	N	C	E	S	A	B
F	L	I	G	H	T	S	H	U	T	T	L	E	S
S	R	A	M	I	S	S	I	O	N	S	I	R	T
F	L	O	R	I	D	A	K	E	A	Y	F	O	E
A	P	O	L	L	O	A	M	Y	S	G	T	L	K
S	A	T	U	R	N	N	P	L	A	O	O	P	C
T	Y	R	U	C	R	E	M	H	C	L	F	X	O
R	E	G	N	E	L	L	A	H	C	O	F	E	R
O	G	C	V	O	N	W	O	D	T	N	U	O	C
N	O	O	M	Y	R	O	T	S	I	H	U	O	O
A	G	L	V	A	I	R	F	O	R	C	E	A	R
U	E	U	T	D	I	S	C	O	V	E	R	Y	L
T	M	M	T	E	T	I	L	L	E	T	A	S	A
S	I	B	K	E	N	N	E	D	Y	A	W	E	N
G	N	I	N	I	A	R	T	O	U	R	S	I	D
F	I	A	O	R	B	I	T	E	R	O	W	R	O

Kennedy Space Center

E	G	D	E	W	O	O	D	S	Q	K	C	T	R
L	R	M	G	R	R	O	U	G	H	S	N	R	W
M	A	G	R	S	E	I	D	D	A	C	C	A	A
G	S	T	R	O	K	E	S	T	Y	O	T	C	L
A	S	H	O	E	S	C	S	D	U	E	S	A	K
Y	E	M	A	C	E	U	L	R	R	U	G	H	M
K	W	A	S	N	G	N	S	U	U	I	D	O	N
F	K	S	G	U	D	E	S	M	B	D	V	L	B
P	F	T	A	L	S	I	F	C	N	S	Z	E	D
X	V	E	L	N	E	G	C	A	H	B	N	S	R
H	P	R	F	L	D	H	L	A	I	I	I	R	A
Y	P	S	P	U	T	T	E	R	P	R	P	E	Z
B	Y	N	Z	G	O	E	R	U	U	D	W	Y	A
B	O	O	Z	C	A	E	E	A	U	I	G	A	H
E	Z	R	S	W	I	N	G	S	P	E	K	L	Y
F	W	I	O	O	E	R	O	G	T	R	O	P	S

Golf Vacation

F	E	D	E	X	B	U	S	I	N	E	S	S	R
A	B	K	I	M	P	O	R	T	A	N	T	I	E
S	E	L	A	C	S	P	U	D	X	N	H	G	N
T	E	X	P	E	N	S	I	V	E	C	G	N	N
R	E	G	N	E	S	S	E	M	N	O	I	A	U
A	D	H	L	S	T	S	U	O	F	W	N	T	R
C	N	P	Y	A	E	C	E	F	T	X	R	U	Y
K	E	A	N	J	O	G	I	R	T	O	E	R	Q
I	S	C	A	D	I	C	A	L	P	B	V	E	N
N	E	K	P	P	E	V	G	S	E	X	O	I	O
G	R	A	M	W	E	L	N	D	S	C	E	R	S
V	V	G	O	L	R	A	I	U	P	E	R	R	R
G	I	E	C	O	R	O	N	V	E	L	M	A	E
Q	C	S	Y	T	I	R	U	C	E	S	I	C	P
N	E	L	C	Y	C	I	B	T	D	R	N	A	V
B	S	B	I	K	E	C	A	F	E	P	Y	T	M

Courier

O	C	A	N	O	M	N	E	V	A	D	A	O	T
D	P	Q	S	S	E	G	A	R	I	M	E	I	T
D	E	R	H	E	R	E	N	O	T	U	F	O	R
S	O	E	O	C	W	Z	J	I	N	N	U	K	O
W	P	Y	P	U	B	S	P	E	M	R	C	S	S
M	L	A	P	R	L	R	V	F	I	A	O	P	E
I	E	L	I	I	Z	E	O	S	J	B	G	O	R
N	C	P	N	T	R	S	T	K	N	E	Q	R	E
D	N	B	G	Y	S	T	C	T	E	T	S	T	K
I	A	M	A	D	N	A	H	Y	E	T	E	S	O
A	H	H	M	C	L	U	G	Z	R	I	N	E	P
N	C	O	B	B	C	R	A	E	W	N	I	L	N
I	R	T	L	Y	F	A	C	G	V	G	H	B	H
W	A	E	I	U	M	N	R	X	C	S	C	A	A
G	P	L	N	O	O	T	T	A	N	C	A	T	D
H	S	S	G	C	N	S	L	O	T	J	M	L	E

Casino

I	V	W	B	U	S	T	C	A	P	M	O	C	E
G	A	S	K	E	T	S	P	O	N	Y	C	A	R
R	I	A	V	R	O	C	Y	Y	G	G	U	B	V
E	I	D	O	O	W	B	O	D	Y	W	O	R	K
A	T	A	C	H	O	M	E	T	E	R	I	I	S
R	S	T	U	D	E	B	A	K	E	R	L	O	T
E	E	J	O	D	O	M	E	T	E	R	C	L	R
T	L	S	T	H	G	I	L	D	A	E	H	E	U
S	X	G	T	E	N	I	G	N	E	V	A	T	T
O	A	A	T	S	F	B	E	A	R	I	N	G	S
R	S	S	N	R	T	U	N	E	U	P	G	H	P
F	N	G	I	I	P	O	T	G	A	R	E	O	A
E	A	A	O	P	M	U	P	L	E	U	F	T	C
D	R	U	J	S	N	G	I	S	D	A	O	R	B
Q	T	G	V	E	L	T	T	O	R	H	T	O	U
M	R	E	C	T	R	A	N	S	A	M	D	D	H

Passenger Vehicle

L	C	M	G	E	O	L	O	G	Y	S	K	U	U
A	F	O	R	E	S	T	A	T	I	B	A	H	N
K	B	I	S	E	Q	U	O	I	A	S	U	A	M
E	F	T	U	O	L	U	M	N	E	J	Q	L	O
S	R	U	D	E	T	C	E	T	O	R	P	F	U
W	R	E	N	I	P	L	A	B	U	S	N	D	N
V	I	S	I	T	O	R	S	P	E	O	U	O	T
Y	U	L	T	R	A	I	L	S	I	A	I	M	A
R	M	A	D	R	A	V	L	T	R	T	R	E	I
O	N	M	D	E	O	A	A	R	A	O	A	S	N
T	H	I	Y	L	R	T	F	E	N	U	G	N	S
S	O	N	C	E	E	N	R	A	G	R	N	O	T
I	J	A	D	G	L	C	E	M	E	I	I	Y	N
H	N	A	E	R	E	L	T	S	R	S	K	N	A
O	M	V	E	R	U	T	A	N	S	T	I	A	L
E	F	I	L	D	L	I	W	V	P	S	B	C	P

Scenic Yosemite

W	D	P	O	R	T	Q	G	C	S	A	N	D	S
E	O	D	O	F	B	Q	O	W	W	A	V	E	S
S	C	C	T	O	U	R	I	S	T	S	D	F	S
T	K	U	R	A	A	M	F	D	R	I	X	E	H
Y	E	D	S	L	M	A	P	N	T	I	H	Q	S
K	E	L	U	I	N	N	U	A	S	C	V	N	H
R	A	I	N	R	O	F	I	L	A	C	A	E	O
G	Y	G	B	I	I	V	Y	E	O	E	X	B	R
N	F	C	A	R	S	A	B	D	C	H	R	O	E
I	L	I	T	O	O	S	T	O	T	O	B	A	E
F	E	F	H	G	R	F	I	L	S	R	V	T	C
R	V	I	I	K	E	F	S	E	A	W	E	E	D
U	E	C	N	G	K	I	W	H	E	N	O	Z	C
S	E	A	G	U	L	L	S	E	W	A	T	E	R
L	B	P	K	L	H	C	G	N	I	H	S	I	F
K	H	Z	G	F	E	M	J	R	D	V	X	D	C

Coastline

E	B	N	I	L	K	N	A	R	F	N	E	B	F
R	R	B	B	C	R	I	G	P	T	S	V	S	D
U	F	A	E	O	O	V	H	O	N	K	O	E	I
T	R	S	T	N	C	X	I	P	I	R	L	T	N
C	E	K	S	S	K	S	S	U	M	A	Y	A	D
E	S	E	Y	T	Y	O	T	L	W	P	L	T	E
T	H	T	R	I	T	C	O	A	M	T	R	S	P
I	P	B	O	T	I	I	R	T	I	N	E	D	E
H	R	A	S	U	S	E	Y	I	N	U	H	E	N
C	I	L	S	T	R	T	S	O	Q	O	T	T	D
R	N	L	G	I	E	Y	E	N	U	M	O	I	E
A	C	A	V	O	V	H	L	K	I	R	R	N	N
O	E	E	B	N	I	I	G	C	R	I	B	U	C
G	R	E	E	N	N	L	A	I	E	A	C	A	E
N	O	R	T	H	U	L	E	T	R	F	M	Z	N
W	E	L	I	B	E	R	T	Y	B	E	L	L	M

Philadelphia

S	M	O	E	L	T	O	T	S	I	R	A	M	W
U	Y	D	N	A	L	E	X	A	N	D	E	R	S
R	T	R	E	P	U	B	L	I	C	R	S	E	N
P	H	A	N	M	Y	E	K	R	U	T	N	G	I
Y	O	M	I	G	O	D	S	T	W	S	A	A	A
C	L	A	S	S	I	C	A	L	I	T	E	U	T
O	O	H	I	O	R	R	R	L	R	N	G	G	N
R	G	H	U	Z	E	H	O	A	I	T	E	N	U
T	Y	Y	C	T	M	P	P	W	C	X	A	A	O
H	P	H	I	L	O	S	O	P	H	Y	S	L	M
O	O	L	Q	R	H	E	L	L	E	N	I	C	S
D	M	A	C	E	D	O	N	I	A	V	H	G	N
O	H	A	T	P	A	R	T	H	E	N	O	N	E
X	Z	E	U	S	E	U	R	O	P	E	A	N	H
I	R	A	L	U	S	N	I	N	E	P	R	V	T
C	T	R	A	V	E	L	T	N	E	I	C	N	A

Greece

R	E	L	I	A	R	T	A	T	T	L	B	T	E
P	T	H	G	I	E	R	F	R	R	E	R	A	S
T	S	E	F	I	N	A	M	U	A	U	O	N	H
K	H	N	L	Y	S	N	K	C	C	F	K	D	I
I	I	G	A	R	A	S	B	K	T	O	E	E	P
N	P	I	T	T	G	P	L	S	O	L	R	M	P
G	M	N	B	S	B	O	X	T	R	U	C	K	E
P	E	E	E	U	A	R	R	O	A	D	O	K	R
I	N	O	D	D	X	T	U	P	E	R	N	O	E
N	T	V	B	N	L	T	D	M	E	Y	S	O	V
D	P	E	I	I	E	O	U	P	O	E	I	B	I
R	A	R	G	M	C	R	E	V	M	A	G	G	E
I	L	S	R	K	R	E	N	I	A	T	N	O	C
V	L	I	I	A	L	O	I	D	A	R	O	L	E
E	E	Z	G	S	C	A	R	R	I	E	R	U	R
R	T	E	R	M	I	N	A	L	E	S	E	I	D

Trucking Words

S	E	O	U	L	T	O	R	O	N	T	O	F	J
H	I	S	T	O	R	Y	P	K	N	F	I	M	S
A	M	H	O	P	E	R	A	O	G	N	E	Y	I
N	E	W	Y	O	R	K	D	E	A	T	Y	A	N
G	G	O	S	P	U	N	O	N	R	T	E	I	G
H	A	C	I	U	O	G	C	O	I	H	G	R	A
A	C	S	R	L	R	E	P	C	O	B	R	P	P
I	I	O	A	A	P	O	D	N	D	U	A	O	O
O	T	M	P	T	L	L	G	I	R	S	L	R	R
G	Y	H	P	I	R	K	V	B	E	I	A	T	E
A	Y	E	S	O	O	E	A	E	T	N	R	S	C
C	R	M	W	N	R	N	U	I	N	E	U	Y	O
I	O	O	G	S	K	T	C	J	E	S	T	D	N
H	T	R	E	S	A	A	A	I	C	S	L	N	O
C	E	I	N	F	L	U	E	N	C	E	U	E	M
S	C	I	F	F	A	R	T	G	T	I	C	Y	Y

Global Cities

G	V	O	W	M	S	E	I	R	E	S	R	V	S
D	E	W	H	U	M	S	K	C	A	R	T	M	P
E	H	D	E	S	I	G	N	A	S	C	A	R	Y
E	I	Y	E	T	D	N	A	R	B	L	I	B	T
P	C	V	L	A	M	O	D	E	L	S	B	N	F
S	L	E	S	N	K	S	R	O	L	O	C	O	G
E	E	H	M	G	E	B	P	T	H	X	R	T	E
S	S	C	I	S	S	A	L	C	O	D	N	S	N
Y	D	F	U	N	E	R	D	L	I	H	C	A	I
A	C	I	L	P	E	R	S	Y	O	T	C	C	L
V	O	L	K	S	W	A	G	E	N	I	N	E	D
P	L	A	S	T	I	C	C	S	R	A	C	I	E
F	L	A	M	E	R	U	Y	E	V	I	R	D	R
P	M	E	T	A	L	D	M	A	T	T	E	L	R
B	O	Y	S	O	M	A	T	C	H	B	O	X	U
O	O	H	H	S	K	C	U	R	T	S	A	F	A

Hot Wheels

B	I	K	E	S	N	I	A	T	N	U	O	M	K
G	P	G	Y	R	U	J	N	I	S	A	T	B	E
D	E	E	S	T	R	O	P	S	R	R	R	F	X
A	D	V	E	N	T	U	R	E	A	A	I	R	T
O	A	G	N	T	X	W	O	E	E	C	A	E	R
R	L	E	O	K	S	F	T	N	G	I	L	E	E
F	S	Q	I	H	E	I	E	D	B	N	S	R	M
F	S	U	S	T	L	R	C	U	R	G	A	I	E
O	S	I	N	G	L	E	T	R	A	C	K	D	C
S	E	P	E	N	I	R	I	A	K	C	G	E	N
H	N	M	P	E	H	O	O	N	E	O	N	K	A
O	T	E	S	R	N	A	N	C	S	K	I	L	L
E	I	N	U	T	W	D	S	E	V	O	L	G	A
S	F	T	S	S	O	S	E	L	C	Y	C	I	B
R	U	G	G	E	D	E	E	P	S	L	Y	H	M
H	E	L	M	E	T	S	B	M	I	L	C	E	X

Mountain Biking

A	F	I	S	H	T	R	A	N	S	F	A	T	A
N	R	E	S	T	A	U	R	A	N	T	S	A	I
S	E	H	C	I	W	D	N	A	S	P	L	C	T
E	N	K	M	E	A	L	S	G	O	D	T	O	H
I	C	H	C	N	U	L	C	A	M	G	I	B	L
R	H	W	H	I	T	E	C	A	S	T	L	E	J
O	F	E	S	I	H	C	N	A	R	F	O	L	B
L	R	P	I	D	E	C	I	V	R	E	S	L	M
A	I	R	E	D	R	O	D	I	N	N	E	R	C
C	E	E	C	N	E	I	N	E	V	N	O	C	D
H	S	P	A	E	H	C	V	P	I	T	A	S	O
A	P	A	G	N	I	K	R	E	G	R	U	B	N
I	B	R	E	A	K	F	A	S	T	K	F	C	A
N	M	E	N	U	P	I	Z	Z	A	H	U	T	L
S	M	D	H	A	M	B	U	R	G	E	R	S	D
G	R	E	A	S	E	Z	I	S	R	E	P	U	S

Road Food

F	P	G	S	P	E	C	T	A	C	U	L	A	R
J	T	R	Z	Y	E	A	R	T	H	W	C	D	G
S	N	E	D	R	A	G	G	N	I	G	N	A	H
C	E	A	L	A	I	Y	T	S	C	M	T	M	T
O	I	T	R	M	H	T	D	M	H	L	O	A	S
L	C	W	O	I	P	I	I	A	E	A	W	D	E
O	N	A	W	D	O	U	M	U	N	N	E	R	R
S	A	L	L	O	S	Q	A	S	I	A	R	E	E
S	L	L	A	F	A	I	R	O	T	C	I	V	V
U	N	A	V	G	I	T	Y	L	Z	A	E	O	E
S	E	R	E	I	G	N	P	E	A	M	G	O	T
A	V	O	I	Z	A	A	T	U	A	A	Y	H	N
R	E	R	D	A	H	K	A	M	Q	N	P	D	U
T	S	U	E	Z	F	O	E	U	T	A	T	S	O
E	D	A	M	N	A	M	R	L	M	P	M	D	M
P	L	E	A	N	I	N	G	T	O	W	E	R	F

Wonders of the World

H	E	R	U	S	I	E	L	S	H	O	R	E	Z
U	N	E	T	Q	F	Y	E	L	L	A	G	W	F
G	I	D	S	U	O	I	R	U	X	U	L	A	W
E	G	N	A	R	T	O	P	R	I	V	A	T	E
H	N	E	F	I	O	B	L	T	C	P	G	E	A
C	E	K	N	O	I	T	A	E	R	C	E	R	L
I	V	E	W	I	O	O	O	O	U	V	P	C	T
R	M	E	T	S	B	C	P	M	I	F	Y	R	H
A	R	W	S	M	G	U	E	S	S	F	T	A	Y
C	P	A	A	S	L	N	N	A	I	D	L	F	H
A	O	E	M	S	E	E	I	S	N	E	L	T	A
E	T	M	I	K	P	L	H	L	G	C	U	S	R
S	G	O	F	X	B	I	T	V	I	K	H	P	B
H	N	R	E	O	N	S	N	I	B	A	C	O	O
I	W	H	A	G	R	A	C	I	N	G	S	R	R
P	V	T	R	L	C	T	B	A	R	I	X	T	D

Yachting

W	P	Z	D	C	A	B	I	N	C	R	E	W	G
E	V	A	C	U	A	T	I	O	N	D	O	I	K
R	W	D	S	Y	C	O	M	F	O	R	T	J	E
C	I	S	R	S	T	M	J	H	K	J	O	M	A
R	N	T	Z	I	E	S	E	A	T	B	E	L	T
I	G	H	S	R	N	N	O	T	D	R	A	T	L
A	S	G	C	E	J	K	G	H	G	I	S	A	E
U	N	I	F	O	R	M	S	E	R	A	E	I	D
G	A	L	L	E	Y	V	N	L	R	I	N	R	G
L	C	F	V	W	U	C	I	P	S	S	A	P	N
U	O	S	S	K	Y	N	D	C	K	L	L	O	I
G	C	I	T	S	E	M	O	D	E	E	P	R	D
G	K	N	O	S	G	N	I	N	I	A	R	T	R
A	P	G	L	V	S	N	O	I	T	A	I	V	A
G	I	L	I	R	E	S	R	U	P	C	A	R	O
E	T	E	P	D	O	O	F	L	Y	I	N	G	B

Flight Attendants

N	O	O	P	S	E	N	O	C	S	G	M	Z	B
F	E	C	W	L	A	T	T	E	O	G	U	F	Y
T	A	L	K	R	L	S	A	D	F	F	F	A	O
O	O	D	P	H	E	T	K	M	R	O	F	C	R
S	R	E	M	O	T	S	U	C	O	I	I	E	D
S	J	X	Y	L	E	S	T	D	A	I	N	D	E
E	K	A	E	L	I	P	R	A	T	N	S	K	R
R	Q	L	V	C	A	E	H	T	U	K	S	Z	S
P	S	E	M	A	T	I	O	I	C	R	C	B	U
S	I	R	O	N	I	C	C	U	P	P	A	C	Y
E	A	W	U	J	S	A	B	O	D	T	F	N	R
W	S	O	D	I	H	R	Y	Y	S	A	F	W	T
I	C	K	B	C	A	K	L	I	M	T	E	A	S
F	Q	X	O	T	E	N	R	E	T	N	I	R	A
I	C	M	S	O	T	A	B	L	E	S	N	J	P
R	S	N	A	E	B	S	C	O	L	L	E	G	E

Coffee Stop

C	R	I	M	E	K	A	C	E	S	E	E	H	C
T	R	A	F	F	I	C	Y	T	G	L	C	B	O
G	O	T	H	A	M	A	N	Y	N	P	N	W	N
P	K	R	O	Y	W	E	N	E	I	P	A	A	C
Y	F	O	O	D	M	Z	T	N	D	A	N	L	E
T	H	E	A	T	R	E	S	O	L	G	I	K	R
X	N	O	R	B	E	H	T	M	I	I	F	I	T
Z	R	A	B	A	G	E	L	S	U	B	H	N	S
B	P	H	T	U	R	B	A	N	B	E	M	G	T
A	C	A	O	T	O	U	R	I	S	T	S	A	F
C	R	R	F	R	A	N	G	E	R	S	X	U	X
A	O	L	X	Y	S	H	O	P	P	I	N	G	M
B	W	E	B	U	S	I	N	E	S	S	T	E	J
S	D	M	N	O	I	H	S	A	F	E	R	R	Y
A	E	R	U	T	L	U	C	Y	M	C	I	T	Y
I	D	S	U	B	W	A	Y	S	T	H	G	I	L

Gotham

C	W	S	E	L	C	I	H	E	V	D	V	L	I
V	Z	P	I	B	B	I	K	E	N	A	L	M	K
E	L	E	X	U	L	I	C	E	N	S	E	T	T
T	E	E	A	S	P	H	A	L	T	S	T	R	H
U	V	D	T	N	E	M	E	V	A	P	R	A	G
O	A	W	R	R	O	T	C	A	R	T	U	I	I
R	R	U	S	I	O	D	B	I	C	Y	C	L	E
L	T	T	C	D	V	P	O	B	I	F	K	E	R
O	W	R	O	S	M	E	S	O	F	M	E	R	F
G	A	U	O	D	E	B	R	N	F	G	R	D	H
S	H	C	T	O	L	L	R	O	A	D	S	A	E
L	S	K	E	O	M	N	R	I	R	R	U	O	N
E	K	I	R	G	S	E	R	I	T	L	T	L	G
E	C	N	S	O	Y	R	E	V	I	L	E	D	I
H	I	G	H	W	A	Y	S	N	G	I	S	K	N
W	R	I	L	C	M	E	G	D	I	R	B	J	E

Back on the Road

N	T	K	D	P	P	O	T	N	H	N	U	K	A
A	E	J	E	A	O	L	U	W	C	A	N	N	O
E	R	O	S	C	R	O	A	O	R	V	C	O	L
C	R	U	O	I	T	P	N	N	A	I	O	O	S
O	A	R	T	R	U	O	O	K	E	G	V	M	E
T	I	N	O	E	G	C	R	N	S	A	E	N	C
R	N	E	T	M	A	R	T	U	E	T	R	E	R
A	O	Y	K	A	L	A	S	A	R	I	K	W	U
V	I	N	F	O	R	M	A	T	I	O	N	W	O
E	T	J	S	E	I	C	E	P	S	N	S	O	S
L	I	S	C	I	E	N	T	I	F	I	C	R	E
I	D	S	E	A	R	C	H	I	N	G	N	L	R
N	E	A	P	Y	R	E	V	O	C	S	I	D	E
G	P	E	R	U	T	N	E	V	D	A	A	N	V
E	X	P	L	O	R	E	R	S	H	I	P	I	A
G	E	O	G	R	A	P	H	Y	Y	Q	S	F	C

Journey of Discovery

X	G	B	G	N	I	V	I	R	D	C	O	S	T
L	C	N	M	D	Y	V	E	H	I	C	L	E	E
P	L	F	I	G	C	C	G	R	E	E	N	J	V
E	E	A	R	G	H	J	T	S	U	I	R	P	I
G	A	E	M	A	R	C	O	M	P	A	C	T	S
A	N	L	R	S	E	A	D	I	R	B	Y	H	N
E	Y	G	O	L	O	N	H	C	E	T	I	K	E
L	E	P	E	E	F	F	I	C	I	E	N	T	P
I	E	L	I	B	O	M	O	T	U	A	O	A	X
M	P	U	B	Q	S	N	O	I	S	S	I	M	E
U	O	G	U	A	O	A	Y	R	E	T	T	A	B
I	W	I	Q	M	W	Q	G	F	U	T	U	R	E
H	E	N	I	G	N	E	G	N	A	R	L	O	T
T	R	C	S	A	V	I	N	G	S	O	L	T	L
I	A	W	O	L	S	L	E	E	H	W	O	O	O
L	C	A	Y	L	D	N	E	I	R	F	P	M	V

Electric Cars

F	F	H	H	Y	O	I	K	N	P	G	O	T	F
F	M	K	S	S	Q	L	B	E	A	C	H	E	S
P	I	I	U	S	K	Y	L	A	T	I	P	A	C
W	L	Y	L	E	Z	K	R	A	H	O	X	L	E
E	S	E	T	N	X	O	K	C	S	D	A	Y	Z
K	U	W	A	I	T	P	I	H	Y	I	U	Z	L
W	M	Z	N	S	C	R	E	H	C	P	V	B	S
F	A	M	O	U	S	I	T	N	D	L	O	G	A
U	M	R	V	B	K	L	A	R	S	D	N	H	N
B	Y	H	C	R	A	N	O	M	I	I	S	O	D
U	P	O	F	E	I	G	E	L	D	V	V	T	D
R	Z	R	W	F	O	N	L	L	T	E	H	E	U
J	A	S	H	O	P	P	I	N	G	R	E	L	N
O	S	T	S	I	R	U	O	T	N	S	A	S	E
R	E	T	A	W	B	X	R	H	A	E	T	D	S
Y	R	Y	V	Q	I	V	W	H	O	J	W	T	E

Dubai

G	I	S	L	A	N	D	R	A	W	D	E	C	E
D	V	E	Y	T	N	E	M	A	I	L	R	A	P
D	R	M	C	R	I	C	K	E	T	I	N	M	O
D	I	A	N	A	O	L	C	O	E	V	K	B	R
N	T	H	U	U	S	T	N	H	F	E	I	R	U
U	O	T	N	G	T	J	S	M	I	R	N	I	E
O	U	T	I	Y	O	C	I	I	S	P	G	D	P
P	R	E	O	H	N	I	A	R	H	O	S	G	I
Y	I	C	N	C	E	H	A	S	E	O	L	E	N
B	S	A	J	R	H	B	E	A	T	L	E	S	T
G	M	L	A	A	E	S	C	G	A	L	A	N	G
U	C	A	C	N	N	A	O	B	U	P	E	N	W
R	I	P	K	O	G	T	T	C	B	C	H	S	D
E	R	I	P	M	E	O	E	H	C	R	U	H	C
D	N	A	L	T	O	C	S	A	S	E	L	A	W
J	A	O	X	F	O	R	D	N	W	O	R	C	T

English Holiday

H	L	R	I	G	W	O	C	A	T	T	L	E	C
H	T	G	I	B	L	U	B	B	O	C	K	H	S
N	S	R	G	O	E	G	E	L	L	O	C	N	D
O	A	D	O	A	G	L	L	A	B	T	O	O	F
T	O	M	Y	W	L	R	I	S	O	R	T	S	A
T	C	O	U	T	T	V	A	O	J	D	S	H	R
O	F	E	S	E	I	R	E	N	I	F	E	R	M
C	L	G	L	A	L	S	O	S	D	A	V	A	I
H	U	O	O	D	P	O	R	F	T	E	I	N	N
K	G	M	N	R	N	L	R	E	V	O	L	C	G
A	M	A	G	E	O	A	E	T	V	C	N	H	H
U	E	L	H	D	S	D	H	G	E	I	I	E	T
S	X	A	O	R	A	T	E	N	R	P	N	S	U
T	I	E	R	O	I	J	A	O	A	A	C	U	O
I	C	H	N	B	S	P	U	R	S	P	L	A	S
N	O	T	S	U	O	H	D	E	S	E	R	T	W

The Lone Star State

J	I	R	A	R	R	E	F	A	M	I	L	Y	V
F	O	O	D	Q	Y	R	O	T	S	I	H	P	E
R	S	M	U	E	S	U	M	O	L	A	T	I	N
M	L	E	V	A	R	T	O	E	F	L	A	G	I
E	I	W	I	N	E	L	J	E	S	E	E	H	C
P	B	L	E	G	A	U	G	N	A	L	X	C	E
O	O	F	A	S	X	C	A	A	A	W	A	M	E
R	O	M	A	N	T	I	C	T	T	T	S	F	T
U	T	G	D	S	L	C	O	C	H	I	L	U	N
E	N	A	R	A	H	J	U	O	R	O	S	O	A
A	R	S	T	B	V	I	L	U	R	C	I	K	D
Y	L	I	C	I	S	I	O	E	A	I	F	A	M
P	O	P	E	I	C	T	N	N	A	P	L	E	S
Y	R	T	N	U	O	C	Y	C	A	T	S	A	P
W	N	E	H	B	E	O	E	L	I	L	A	G	L
K	N	A	Z	Z	I	P	R	U	I	N	S	S	A

Italian Tour

S	H	A	R	E	M	A	R	F	D	J	D	F	V
L	C	O	L	O	R	S	K	I	O	E	A	R	T
I	R	A	C	B	M	E	G	K	V	C	P	P	S
D	R	E	P	B	U	I	T	E	E	T	U	O	T
E	E	V	P	E	T	M	L	U	I	N	Z	S	I
L	C	I	M	A	R	O	N	A	P	E	M	I	L
E	O	T	L	U	P	T	R	G	S	M	O	N	L
N	R	A	I	T	K	T	U	E	C	U	O	G	E
S	D	G	F	Y	R	J	R	R	U	C	R	C	D
O	I	E	Q	O	R	U	Y	U	E	O	K	A	O
P	M	N	P	O	T	R	U	S	N	D	R	P	M
F	A	I	S	C	O	T	L	O	A	Y	A	T	E
L	G	N	I	T	N	I	R	P	T	R	D	U	N
A	E	P	S	E	G	V	A	X	U	O	B	R	E
S	S	I	V	H	C	A	M	E	R	A	H	E	C
H	H	E	T	Q	E	L	P	O	E	P	L	P	S

Take Pictures

O	C	E	A	N	I	A	T	P	A	C	V	S	E
L	A	C	I	P	O	R	T	A	O	B	H	K	U
C	M	Q	Q	S	H	I	P	W	R	E	C	K	C
Y	A	G	C	S	C	A	S	T	A	W	A	Y	S
D	R	D	I	L	T	R	M	I	O	B	E	P	E
E	Y	H	V	L	A	H	U	M	V	U	B	R	R
M	A	E	Q	E	L	S	E	I	O	E	R	O	M
O	N	Y	V	W	N	I	S	M	S	C	L	F	R
C	N	S	M	O	W	T	G	I	I	E	K	E	O
O	O	T	O	H	L	O	U	A	C	N	V	S	T
C	O	R	C	R	O	R	H	R	N	N	N	S	S
O	G	A	T	M	R	A	T	S	E	I	V	O	M
N	A	N	I	S	L	A	N	D	V	S	T	R	W
U	L	D	S	B	A	M	B	O	O	T	S	O	L
T	H	E	M	E	S	O	N	G	I	N	G	E	R
O	I	D	A	R	B	S	K	I	P	P	E	R	F

Stuck on Gilligan's Island

S	P	O	H	F	I	N	A	M	R	E	G	J	M
P	K	W	G	R	A	I	N	S	V	N	A	E	A
I	T	C	I	B	M	A	L	I	S	G	L	E	L
C	I	D	E	R	I	P	S	R	R	A	T	L	T
E	U	S	E	G	I	C	E	A	N	P	B	A	S
D	R	S	L	L	O	G	V	W	C	M	I	D	A
E	F	E	S	S	A	I	O	A	O	A	E	E	E
W	B	N	I	L	T	R	W	P	L	H	R	R	Y
E	E	T	A	Y	B	A	E	V	O	C	B	E	R
R	Y	E	M	I	K	C	O	B	R	R	R	E	A
B	L	E	E	F	H	T	U	O	M	E	T	B	M
T	H	W	R	K	I	P	A	L	E	A	L	E	O
H	N	S	I	R	D	A	E	H	W	M	W	Y	R
G	T	R	C	A	S	S	Y	R	I	A	N	R	A
I	E	L	A	D	L	O	H	O	C	L	A	Q	D
L	E	K	N	U	D	H	T	G	N	E	R	T	S

Beers Around the World

G	O	N	D	O	L	A	E	N	I	G	N	E	Z
E	L	I	F	T	H	I	S	T	O	R	Y	Q	E
R	N	S	Y	G	O	L	O	N	H	C	E	T	P
M	E	A	P	M	R	A	I	R	P	O	R	T	P
A	G	M	L	M	F	U	H	S	A	R	C	R	E
N	O	V	N	P	I	U	B	B	S	F	O	E	L
Y	R	A	O	O	R	L	E	N	S	P	K	W	I
U	D	I	R	I	G	I	B	L	E	S	G	D	N
T	Y	R	K	E	C	E	A	L	N	D	E	A	S
A	H	C	A	W	S	F	L	O	G	R	N	V	S
T	U	R	B	U	L	E	N	C	E	I	O	I	T
S	W	A	U	O	R	T	A	W	R	A	O	A	H
O	I	F	A	S	O	T	O	R	S	T	L	T	G
R	N	T	U	L	T	P	N	S	C	O	L	I	I
E	G	N	I	D	N	A	L	K	N	H	A	O	L
A	S	P	T	U	T	N	A	Y	O	U	B	N	F

Airships

B	I	K	E	L	Q	S	V	D	D	G	F	R	N
K	C	O	L	J	T	H	L	G	B	R	P	I	T
B	U	S	X	R	C	A	N	R	A	R	A	A	D
V	I	U	A	T	D	I	A	M	E	T	E	R	F
X	X	P	A	E	L	K	E	S	N	S	O	A	R
B	M	P	P	L	E	D	S	U	S	P	S	C	Z
Q	B	O	O	S	A	U	O	G	O	T	T	I	R
C	O	R	T	O	R	M	K	U	N	V	U	N	U
A	L	T	R	E	R	O	T	A	T	I	N	G	B
A	T	A	A	C	K	S	R	O	U	N	D	L	B
H	S	F	C	E	L	C	Y	C	I	B	A	I	E
W	D	O	T	I	I	D	O	G	B	T	N	G	R
Z	A	R	I	K	N	J	W	R	E	N	C	H	I
S	E	K	O	P	S	G	I	M	P	A	R	O	M
H	R	I	N	F	L	A	T	E	A	S	R	S	S
M	T	V	A	L	V	E	M	D	E	E	P	S	M

Bicycle Wheels

A	H	T	O	L	S	B	S	R	A	U	G	A	J
H	O	R	U	O	J	A	K	N	I	K	S	R	M
N	Q	T	C	O	I	N	A	M	R	S	I	B	P
A	W	E	O	T	B	A	N	Y	A	N	P	O	H
R	K	R	A	A	V	N	R	S	R	R	A	C	A
I	S	M	T	K	M	A	S	E	E	E	K	H	R
P	I	I	I	C	W	S	E	L	W	F	O	B	M
R	L	T	X	O	F	G	N	I	Y	L	F	I	A
O	I	E	S	C	I	A	I	D	P	T	M	N	C
T	S	S	E	B	G	N	P	O	S	A	A	T	Y
E	A	Z	B	B	O	T	U	C	E	P	C	U	O
C	B	O	S	O	R	E	C	O	N	I	H	R	P
T	N	P	S	U	C	A	R	R	I	R	E	O	A
E	L	N	M	M	F	T	O	C	V	S	T	N	K
D	O	E	T	A	R	E	P	M	E	T	E	G	A
M	L	X	G	N	I	R	A	E	L	C	A	K	K

Jungle Journey

E	C	L	S	I	S	T	A	T	U	S	M	I	R
D	F	A	E	N	V	E	R	E	H	T	A	E	L
I	W	C	D	F	J	A	G	U	A	R	S	J	S
R	Q	O	A	I	C	R	O	I	R	E	P	U	S
F	F	M	N	N	L	E	L	Y	T	S	A	F	A
M	O	F	W	I	Z	L	E	X	U	S	C	E	L
W	E	O	O	T	N	B	A	S	F	R	E	R	C
E	T	R	R	I	L	A	E	C	L	V	S	R	I
A	W	T	C	N	P	R	E	M	I	U	M	A	P
L	A	R	G	E	U	I	A	S	M	N	O	R	O
T	U	D	V	T	D	S	N	R	O	L	O	I	R
H	D	N	A	R	B	E	T	I	U	O	T	M	S
Y	I	E	L	I	P	D	S	C	S	C	H	O	C
H	F	L	U	X	U	R	Y	H	I	N	A	N	H
W	M	B	E	N	T	L	E	Y	N	I	F	E	E
B	F	A	S	T	N	A	S	A	E	L	P	Y	X

Luxury Vehicles

T	O	I	L	E	T	S	K	Y	I	D	O	O	F
O	G	A	S	E	L	B	A	T	H	R	O	O	M
U	N	R	E	T	A	W	O	R	M	I	D	H	S
R	I	O	P	A	E	S	E	A	X	V	I	C	P
I	D	A	A	E	T	S	T	V	C	E	R	T	U
S	N	D	R	C	N	M	A	E	A	R	E	E	B
T	E	F	K	I	A	O	T	L	M	X	C	R	L
R	V	G	I	V	R	O	S	E	P	T	T	T	I
E	S	H	N	R	U	R	R	R	C	P	I	S	C
F	C	I	G	E	A	T	E	S	O	O	O	P	I
U	E	G	B	S	T	S	T	P	F	T	N	L	N
E	N	H	R	Y	S	E	N	A	F	S	S	A	C
L	I	W	E	W	E	R	I	M	E	T	R	Z	I
I	C	A	A	I	R	E	G	N	E	S	S	A	P
I	J	Y	K	Z	T	R	U	C	K	E	R	S	C
F	F	L	N	F	E	K	I	P	N	R	U	T	L

Rest Areas

T	H	N	D	H	O	L	D	Y	R	O	P	E	S
J	M	A	R	E	I	R	R	A	C	S	G	S	D
X	E	P	R	N	C	O	T	M	V	R	C	C	O
G	R	S	E	B	T	K	A	H	A	E	O	E	O
N	C	R	S	N	O	S	O	B	G	N	M	X	G
I	H	E	E	O	R	R	B	W	T	I	M	P	A
P	A	V	I	I	E	E	L	A	A	R	E	O	G
P	N	I	R	T	G	G	I	T	N	A	R	R	C
I	T	R	R	A	D	N	A	E	K	M	C	T	F
H	U	L	E	E	E	E	S	R	E	W	E	R	C
S	G	E	F	R	R	S	C	C	R	U	I	S	E
L	B	V	S	C	D	S	D	R	S	K	C	O	D
A	O	A	T	E	T	A	P	A	C	I	F	I	C
N	A	R	A	R	O	P	R	F	O	C	E	A	N
A	T	T	O	L	Y	R	A	T	I	L	I	M	U
C	L	P	B	I	M	P	O	R	T	H	U	L	L

On a Ship

A	M	R	U	B	B	E	A	S	T	E	R	N	I
N	A	T	U	H	B	C	U	L	T	U	R	E	S
Z	N	Y	M	O	N	O	C	E	G	R	A	L	L
T	T	A	E	T	L	S	R	I	L	A	N	K	A
B	E	I	I	U	H	O	N	G	K	O	N	G	M
U	I	L	P	S	P	P	E	O	P	L	E	X	A
D	V	O	Y	A	A	I	S	E	N	O	D	N	I
D	P	G	G	S	E	G	A	U	G	N	A	L	S
H	I	N	D	U	I	S	M	R	N	A	I	A	Y
I	I	O	Z	N	N	Y	A	A	E	T	D	T	A
S	U	M	A	A	A	P	C	S	P	S	O	N	L
M	S	P	W	N	H	L	H	I	A	I	B	E	A
R	A	I	M	Y	A	M	I	A	L	K	M	I	M
J	A	A	K	O	K	G	N	A	B	A	A	R	V
T	R	U	S	S	I	A	A	U	H	P	C	O	K
E	N	I	S	I	U	C	O	U	N	T	R	Y	J

Around Asia

G	R	A	Z	G	N	I	C	A	R	A	S	O	R
G	U	S	C	P	C	R	A	F	T	I	N	G	S
N	N	K	S	T	L	G	N	I	M	M	I	W	S
I	N	I	G	N	I	N	O	O	L	L	A	B	G
T	I	I	H	T	M	V	E	E	R	U	T	A	N
N	N	N	W	S	B	F	I	T	G	A	N	C	I
U	G	G	T	Z	I	G	N	T	N	D	U	K	K
H	D	N	N	T	N	F	G	G	I	V	O	P	L
G	E	L	N	I	G	P	N	N	L	E	M	A	A
T	N	E	D	F	P	I	I	I	C	N	S	C	W
G	S	I	X	S	K	M	K	V	Y	T	A	K	G
S	L	S	G	K	A	R	A	A	C	U	I	H	N
G	V	U	E	G	A	F	Y	C	I	R	L	C	I
S	P	R	X	P	O	Q	A	T	B	E	I	A	K
F	T	E	M	K	B	J	K	R	Y	X	N	E	I
S	P	O	R	T	S	U	R	F	I	N	G	B	B

Outdoor Recreation

D	N	U	O	R	G	R	E	D	N	U	G	Y	L
Y	A	A	N	S	R	E	H	S	A	R	H	T	S
H	T	P	L	I	M	O	D	E	R	N	O	N	K
T	I	N	H	O	T	O	U	R	I	S	M	E	Y
E	L	S	U	I	C	E	L	A	R	G	E	M	S
D	O	C	T	O	L	A	D	B	U	H	D	N	C
T	P	I	A	O	C	I	C	S	C	P	E	I	R
U	O	V	I	S	R	N	P	O	T	N	P	A	A
R	R	I	R	P	N	I	O	S	C	A	O	T	P
N	T	L	P	O	A	H	C	T	A	B	T	R	E
E	E	W	O	R	A	U	S	A	L	R	X	E	R
R	M	A	R	T	R	A	V	E	L	U	E	T	S
H	A	R	T	S	F	I	E	L	D	O	F	N	D
K	R	A	P	T	N	O	M	D	E	I	P	E	A
R	H	D	L	E	I	F	R	E	N	R	U	T	I
C	I	T	Y	P	E	A	C	H	T	R	E	E	G

Atlanta

O	E	G	T	M	C	F	S	I	A	Q	I	N	Z
W	G	N	D	E	C	K	S	O	P	E	K	H	M
T	N	T	I	R	G	N	I	L	I	A	S	D	W
R	I	R	U	G	P	L	A	C	I	T	U	A	N
A	H	I	E	I	N	E	O	N	A	C	W	N	O
V	S	P	H	T	F	E	R	R	Y	B	O	A	T
E	I	S	R	L	S	K	B	R	O	I	S	U	A
L	F	O	A	M	I	O	V	D	T	E	A	R	O
N	P	H	O	L	A	F	D	A	L	T	I	D	L
W	A	T	E	R	G	O	E	D	S	F	L	A	F
W	O	O	D	E	N	R	D	B	C	A	B	I	N
R	E	L	B	N	C	A	E	L	O	R	O	K	U
O	H	E	A	E	P	M	C	B	O	A	A	L	S
W	G	E	R	E	V	I	R	W	I	Y	T	L	R
P	C	H	G	L	A	K	E	N	A	F	Y	U	Q
O	M	W	E	R	B	O	W	K	Y	A	C	H	T

Watercraft

Z	S	E	I	T	I	C	E	L	A	N	D	M	V
S	N	A	C	I	T	A	V	C	K	I	N	G	S
G	E	R	M	A	N	Y	B	O	R	D	E	R	S
Y	H	U	S	C	O	T	L	A	N	D	S	U	D
H	Q	N	R	S	D	N	A	L	N	I	F	O	N
C	R	I	P	A	A	E	S	K	C	A	L	B	A
R	U	L	C	T	S	N	I	A	P	S	L	M	L
A	A	R	O	O	A	I	R	T	S	U	A	E	E
N	E	E	R	I	U	T	A	Y	I	D	G	X	R
O	N	B	T	E	N	N	R	S	R	P	U	U	I
M	G	A	E	E	N	O	T	E	A	T	T	L	E
B	L	Y	I	L	T	C	T	R	P	H	R	O	C
Y	A	C	B	S	G	S	Y	B	I	N	O	N	N
H	N	J	I	E	M	I	C	I	K	E	P	D	A
A	D	H	L	A	N	G	U	A	G	E	S	O	R
P	O	L	A	N	D	E	N	M	A	R	K	N	F

Around Europe

M	I	D	W	E	S	T	O	U	R	I	S	M	W
L	I	G	H	T	S	R	A	C	Y	J	A	Z	Z
W	O	N	S	Q	E	W	H	I	T	E	S	O	X
Z	S	S	S	G	N	I	D	L	I	U	B	L	C
L	E	N	U	B	I	R	T	I	S	E	A	L	I
L	U	A	C	E	S	B	Y	K	R	K	N	A	F
A	L	M	R	L	U	M	W	D	E	A	F	B	F
B	B	E	I	A	B	A	P	F	V	W	G	T	A
T	U	R	M	L	H	O	R	Y	I	G	O	O	R
E	L	I	E	K	L	O	P	N	N	F	D	O	T
K	L	C	C	I	N	I	D	L	U	I	T	F	D
S	S	A	T	T	E	Y	N	A	D	R	O	J	A
A	L	I	C	R	C	P	O	O	L	E	H	T	L
B	C	O	E	I	K	L	A	C	I	S	U	M	E
S	L	E	T	D	R	I	N	D	U	S	T	R	Y
D	J	Y	A	Z	Z	I	P	N	A	B	R	U	Z

The Windy City

A	V	L	E	T	O	H	M	Z	A	P	G	R	U
M	W	A	V	E	S	O	Z	L	U	I	U	A	M
A	W	A	L	S	U	C	O	C	O	N	U	T	R
B	O	E	S	N	Q	L	W	A	T	E	R	H	I
O	B	T	T	U	E	N	A	C	R	A	G	U	S
G	N	A	I	S	E	N	Y	L	O	P	M	A	L
J	I	M	Q	E	U	T	K	U	S	P	A	A	A
N	A	I	W	O	I	A	O	A	J	L	M	S	N
H	R	L	L	N	U	W	N	U	O	E	C	I	D
U	I	C	K	A	L	D	L	H	R	I	I	C	S
M	T	S	I	C	V	U	A	I	P	I	W	U	E
I	N	R	T	L	L	A	C	O	N	H	S	L	Q
D	U	H	A	O	I	A	R	E	S	O	R	T	S
N	S	E	N	V	R	T	G	N	I	F	R	U	S
A	S	O	Z	S	E	Y	R	O	U	U	Z	R	J
R	H	Y	H	Y	I	L	C	O	F	F	E	E	N

Visit Hawaii

K	Y	S	D	O	N	I	L	K	N	A	R	F	B
A	R	C	N	U	S	W	Z	C	E	M	G	C	R
I	E	O	A	A	T	N	O	T	S	O	B	O	I
N	N	N	Y	R	T	C	E	T	V	D	G	T	T
I	G	G	I	W	C	I	H	E	S	E	N	T	I
G	L	R	N	A	E	O	R	X	T	E	O	O	S
R	A	E	O	V	P	N	M	U	M	R	M	N	H
I	N	S	T	A	M	S	G	E	P	F	I	A	T
V	D	S	G	E	E	N	L	L	D	K	S	H	J
B	E	V	N	O	I	T	U	L	O	V	E	R	T
R	L	T	I	K	T	R	E	L	I	G	I	O	N
I	A	R	H	E	M	A	R	Y	L	A	N	D	M
T	W	A	S	M	I	R	G	L	I	P	O	B	E
A	A	D	A	G	H	T	U	O	M	Y	L	P	L
I	R	E	W	O	L	F	Y	A	M	Q	O	F	A
N	E	T	A	X	A	T	I	O	N	Y	C	M	S

Colonial Tour

R	E	E	T	S	L	O	E	L	D	D	A	S	K
C	C	R	O	P	S	O	C	A	T	T	L	E	E
S	A	X	E	T	R	C	O	O	Z	E	E	S	U
A	L	N	A	A	E	O	W	W	U	G	P	R	Q
G	F	G	I	E	M	R	B	E	B	N	L	O	T
H	N	N	O	M	R	R	O	S	J	I	T	H	R
O	J	I	E	L	A	A	Y	T	V	H	G	R	T
B	I	Z	D	A	F	L	S	E	K	C	G	D	Y
E	E	A	O	N	E	P	S	R	I	N	N	L	A
E	I	R	R	D	A	T	K	N	N	A	I	E	X
F	R	G	U	S	O	R	Y	A	H	R	M	I	V
E	I	D	T	C	S	I	B	W	B	P	R	F	X
N	A	U	K	A	O	J	O	U	I	E	A	A	R
C	R	S	M	P	U	C	D	X	S	E	F	L	I
E	P	D	A	E	T	S	E	M	O	H	E	R	D
S	L	L	U	B	H	N	G	E	N	S	X	B	E

Dude Ranch

Y	G	P	U	C	C	B	E	P	O	L	S	U	X
S	A	Q	T	R	A	X	D	H	E	I	D	A	F
O	M	H	O	K	P	M	A	W	S	G	Z	D	H
U	K	C	J	J	E	M	E	A	H	R	D	C	N
N	K	R	B	N	Y	C	O	G	K	U	A	I	S
D	K	A	I	I	O	L	D	F	N	E	S	M	R
R	C	C	G	V	S	M	L	E	B	A	Y	O	U
O	B	D	E	L	E	T	T	U	B	T	R	X	F
J	D	U	N	S	A	R	H	O	G	O	G	F	E
F	S	E	A	A	U	C	N	M	X	L	I	T	E
F	I	O	L	J	L	A	I	V	U	L	F	R	R
K	X	E	I	T	C	S	E	E	C	S	E	E	V
C	Y	E	L	L	A	V	I	T	R	T	V	S	I
R	A	L	O	D	N	O	Y	N	A	C	A	E	S
M	I	V	E	N	I	V	A	R	U	L	C	D	S
H	W	T	U	M	O	H	C	Z	C	P	P	W	E

Landforms along the Way

E	T	U	M	M	O	C	S	T	I	C	K	S	I
R	I	S	O	L	L	A	M	T	O	K	G	F	H
U	A	T	V	G	R	O	U	N	D	E	N	E	S
S	G	R	E	P	E	C	N	A	L	A	B	E	H
I	E	E	M	G	E	C	A	P	T	T	L	T	R
E	C	N	E	N	F	U	N	U	R	I	A	K	O
L	C	G	N	I	H	C	R	A	M	P	S	L	A
G	F	T	T	G	E	E	V	S	T	I	E	A	D
N	S	H	U	G	A	E	P	O	R	S	I	W	W
I	L	I	O	O	L	E	O	B	I	D	I	E	A
N	O	K	K	J	T	F	R	C	E	P	L	D	T
N	W	I	R	S	H	J	R	E	Q	L	G	I	E
U	F	N	O	A	Y	E	P	K	N	E	E	S	R
R	J	G	W	V	X	S	S	E	N	T	I	F	S
N	P	O	W	E	R	C	S	E	L	C	S	U	M
X	E	D	I	R	T	S	L	I	A	R	T	A	F

Walking

U	N	I	V	E	R	S	I	T	Y	G	L	Y	S
D	B	R	E	W	E	R	S	T	R	A	N	U	P
N	O	R	T	H	E	R	N	E	K	I	M	F	O
A	D	L	E	I	F	U	A	E	B	M	A	L	R
L	C	Y	H	I	O	T	M	O	E	R	Y	E	T
Y	O	U	B	C	L	I	R	R	M	E	E	S	S
R	L	B	R	A	C	O	F	I	R	B	D	L	U
I	D	O	K	H	D	E	N	U	A	A	L	S	G
A	O	E	I	K	S	G	T	W	E	I	K	R	A
D	S	G	Y	T	S	L	E	H	M	I	N	E	R
L	A	K	E	S	U	P	E	R	I	O	R	V	M
N	W	A	K	C	P	S	E	N	S	M	O	I	A
I	P	C	I	I	E	P	G	V	W	T	C	R	P
U	U	R	H	E	A	F	O	O	T	B	A	L	L
B	G	C	H	P	K	E	N	O	S	H	A	T	E
A	I	C	E	F	I	S	H	I	N	G	X	G	E

Wisconsin

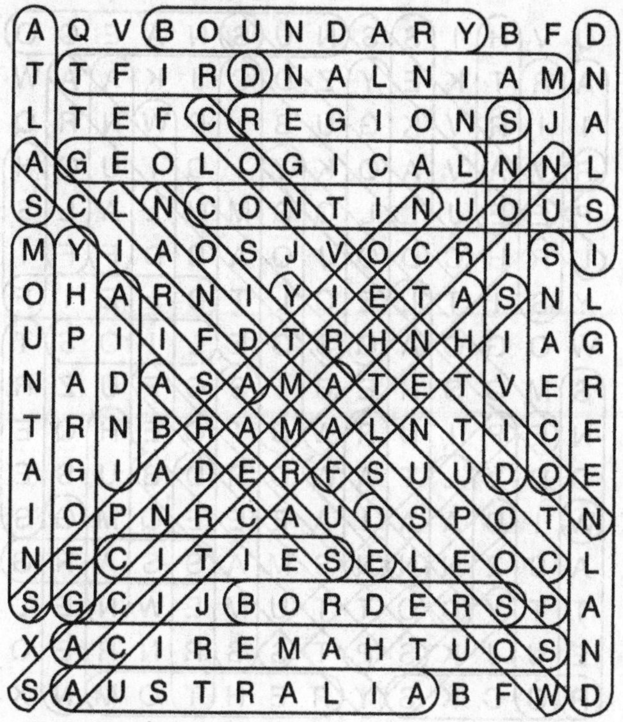

Continents

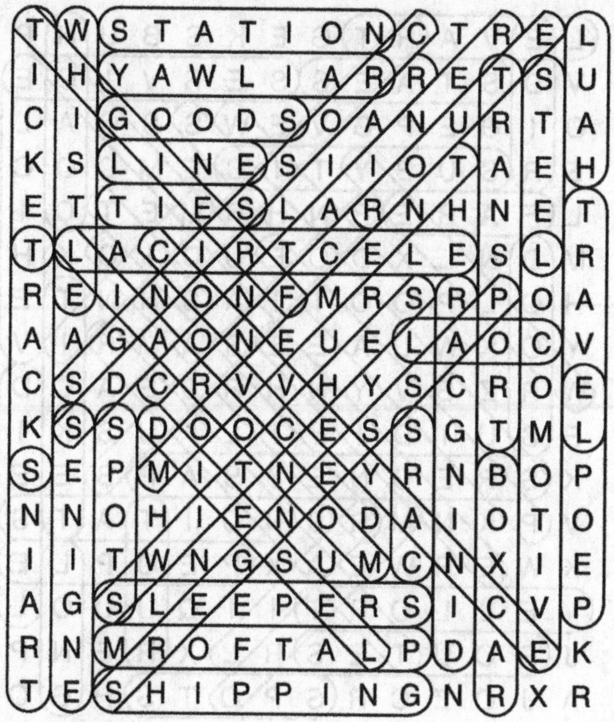

By Rail

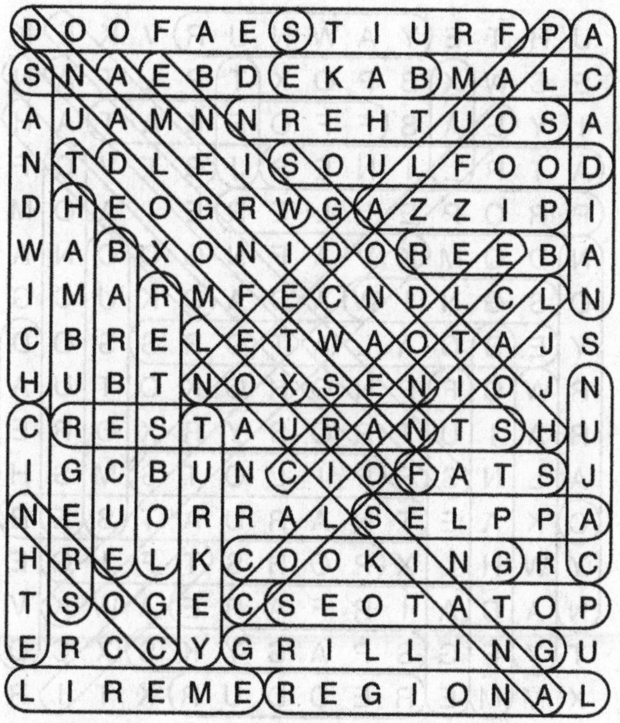

Cuisine Across the U.S.

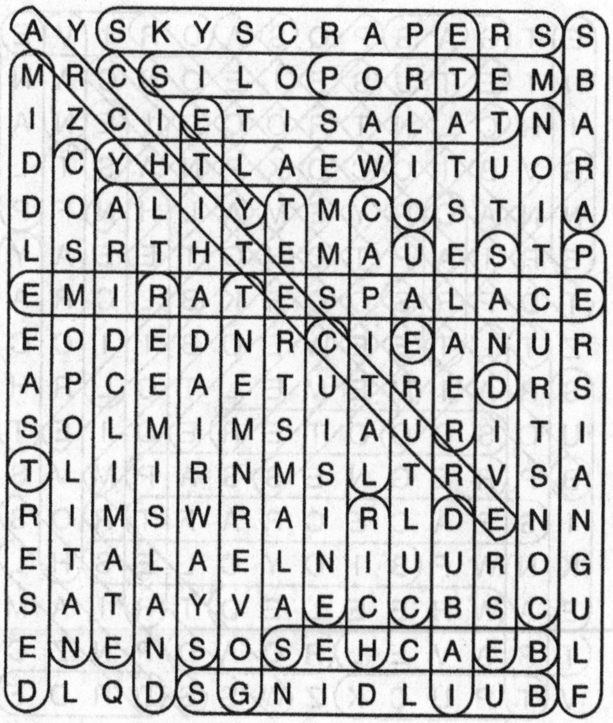

Abu Dhabi

L	E	V	A	R	T	G	E	K	S	B	U	H	P
V	D	S	T	A	E	S	S	E	R	V	I	C	E
O	I	G	E	P	G	V	E	W	S	S	O	A	L
E	R	S	U	B	Y	T	I	C	E	M	C	O	C
L	F	A	R	E	P	N	H	R	M	E	T	C	I
M	D	N	L	X	D	O	E	U	D	I	C	K	H
H	O	L	P	O	O	T	T	A	S	H	N	T	E
Y	O	K	W	L	A	E	E	S	A	M	R	I	V
W	R	Z	B	V	Y	N	H	R	S	E	A	C	D
E	S	U	I	D	I	Y	T	L	F	U	S	K	I
K	S	R	E	G	N	E	S	S	A	P	B	E	E
V	P	K	N	M	R	S	N	O	I	T	A	T	S
K	W	E	R	W	E	A	X	P	E	O	P	L	E
Y	E	L	L	O	R	T	I	I	Q	U	U	O	L
J	R	O	U	T	E	S	R	L	X	R	E	N	P
A	J	O	Z	C	R	S	P	O	T	S	H	G	O

Bus Trip

U	V	H	I	S	S	N	U	S	N	A	E	C	O
A	R	T	K	E	Y	Z	D	C	J	K	A	A	W
I	I	R	V	K	G	U	B	L	P	W	N	R	Q
R	V	A	V	A	O	K	Y	I	O	I	U	O	H
P	E	E	J	L	L	G	G	M	M	L	A	L	S
L	R	H	C	D	O	J	O	A	B	D	F	F	I
Y	S	I	T	L	E	G	L	T	D	L	E	I	F
W	O	G	O	A	G	S	O	E	L	I	O	S	T
S	M	C	S	R	E	B	I	S	Q	F	U	Z	R
N	E	P	I	U	R	W	B	T	O	E	H	Q	E
O	D	V	L	T	A	W	D	R	D	B	U	S	E
W	I	D	A	A	I	A	E	E	E	Q	M	G	S
A	S	Z	N	N	N	S	M	A	S	S	A	R	G
T	T	Y	D	O	T	T	U	M	E	W	N	E	L
E	U	J	K	S	P	T	S	S	R	N	R	E	Q
R	O	C	K	S	Y	R	E	H	T	O	M	N	X

See Nature

E	T	G	A	S	P	Q	S	A	D	R	I	V	E
N	T	E	T	U	S	E	I	E	O	N	C	A	N
I	R	C	L	N	T	R	O	C	D	I	E	N	A
G	V	B	I	C	C	O	K	P	N	A	S	T	L
N	N	A	C	R	Y	E	M	A	L	H	N	F	P
E	R	I	A	P	T	C	H	O	T	E	E	A	Y
T	D	F	R	S	O	C	R	K	B	L	C	R	A
Z	T	L	T	E	E	W	E	O	B	I	I	C	C
S	R	A	I	M	E	M	E	L	T	C	L	R	H
U	O	S	C	O	O	T	E	R	E	O	I	E	T
B	P	R	E	G	N	E	S	S	A	P	M	V	S
I	S	P	A	C	E	C	R	A	F	T	R	O	S
K	N	W	F	B	I	C	Y	C	L	E	S	H	L
E	A	W	H	E	E	L	E	D	T	R	I	A	M
T	R	A	V	E	L	R	O	A	D	P	N	Z	C
V	T	R	U	C	K	Z	W	S	S	D	R	O	F

Vehicles

U	H	T	E	Y	A	W	N	U	R	V	K	E	K
E	C	W	X	B	P	O	X	T	P	L	T	A	N
I	Y	E	A	S	F	F	O	E	K	A	T	A	H
A	I	R	L	I	N	E	S	J	G	T	V	C	F
P	R	O	P	E	L	L	E	R	E	I	A	O	M
N	D	Q	M	K	V	A	F	N	G	O	C	N	A
O	S	G	N	I	W	A	D	A	C	K	U	C	G
Y	E	S	C	A	L	A	T	O	R	S	S	O	D
R	W	C	F	P	N	O	H	O	K	Q	T	U	A
R	A	I	U	T	R	O	S	Y	R	X	O	R	E
A	L	N	S	S	P	I	L	O	T	S	M	S	H
C	K	A	E	T	N	A	R	U	A	T	S	E	R
Y	W	H	L	X	P	O	H	S	T	F	I	G	E
N	A	C	A	I	R	F	A	R	E	A	W	K	V
T	Y	E	G	S	P	A	C	Y	K	S	X	C	O
X	M	M	E	R	E	D	D	U	R	K	T	I	R

Around the Airport

X	S	S	Y	N	A	L	P	S	Q	F	W	D	N
M	E	S	N	R	L	U	C	E	R	N	E	W	S
C	H	O	C	O	L	A	T	E	O	K	U	E	S
I	C	R	N	H	W	C	N	R	C	R	R	A	K
L	T	C	E	R	E	C	O	O	A	T	O	L	I
B	A	D	U	E	H	E	L	L	P	V	P	T	I
U	W	E	T	T	Y	D	S	I	D	I	E	H	N
P	Y	R	R	T	N	S	R	E	I	C	A	L	G
E	K	I	A	A	Y	Y	J	S	W	I	N	E	N
R	S	T	L	M	O	U	N	T	A	I	N	S	I
F	Y	A	I	S	D	B	S	S	I	W	S	P	K
R	E	L	T	N	E	M	A	I	L	R	A	P	N
A	L	I	Y	R	L	G	E	R	M	A	N	Y	A
N	L	A	N	N	I	C	O	U	N	T	R	Y	B
C	A	N	T	O	N	S	F	O	N	D	U	E	S
A	V	E	N	E	G	N	A	T	I	O	N	U	F

Switzerland

P	O	L	I	T	I	C	S	A	M	R	U	B	G
Y	G	C	U	I	S	I	N	E	F	O	O	D	H
R	N	Y	Q	U	Q	A	I	D	O	B	M	A	C
R	I	N	H	F	R	I	E	N	D	L	Y	U	A
U	X	R	I	C	E	S	R	H	A	W	L	Y	E
C	O	U	N	T	R	Y	I	O	T	T	U	R	B
K	B	C	F	E	B	A	S	A	U	U	R	O	C
D	I	T	L	C	A	L	N	R	M	W	O	T	I
S	L	N	U	N	N	A	E	O	A	S	N	S	F
S	E	E	G	A	G	M	N	T	M	D	G	I	I
E	V	I	Y	D	K	S	E	S	E	N	I	H	C
L	A	C	I	P	O	R	T	J	K	A	E	D	A
P	R	N	B	O	K	M	F	U	O	L	R	D	P
M	T	A	N	Z	A	S	I	A	N	S	O	U	T
E	H	S	T	R	O	P	X	E	G	I	F	B	O
T	O	U	R	I	S	M	A	N	T	E	I	V	H

Thailand

S	B	I	N	T	E	R	N	E	T	X	F	T	Y
T	Y	G	O	L	O	N	H	C	E	T	H	F	Y
A	E	G	C	A	L	I	F	O	R	N	I	A	N
N	R	B	U	S	I	N	E	S	S	E	G	C	A
F	A	I	I	M	O	N	E	Y	A	M	H	E	P
O	W	N	Y	T	B	O	N	H	N	I	T	B	M
R	T	D	A	A	R	V	G	O	J	R	E	O	O
D	F	U	H	P	S	A	I	B	O	E	C	O	C
H	O	S	O	P	M	T	N	A	S	P	H	K	O
C	S	T	O	L	N	O	E	S	E	X	I	R	M
R	O	R	L	E	E	R	E	V	I	E	P	A	P
A	R	Y	V	A	A	S	R	E	E	S	H	D	U
E	C	N	Z	Y	O	C	S	I	C	J	T	I	T
S	I	Y	A	B	E	L	G	O	O	G	O	O	E
E	M	B	N	A	D	V	A	N	C	E	D	B	R
R	O	S	S	E	C	O	R	P	T	A	Q	V	S

Silicon Valley

N	A	S	C	A	R	A	T	S	D	N	I	W	J
M	D	S	E	L	C	I	H	E	V	M	B	P	O
O	Z	M	O	S	Q	U	A	L	I	T	Y	D	B
T	A	U	C	U	T	R	A	C	T	O	R	S	S
O	M	S	N	C	B	F	H	M	M	R	O	Y	E
R	O	T	O	O	C	I	S	V	E	E	T	L	P
S	D	A	R	F	G	H	U	E	R	R	S	B	A
M	E	N	B	A	Y	F	R	N	C	O	I	M	C
E	L	G	N	B	D	V	U	A	U	L	H	E	S
L	T	S	R	A	C	I	A	L	R	P	O	S	E
A	I	I	N	D	U	S	T	R	Y	X	P	S	S
T	D	N	O	U	N	A	C	I	R	E	M	A	C
S	X	U	C	R	V	M	G	A	O	N	E	F	O
E	E	Y	R	O	T	C	A	F	Z	N	T	W	R
I	E	D	S	E	L	E	N	G	I	N	E	R	T
F	U	S	I	O	N	N	D	R	I	V	I	N	G

Drive a Ford

```
S T O P A T E K C I T T K I
R R L S E S U B W A Y O C V
E A C I R T C E L E N U O E
V V I D I E S E L P O R N H
I E F L A A G L A E I Y D I
R L F I L M O N G D T A U C
D C A G U R T A E S A W C L
W I R H T O I L N S T L T E
S L T T G R O I I B S I O N
L B O R R C A B L E C A R C
E U A A W R R N T S F R P I
E P C I T I H U S K C A R T
H T R L T C M J Z P R B R I
W E U I A M N O D N O L U E
K A S O O F A S T E E R T S
J H C C R N Y A W M A R T A
```

Trams

```
E L F L I G H T S T O L I P
T A K E O F F T L A H P S A
A N O V E R R U N S T E J R
X I P Y T A V I A T I O N A
I M A L I G H T I N G A T E
W R T G J A P P R O A C H G
A E H N D I R E C T I O N L
Y T S I E R U T R A P E D E
G R A D G P U O A R M S T L
G O F N R L L U F M A E N L
N P E A A A T C T A R C E A
I R T L V N A H G C K U M R
Y I Y I E E L D N Y I R E A
L A R M L S F O O K N I V P
F R E W O T C W L S G T A R
A C D I S T A N C E S Y P K
```

Runway

```
P G N I T H G I L S I R A P
E B C N O I T A C U D E T G
L S H O P S C I M A R E C A
P M T I L I A R T I S T S L
O O B I S L E T S A P N C L
E N P S B T E C U L T U R E
P A A E H I O C A X S L X R
I L I R I P H R T M K O V Y
C I N U E M A X Y I O V U S
A S T T R A N R E D O M G E
S A I P V N V S G W B N L R
S S N L U Y E R N O I Y D U
O M G U O T K R O W T R A T
K E S C L I L C A S W O K C
Z Q N S J C U R A T O R H I
S T N I R P D I S P L A Y P
```

Art Museum Tour

```
A T S P I H C R S M A L L B
H C E N I L O S A G X E O G
R L Z E A S E E P R U L S U
P E S A H C R U P F P O A M
M R T O N C K M S O S T N I
U K G A E F A S T P K T D L
P S N C W P P S U T N E W K
Y E I E S O S R N O I R I C
S I P G P R E E H B R Y C I
A R P A A E I M G A D E H U
E T O R P N R O U C A N O Q
E E H E E R E T O C E O T D
F L S V R O C S D O R M D O
F I N E S C O U E X B P O O
O O W B C I R C L E K I G F
C T A T M A G A Z I N E S R
```

Convenience Store Stop

W	L	E	N	N	U	T	B	H	C	T	I	D	L
M	P	A	S	L	A	N	A	C	E	I	R	E	A
B	E	A	S	T	R	A	N	S	P	O	R	T	K
S	E	Q	M	U	A	B	K	V	E	N	I	C	E
F	D	U	P	S	E	O	B	R	I	D	G	E	S
L	A	E	G	D	T	Z	B	D	A	N	A	A	C
O	M	D	C	Q	S	E	C	R	M	A	T	B	A
W	N	U	O	V	K	H	R	A	A	L	I	Y	R
C	A	C	M	K	C	O	L	D	N	U	O	P	G
B	M	T	M	N	O	S	T	H	A	A	N	H	O
G	J	S	E	B	L	E	N	R	P	M	L	L	R
O	A	R	R	R	K	G	K	A	A	E	E	W	O
O	T	T	C	O	W	R	S	R	E	V	I	R	U
D	S	L	E	N	N	A	H	C	E	C	E	J	T
S	B	N	I	S	A	B	Y	L	N	H	O	L	E
V	G	N	I	P	P	I	H	S	U	P	P	L	Y

Down a Canal

S	T	A	R	S	C	W	E	C	N	E	I	C	S
T	H	D	J	S	N	O	O	M	A	R	S	C	T
U	G	C	P	U	Y	A	W	Y	K	L	I	M	E
D	I	C	R	N	P	R	B	N	A	S	A	S	N
Y	N	O	K	A	E	I	M	I	Y	T	G	A	A
S	E	S	G	R	E	S	T	H	G	I	A	T	L
U	B	M	D	U	A	S	P	E	Q	B	L	U	P
N	U	O	U	I	E	V	E	I	R	R	A	R	T
E	L	S	M	L	O	N	O	R	L	O	X	N	H
V	A	D	E	M	O	R	D	N	A	C	I	N	G
L	E	C	R	M	E	T	E	O	R	S	E	E	I
E	A	O	C	S	L	D	P	T	A	E	S	P	L
C	R	M	U	N	I	V	E	R	S	E	P	T	Y
A	T	E	R	E	L	B	B	U	H	A	C	U	K
P	H	T	Y	L	A	N	H	E	A	V	E	N	S
S	E	S	A	G	G	R	A	V	I	T	Y	E	X

Space Journey

S	D	R	I	V	I	N	G	T	S	E	R	O	F
T	D	A	E	L	C	Y	C	R	O	T	O	M	S
Y	R	O	N	O	I	T	A	E	R	C	E	R	P
S	A	A	O	G	E	B	O	G	G	I	N	G	O
P	Y	M	I	W	E	K	I	B	T	R	I	D	R
E	T	D	A	L	I	R	I	V	T	A	G	O	T
E	E	U	D	H	S	L	O	B	H	A	N	F	M
D	F	N	I	U	A	V	D	U	D	O	E	H	O
J	A	E	K	T	M	C	A	E	S	A	G	S	T
H	S	B	A	G	N	I	C	A	R	U	U	S	O
E	S	U	S	P	E	N	S	I	O	N	A	Q	C
L	L	G	A	D	N	O	H	R	D	F	E	W	R
M	L	G	W	N	E	L	C	I	H	E	V	S	O
E	I	Y	A	A	S	T	E	E	R	I	N	G	S
T	H	Z	K	S	S	W	H	E	E	L	S	T	S
S	U	Z	U	K	I	N	P	O	L	A	R	I	S

All-Terrain Vehicles

E	C	I	V	R	E	S	R	E	G	R	A	H	C
S	M	L	S	S	K	L	A	T	A	D	L	R	O
E	P	E	I	P	S	G	N	I	M	A	O	R	N
M	L	Y	S	A	R	E	E	L	O	T	R	P	N
A	A	R	E	S	M	I	L	L	D	M	O	F	E
G	N	E	I	L	A	E	N	E	E	O	T	A	C
G	I	T	P	Q	B	G	G	T	R	B	O	M	T
N	C	T	E	I	I	A	E	A	N	I	M	I	A
U	Q	A	S	N	C	K	T	S	R	L	W	L	R
S	K	B	L	I	N	T	E	R	N	E	T	Y	E
M	B	I	L	L	G	A	U	Y	O	O	V	P	M
A	T	E	X	T	I	N	G	R	B	P	K	O	A
S	R	E	B	M	U	N	A	P	E	O	I	I	C
K	E	Y	P	A	D	F	G	L	S	S	A	L	A
I	P	H	O	N	E	G	R	A	H	C	E	R	F
L	E	V	A	R	T	D	S	I	M	C	A	R	D

Mobile Phone

R	S	P	O	L	I	T	I	C	A	L	T	G	F
E	T	T	A	J	M	A	H	A	L	N	N	S	E
W	N	Y	T	R	E	B	I	L	A	I	L	C	U
O	E	N	N	M	T	C	Y	T	N	A	A	U	P
T	V	R	O	N	O	H	R	A	N	L	N	L	Y
N	E	E	T	N	L	O	E	D	P	O	C	P	R
O	R	G	G	Z	P	M	M	N	Y	I	I	T	A
I	U	R	N	M	M	A	U	S	O	L	E	U	M
T	T	A	I	E	R	O	Y	S	E	N	N	R	I
A	C	L	H	K	H	E	N	A	E	V	T	E	D
C	U	C	S	F	M	E	M	O	R	I	A	L	S
O	R	N	A	T	I	O	N	A	L	C	T	R	V
L	T	M	W	S	D	N	U	O	M	I	H	I	G
D	S	K	S	I	L	E	B	O	T	G	T	E	C
J	X	P	L	A	C	I	R	O	T	S	I	H	S
S	C	E	N	O	T	A	P	H	T	O	M	B	S

Monuments

H	H	H	I	S	T	O	R	Y	L	I	M	A	F
U	B	O	S	R	E	L	T	T	E	S	A	N	B
N	U	E	R	U	T	N	E	V	D	A	P	O	N
T	F	X	E	S	R	E	E	N	O	I	P	G	N
I	F	P	N	U	E	D	R	A	W	T	S	E	W
N	A	E	I	R	U	S	L	R	J	I	X	R	G
G	L	D	M	I	D	A	H	O	I	O	D	O	N
N	O	I	S	N	A	P	X	E	G	T	A	V	I
I	S	T	R	A	N	C	H	E	R	S	O	E	M
P	U	I	E	S	A	E	S	I	D	M	R	R	O
M	P	O	L	J	O	U	R	N	E	Y	L	L	Y
A	P	N	E	R	D	L	I	H	C	Q	I	A	W
C	L	Y	V	Q	B	X	I	N	D	I	A	N	S
A	I	M	A	M	E	R	I	C	A	N	R	D	O
N	E	B	R	A	S	K	A	R	E	L	O	H	C
A	S	D	T	R	A	P	P	E	R	S	U	N	M

On the Oregon Trail

E	J	P	L	A	T	F	O	R	M	S	R	A	C
M	N	L	T	R	O	P	S	N	A	R	T	U	A
E	E	G	A	G	G	U	L	B	A	E	H	X	L
T	R	A	I	N	S	G	D	O	R	G	G	R	U
R	U	L	I	N	E	S	E	A	R	N	I	O	K
O	S	W	P	H	E	J	P	R	I	E	E	U	A
K	Y	N	T	U	N	E	A	D	V	S	R	T	P
D	A	O	R	L	I	A	R	I	A	S	F	E	S
B	W	I	A	L	C	B	T	N	L	A	O	S	N
A	L	T	V	S	O	O	U	G	C	P	W	K	G
G	I	A	E	P	M	C	R	I	L	I	A	C	I
G	A	T	L	O	M	K	E	E	L	N	I	A	S
A	R	S	C	T	U	U	F	O	O	D	T	R	C
G	D	O	J	S	T	S	T	E	K	C	I	T	Y
E	L	B	A	T	E	M	I	T	Y	U	N	N	K
S	U	N	I	M	R	E	T	A	L	T	G	M	G

Train Stations

P	A	R	E	F	A	S	D	D	L	T	S	A	F
H	T	O	L	L	S	R	E	E	U	Y	I	E	A
V	L	A	C	C	I	D	E	N	T	A	G	A	S
T	M	D	R	V	W	T	D	A	I	W	N	T	K
R	E	S	I	O	E	E	X	L	X	K	S	U	C
A	R	N	R	R	R	W	Q	W	E	R	C	R	U
F	G	C	C	P	A	U	T	O	B	A	H	N	R
F	E	N	A	I	D	E	M	L	R	P	Y	P	T
I	O	S	T	L	A	H	P	S	A	B	A	I	R
C	S	S	R	E	B	M	U	N	F	R	W	K	A
O	R	A	M	P	S	S	E	L	C	I	H	E	V
M	E	P	S	D	E	D	I	V	I	D	G	T	E
M	V	R	E	I	R	R	A	B	N	G	I	U	L
U	I	E	N	U	P	O	L	I	C	E	H	O	S
T	R	V	A	W	A	C	C	E	S	S	E	R	N
E	D	O	L	Y	T	I	C	R	A	C	E	H	M

Highways

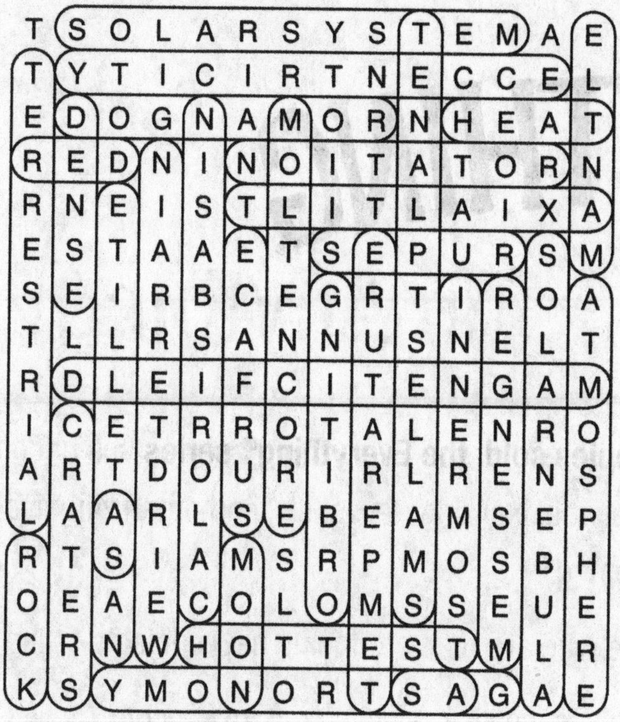

Trip to Mercury

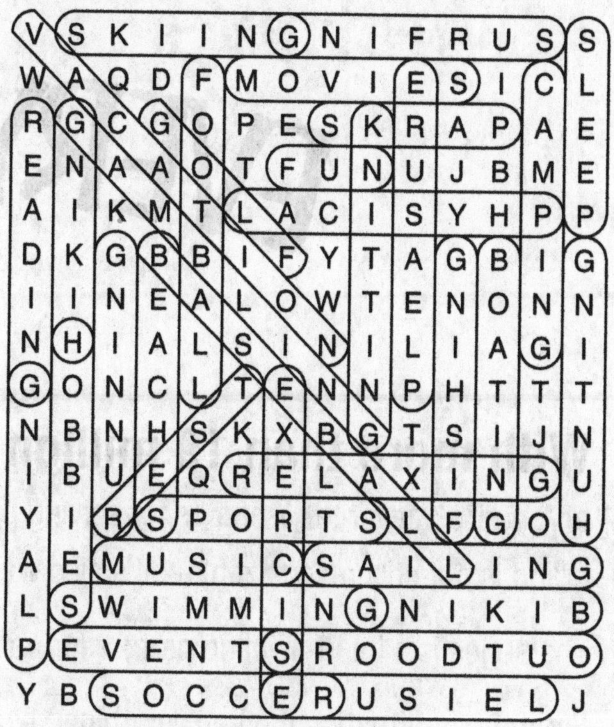

Recreational Travel